Nahum, Habakkuk and Malachi

Readings, A New Biblical Commentary

Nahum, Habakkuk and Malachi

Graham S. Ogden

Sheffield Phoenix Press

2023

Copyright © 2023 Sheffield Phoenix Press

Published by Sheffield Phoenix Press
Sheffield Centre for Interdisciplinary Biblical Studies (SCIBS),
University of Sheffield, S10 2TN

www.sheffieldphoenix.com

All rights reserved.
No part of this publication may be reproduced or transmitted in any form or by any means, electronic or mechanical, including photocopying, recording or any information storage or retrieval system, without the publishers' permission in writing.

A CIP catalogue record for this book
is available from the British Library

ISBN 978-1-914490-25-5 (hardback)
ISBN 978-1-914490-26-2 (paperback)

This volume is dedicated to my wife, Lois, whose unwavering love and support over these many years has sustained our family and made work such as this possible.

Contents

Author's Preface	xi
Acknowledgments	xv
Abbreviations	xvii

Nahum: A Commentary

Introduction	1
Contents and Structure	2
Massa'—an Oracle?	2
Authorship	4
Nahum—Who or What Was He?	5
Date	6
Literary Features	7
Assyria in the Old Testament	9
Nineveh the City	10
Foreign Nation Oracles	11
Nahum's Theological Ideas	12
Reading Strategy	13
Exegesis	15
1.1 Title	15
1.2-6 The Character of YHWH	16
1.7-11 Plot Against YHWH?	21
1.12-15 (2.1) Relief for Judah	25
2.1-13 (2.2-14) Against Assyria	29
2.1-9 (2-10) Assyria under Threat	30
2.11-13 (12-14) Against Assyria	34
3.1-7 Woe to Nineveh	36
3.8-13 Nineveh Will be Devastated	41
3.14-19 Assyria's End	45

Habakkuk: A Commentary

Introduction	49
Outline of Contents	50
Structure	50
A Reading Strategy	51
Authorship and Unity	54
Historical Setting	56
Habakkuk's Place in the Scroll	56
Relationship to Other Books	57
Literary Features of Habakkuk	58
Textual Issues	59
Theological Basis of Habakkuk	60
Exegesis	62
1.1 Superscription	62
1.2-4 Habakkuk's Lament—Part A	63
1.5-11 God's Response?	66
1.12-17 Habakkuk Challenges God	72
2.1 Habakkuk Awaits God's Reply	76
2.2-5 God's Reply	77
2.6-20 'Woe to you who…'	81
2.6-8 First 'Woe' Oracle	82
2.9-11 Second 'Woe' Oracle	85
2.12-14 Third 'Woe' Oracle	87
2.15-17 Fourth 'Woe' Oracle	89
2.18-20 Fifth 'Woe' Oracle	92
3.1-19 Habakkuk's Lament—Part B	94
3.1 Title	95
3.2-15 Confession of Trust	96
3.16 The Petition	104
3.17-19 Song of Praise	105
Conclusion	109
On the Reading Thesis	109
On Habakkuk 2.4 as the Core Text	110
On Prophets and Sages	111
On Violence and Theology	111
Select Bibliography	113

Preface   115

Malachi: A Commentary

Historical Situation   119
Authorship   120
Date   120
From Spoken to Written   121
Structure and Contents   122
Literary Characteristics   125
Malachi's Concerns   126
Relationship to Deuteronomy   128
On Reading Malachi   129
Access to Malachi the Book   132
Nature of the Book   133
Outline   134

Exegesis   135
  1.1 Title   135
  1.2-5 On God's Love-in-Reverse   136
  1.6–2.9 On Priestly Failures   139
  2.1-9 The Levi Covenant   148
  2.10-16 Opposing Foreign Marriages   153
  2.17–3.5 Refining the Community   160
  3.6-12 Guaranteeing a Land of Plenty   166
  3.13–4.3 Is Serving God of Benefit?   172
  4.4-6 (3.22-24) In Conclusion   180

Postscript   183
  On Translating and Interpreting Malachi   184
  Select Bibliography   187

Conclusions   189
  On Prophets and Prophecy   189
  A Final Note on Translation and Interpretation   190

Author's Preface

This commentary on the books of Nahum, Habakkuk and Malachi has been sparked by a growing sense of the importance for ancient Israel's story of the period just prior to the end of Assyrian power in c. 612 BCE, through the years of the Babylonian Empire (611–538 BCE), and into the Medo-Persian period that replaced the Babylonian. The so-called prophetic books that witness to this period each give some insight into the changes that evolved in so many areas of Israel's life—theological challenges, social changes, linguistic revolution, political developments, religious upheavals, and national identity tension—all were in flux. In the collection of materials that comprised the Scroll of the Twelve, or Minor Prophets, the very nature and definition of a 'prophet' is seen to be evolving, as a book like Jonah, a narrative built around a figure from the past, challenges the more traditional notion of prophecy as reported prophetic speeches. These three 'books' that have been written into the Scroll of the Twelve are important witnesses to the changes that were taking place.

The period in which the three books are assumed to locate was one of growing diversity of theological view, though still dominated by that of the Deuteronomic cohort. The hard line or narrow view of those who believed in blessings for obedience and curses for disobedience, such as Haggai, was challenged by those who were less inclined to see life as so simply argued—men like Zerubbabel, and the Sages. For Nahum the Visionary his personal testimony and insights present the first challenge to the issue of prophetic identity. In the case of Habakkuk and Malachi, it is evident how foreign influence, due to extended residence in Babylonia and accommodation to Persian interests, led to a broader perspective on one's identity and beliefs. The loss of a royal tradition and a democratization of kingship was replaced by a more secular administration, and resulted in a more diversified leadership.

The three books, Nahum, Habakkuk and Malachi, are each identified as a *Massa'*—normally translated as 'Oracle'—as are two chapters of Zechariah, 9.1 and 12.1. This same descriptor is applied to speeches directed against foreign nations in Isa. 13.1; 15.1 and 17.1, as well as to Wisdom materials in Prov. 30.1 and 31.1. One of our tasks in this commentary is to seek a definition of the *Massa'* term that matches its use, with the suggestion that it not only indicates a new emerging literary trope, but along with that, it demonstrates a shift in the very nature of 'prophecy' as it merges with the teaching mission of the Sage.

On Translating and Interpreting Biblical Texts

Reading these three books closely has raised again for this reader some interesting practical questions that during years spent as a UBS Translation Consultant were always front of mind. A little like the chicken-and-egg conundrum, the relationship between a translator's theological starting point or ideology and the translation arrived at is always fraught. Which is prior—the theological and cultural assumptions of the translator, or the translation decided upon that then determines or influences the interpretation adopted? The specific term chosen to include in the translation, especially when the Hebrew noun or verb is multivalent, is not always an objective decision but one influenced by other factors such as the translator's personal preference, the potential for an audience to reject one's translation if a reader's favourite word is not used—think of the great debate over the use of 'young woman' in lieu of KJV's 'virgin' in Isa. 7.14—along with socio-cultural or nationalistic pressures, such as deciding in Song 1.5 whether the girl is 'black and beautiful' or 'black but beautiful'. (The *waw* that joins the two adjectives here can have either function, but which rendering of this tiny particle should be used becomes a serious matter for the interpreter and the audience.) Whatever term is chosen by the translator, it becomes one marker in the task of interpreting the text, and one that may have undue influence on the interpretation of the book overall. Assuming that the three books to be considered here represent the words of traditional prophets concerned about the future will influence how some of the verbs are rendered in translation and shape the readers' general approach to their interpretation.

The adage, '*What one says is not necessarily what one means*', needs to be recognized as a cornerstone of much social interaction. Rhetorical Questions and Hyperbole are just some elements in the communication toolbox. So much of spoken and written communication depends on being sensitive to what is intended in a form of words, in order to be able to correctly 'read' or 'hear' what is being communicated. Misunderstandings are always possible, and across the English-speaking world, for example, are very common when other national traits enter the communication, especially when using comedy and irony—they rarely translate across the Atlantic! Appreciating language within its cultural setting is essential to understanding the message that is being sent. Reading figurative or metaphorical language as literally so, being unaware of a localized idiomatic expression, or questioning the honesty in the highly formalized wording required in some honourific languages that sound elitist, will inevitably lead to unusual and inappropriate conclusions about what a speaker/writer intends. A translator or participant in a conversation must recognize, then interpret, what is meant, often despite the specific words that are used to convey that meaning.

Unfortunately, many readers and commentators on the text of Scripture seem to be able to read only the surface words and read them as literal truths or as actual fact. Such a reading, perhaps based on a theological notion regarding the words of Scripture, fails to 'hear' what is being said or written. Appreciating that every language and culture has its way of using the range of its rhetorical features to convey its message, interpreters of the ancient OT text must take great care to avoid literal readings and translations, along with attendant interpretations, when hyperbole, metaphor and figurative language are clearly involved.

These are some of the issues that have engaged this writer now that Israel's oral traditions were put into written form in the traditional Hebrew language while the community in general had moved to the new *lingua franca* of Aramaic. As a result, many Judaeans in the late exilic and postexilic periods did not have access to materials in Hebrew, whether oral or written. There will always remain the question as to how widespread was knowledge of, and access to, this written material within the community. With all materials hand-written, both the number of copies available and their distribution was severely limited; few could read and write and so most were dependent on hearing the stories, and where available, on having documents read to them. Modern readers who begin with a complete, re-ordered, sixty-six book canon called a Bible can easily make assumptions about these ancient materials that are very far from the reality faced by those for whom it was a living experience. The reading being offered here aims to read and understand these three small 'books' in a manner that acknowledges their ancient cultural, linguistic and religious context.

Acknowledgments

I am deeply grateful to Sheffield Phoenix Press for another opportunity to contribute to the Readings series. This volume is offered in the sincere hope that readers will find it a challenging, yet fruitful, perspective on what these three books can offer our understanding of the period without having to wade through some of the distracting minutiae found in many commentaries.

I would also wish to acknowledge with gratitude my many former colleagues in the United Bible Societies' Translation Programme for insights, friendships, fun and great collegiality.

Graham Ogden
Ballarat, Vic., Australia
September 2022

ABBREVIATIONS

AB	Anchor Bible
ANE	Ancient Near East
BDB	F. Brown S.R. Driver, and C. Briggs, *A Hebrew and English Lexicon of the Old Testament* (Oxford: Clarendon Press, 1907, repr. 1957)
BHS	*Biblia Hebraica Stuttgartensia* (ed. K. Elliger and W. Rudolph; Stuttgart: Deutsche Bibelstiftung, 1968–77)
BT	*Bible Translator*
DH	Deuteronomic History
IB	*The Interpreter's Bible*
ITC	International Theological Commentary
JBL	*Journal of Biblical Literature*
KJV	King James Version
LXX	Septuagint
MT	Masoretic Text
NCBC	New Century Bible Commentary
NICOT	New International Commentary on the Old Testament
NRSV	New Revised Standard Version
NT	New Testament
OT	Old Testament
OTE	*Old Testament Essays*
TDOT	*Theological Dictionary of the Old Testament* (ed. G. Botterweck, H. Ringgren and H.-J. Fabry; trans. D. Green *et al.*; Grand Rapids, MI: Eerdmans, 1974–98)
WBC	Word Biblical Commentary

NAHUM: A COMMENTARY

Introduction

The book of Nahum is the seventh book in the Hebrew Bible's *Scroll of the Twelve*, otherwise known as the Minor Prophets. The Superscription or Title identifies it as a '*Massa*' of Nineveh', normally translated as 'An oracle concerning Nineveh'. It is then subtitled, 'the Book of the Vision of Nahum of Elkosh', an introduction to an OT text unlike most others included in the Scroll; it makes no reference to a specific occasion upon which Nahum received a vision, nor circumstances surrounding it. It makes no reference to a regnal period in Israel, nor to the claim that it is a 'word of the Lord' that came to Nahum. It is unique in that it is described as a 'book' (Heb. *sepher*), when it contains only 48 verses now copied onto the middle of the Scroll. Even more important to note is that Nahum is never identified as a Prophet (Heb. *nabi'*). There is much about Nahum the book that makes it stand out for special attention, not least of which is to seek a reason for its inclusion in the so-called Minor Prophets scroll rather than in some other part of the collection.

Nahum the book presents itself as the report of a vision that one man had for the people of Judah regarding the city of Nineveh and the Assyrians more generally. Nahum was an individual with a vision for his people over against the dominant and fearsome power of the Assyrian Empire.

The Book of Nahum in its current form witnesses to the relationship between Israelites and Assyrians in the period of Assyria's late revival that began under Adad-Nirari III (810–783 BCE). His son Tiglath-Pileser III (747–727) led the last great stage of Assyrian domination, expanding territory into Syria, Phoenicia and southern Palestine as far as Gaza. Once established, Tiglath-Pileser III set about dispersing captured peoples throughout the Empire. His successor, Shalmaneser V (726–722 BCE) laid siege to Samaria, the northern Israelite capital that was captured in 721 BCE by Sargon II (722–705), deporting large numbers of the population, and settling non-Israelite tribal peoples in their place. Sargon built a new capital north of Nineveh, but it was soon abandoned. However, the following king, Sennacherib (704–681 BCE) re-established Nineveh as the capital, bridging the Tigris river, built an elaborate system of canals to water the city and its extensive gardens. Despite these achievements he was brutally murdered by his sons. Esarhaddon (680–669) was followed by Assurbanipal (668–627) who waged successful battles against Egypt, but constant rebellion in the Babylonian province weakened the vast Empire and led finally to the demise of both Nineveh and Assur in around 612 BCE. It is against this background that the prophet Nahum is said to have spoken of Nineveh and of Assyria's power.

Contents and Structure

1.1	Title
1.2-6	YHWH's character
1.7-11	Plot against YHWH?
1.12-15 (2.1)	Relief for Judah
2.2-9	Assyria Under Threat
	2.10 central verse
2.11-13	Against Assyria
3.1-7	Woe to Nineveh
3.8-13	Nineveh Will be Devastated
3.14-19	Assyria's End

The above outline is based on literary or rhetorical criteria that are specific to each section of text (see more below). The book as a whole is marked by abrupt changes of subject, pronoun references are vague, there are many changes of imagery and some grammatical oddities suggesting that the work is a composite one, put together using terse poetic language. The suggestion that 1.2-8 is part of an acrostic has been widely accepted, though that thesis is here disputed as it involves a high degree of imagination, emendation and flexibility of definition, in contrast to the strictly formal acrostics such as Psalm 119.

One structural feature that is recognized here is the insertion of the numerically central verse, 2.10 (11)—see also Obadiah v. 11, and Joel 2.17.

Massa'—an Oracle?

Each of the three books in this commentary is classified as *massa'*, usually rendered as 'Oracle'.

Apart from its use as a personal name (Gen. 25.14), the Hebrew nominal form *massa'*, has traditionally been thought to derive from the root *ns'*, 'lift up'. It is found a number of times in the OT narrative with a basic contextual meaning of 'burden' (e.g., Isa. 22.25). This sense has been applied traditionally to all OT examples of *massa'*, and in the case of the prophetic literature has led to interpreting it as a 'burden' both to the prophet who now has to deliver hard words to his community, as well as being a burden that is imposed on the community. It is a conclusion that requires investigation.

The *massa'* term occurs in titles of what are identified in standard Bible translations as 'oracles' approximately twenty times in the OT—Isa. 13.1; 14.28; 15.1; 17.1; 19.1; 21.1, 11,13; 22.1; 23.1; 30.6; Lam. 2.4; Ezek. 12.10; 24.25; Nah. 1.1; Hab. 1.1; Zech. 9.1; 12.1; Mal. 1.1. The majority of these relate to pronouncements directed against foreign nations in prophetic books. In addition to these, the term also describes collected wisdom sayings such as in Prov. 30.1-33 and 31.1-31. In other words, they are pointing to a distinctive category among the written forms emerging in the exilic-postexilic world. Whether the notion of 'burden' is appropriate in these specific contexts is the question that needs to be answered. I note that Muller (TDOT article, p. 23) identifies it as distinct from the 'burden' concept, but nevertheless links it still with the root 'lift up/raise'—'a style of speech for which "the voice is raised."' Really?

Linking *massa'* as 'burden' in narrative contexts with its use in book titles or 'oracle' collections raises a red flag when it comes to words directed at foreign nations because there is no sense of the words being a 'burden' to either the prophet or to Israel—hearing that God is going to deal with the enemies is good news; it is something to celebrate, certainly not a burden to be borne by either party. Its use in Prov. 30.1 and 31.1 adds another level of challenge, especially as these are records of non-Israelite personalities and their wise sayings, including numerical proverbs and an acrostic singing the praises of 'a capable wife', that offer advice on practical living. Given the wide variety of literary forms in those chapters prefaced by the *massa'* title, rhetorical forms that are unique to the *massa'* cannot be claimed. So, seeking to define *Massa'* in terms of literary forms is not possible.

One of the first linguistic principles that applies to any translation attempt is that *Context determines meaning, not Etymology*. This principle must be applied to the rendering of a term in every specific context, rather than beginning with one assumed rendering that is then applied in each and every occasion it is found. Each new context challenges the rendering applied elsewhere. If the same term can be applied in a variety of contexts, then its meaning is broad rather than narrow, making its rendering flexible and entirely dependent upon its immediate context.

Furthermore, what appear to be *identical* terms in a language can hide from the non-native speaker what may well be totally different semantic values, each having a different history, with each meaning and connotation readily identified only by native speakers of the language. Foreign students of a language and culture, no matter how proficient, may never enter emotionally or culturally into that other world to the extent that they respond to its ideas as would a native speaker. So, when the noun *massa'* appears as a single-term unadorned descriptor of a written text, I would argue that it is actually a *homograph*—the same spelled or written form but bearing a very different meaning—similar to English homographs like 'to lie' and 'to lie', or 'bear' and 'bear'; *massa'* in this specific literary setting and context has its own unique reference, and does not carry the sense of *massa'* when used in a narrative context. I suggest that it marks an independent category of speech, and as its use in late so-called 'prophetic' works such as Nahum and Habakkuk and wisdom texts like Prov. 30.1 and especially 31.1 indicate, it refers to material that is more general. By prefixing this term to his report, an Editor identifies the book's nature and purpose as having a didactic function.

The word 'oracle' that NRSV uses to render *massa'* in Proverbs 30 and 31 and elsewhere is generic, so some alternative term needs to be found to best represent this literary form. A possible translation is 'Anthology'. See further in 'A Final Note on Translation and Interpretation'.

Authorship

The Title that has been given the book prioritizes the object of the message of this *massa'*, namely the city of Nineveh, representing the Assyrian Empire. That it is a 'book of a vision' of one man hints at a direct connection with Nahum, but it does not imply that he was its author. In the context of the times where literacy rates were so low, it is almost certain that this book is the result of an Editor reporting on what Nahum's message to Judah was. Nahum would have delivered his message orally, and done so frequently in a variety of contexts, but what we read today is a 'frozen' written report of what he is recalled as having said. These fragments have come down to us in a series of highly poetic but short speeches, and each may well reflect an original oral presentation. It is important for modern readers to recognize that in an oral society, various versions of an address would be known and vividly recalled within the community as living and dynamic lessons that circulated freely until a literate editor fixed them in one now-concrete form. Authorship in the modern sense cannot be applied to so many of the ancient materials that remain; the work here is more collaborative with the final collated form determined by the Editor.

Nahum—Who or What Was He?

It has been traditional to regard Nahum as a true representative of Israel's prophetic movement. However, when all the evidence is considered, there is no justification from doing so, and to persist in this prophetic identity demonstrates a lack of attention to the TEXT. Nowhere is Nahum described as a prophet, which surely must be a clue that carries weight. The traditional view also ignores the fact that there were figures other than prophets in Judaean society who had opinions and insights that were highly valued, with perhaps subtle, but nevertheless important, differences from those of a prophet. Nahum was one such individual.

Given the fact that the Editor has clearly, and one might say, deliberately declined to ascribe to Nahum the title and role of 'Prophet', and that the literary and rhetorical evidence throughout the book shows no sign, apart for 3.1-7, that Nahum had any 'prophetic' leanings, it is important at the outset to honour those facts and affirm that Nahum never was a prophet. What then was he? The Editor identifies him, in the Title he provides, as a 'Visionary'. A Visionary is not a prophet, but one who has radical ideas and keen insight based upon considered personal experience and ideals.

There are several important clues as to the Nahum's role and identity:

1. The first clue is in the title of the book as a *massa'*. The *massa'* is a type of literary work that stands somewhere between a prophetic work and a Wisdom collection—see Prov. 30.1; 31.1—as an anthology or collection of materials that have Instruction as one major focus. It is also of a more general nature and should not be read as predictive or as assured promises about divine intervention in human and international affairs. See on *Massa'* above.
2. The second clue is the word 'vision' (Heb. *chazon*), a word not confined to the prophetic role as some have assumed. Nahum's 'vision' was what he saw had happened, and what was threatening on the regional political scene from Egypt to Assyria.
3. A third clue is the almost complete lack of prophetic rhetoric such as the key phrase '*word of the Lord*' that might ascribe his words to a divine source. Yes, he quotes what YHWH is alleged to have said, but see the notes below at 1.12; 2.14 and 3.5. Nahum's words derive from his own vision, his personal assessment of the situation facing Judah at the time.
4. A fourth clue is that there is an absence of what some want to call 'prophetic perfects' from Nahum's language use. He does use the perfective mode of verbs in describing the character of the God he

acknowledges, and the situation with the Assyrians, but does not use it in a predictive sense. Moreover, while his use of Hebrew verbs is dominated by the imperfective verb forms, in those few passages that seem to look forward, they are what are called *Jussives* and *cohortatives* that express a strong hope or longing—like English, 'May such and such happen (to you…)', 'Would that…' Or in the case of first-person speech, 'I would that…happen…'—they mark future hoped-for possibilities for they are <u>volitional</u>. (The core issue of the Hebrew verbal system and the difference between *qatal* and *w'qtal* and *yiqtol* and *wayyiqtol* forms remains unresolved).

In other words, despite the book being included in the Scroll of the Twelve, it is not 'prophetic' in the more narrow, generalized sense; the book is presented as an expression of Nahum's personal hope and longing. This should not be surprising, but it may go against some readers' understanding of a prophet as one who spoke only what the Lord told him to speak. That view is a gross misrepresentation—even the traditionally recognized prophets had a mind of their own and spoke personally about what irritated or moved them; they needed no divine prodding before opening their mouths on many issues that they found unacceptable in Israelite society. And they also often got it wrong, especially when resorting to hyperbole!

Nahum, if that was his name, is related to the Hebrew root meaning 'compassion' or 'comfort', an *ironic* name in that Nahum had no compassion for the Ninevites (see 3.7), and is in marked contrast to the so-called prophet, or anti-prophet, Jonah (see Jon. 4.1-3, 9-11).

Nahum was a visionary who saw the world of his day from inside his faith in YHWH the national God. The book is a report of his pronouncements in Judah in the late seventh century BCE.

Date

Unlike most prophetic books, Nahum's Editor cites no date in his opening Title, nor any connection to a moment or personality in the Israelite story.

The text of the report provides us with very few clues allowing us to propose a date for the material in Nahum other than it referring to Nineveh and Assyria during its domination of the region. No personal names are cited, but the Empire clearly had earned already a reputation as a fearsome fighting force, yet to be challenged, so it paints a picture of Assyria at the height of its powers. While Judah is mentioned specifically (1.15), and Israel in 2.2 has been 'ravaged', it would appear that we are looking at a date after 721 BCE and the fall of the northern kingdom of Israel. These are the only references the book makes to any Israelite or Judaean context. Some have noted the reference to the fall of the Egyptian city of Thebes in 3.8-10, generally dated as 663 BCE which, with the final overthrow of Nineveh and its capture by the Persians and Medes in 612 BCE, means that Nahum's message must be dated closer to the latter date than earlier. Thus, a possible date for the edited report on Nahum can be placed in the second half of the seventh century BCE. This makes it roughly contemporary with Jeremiah, predating Obadiah, Haggai and Zechariah.

If the final verse in the opening chapter of the report in 1.15 (2.1) is accepted as valid, it concludes with a clear statement that whatever the crisis with the Assyrians, it has now passed, for the promise is that *'never again shall the wicked invade you; they are utterly cut off'*. What it indicates is that the report of Nahum's message, whether the hope was realized or not, is to be dated at a point when no further harassment was to be expected from their enemy, i.e., after Assyria had been defeated in 612 BCE.

Literary Features

Nahum is notable for what features aren't used rather than what features are used!

1. First to note is the ascription in 1.1 of the work as a *massa'*, a literary form particularly associated with oracles against foreign powers, as here, that also shares features with Wisdom collections, as in Proverbs 30 and 31.
2. What is missing is the phrase 'word of the Lord' (Heb. *d'bar-yhwh*) as a description of the contents, nor is the phrase 'the word of the Lord came to…' (Heb. *d'bar-yhwh hayah 'el*) used with respect of Nahum. Given these facts, there is no mention as to how Nahum's 'vision' came, meaning that the text implies its was Nahum's own vision, not something from an external source.
3. Furthermore, typical prophetic literary forms such as *'Thus says the Lord…, says the Lord'*, are rarely found; the opening form *'Thus says the Lord…'* is used only once in 1.12, and there are just two occasions when the report uses the concluding form *'…says the Lord'* (Heb. *n'um YHWH*) even though not functioning as a concluding device.
4. The Editor never uses the noun 'prophet' to refer to Nahum, unlike the Editor of Haggai.

5. The literary and rhetorical features of the report make plain that this is not a prophetic book, and as a result there is an impact on the <u>nature of the verb-forms</u> used—they are *volitionals*. Imperfective verbs are not God's 'promises' but express Nahum's hopes and longings, to be rendered as 'I would that…', and 'May he/ they…', NOT as 'I/he/they will…' (See my translation throughout)
6. Nahum is also described with the rare title of 'a book', as the book 'of a vision', which is even more tantalizing when the 51 verses contain no reference to anything of a strictly optical nature. Hence, we see Nahum as one who had a vision for his people and their situation, with 'vision' as a more over-arching concept. Perhaps it is for this reason that the material tends to be expressed in very <u>general terms</u> and with no specific reference to Israel's past or present, to its history, whether in event or personality.
7. The book is essentially made up of <u>smaller poetic pieces</u> each with its own rhetorical features—1.1, 2-6, 7-11, 12-15; 2.1-9, 10-13; 3.1-7, 8-9, 10-15, 16-19—with minimal narrative. It is like an impressionist painting with short brush strokes combining to present an artist's personal insight, full of feeling, a vision of and for his world.
8. <u>High level language, complex ideas</u> expressed in short, terse word combinations and a wide vocabulary range are featured. This work is a wonderful poetic vision of a man driven by his image of his God and his concern for his community under threat of invasion.
9. The <u>numerically central verse</u> in the book, namely 2.10 (11), is evidence of the Editor's role in structuring his report.
10. Perhaps the element in Nahum that causes readers most frustration from the literary point of view is that its <u>use of pronouns</u> is confusing. This issue appears first in 1.9a when 'you' are charged with plotting against God. While it is clear that 'you' (pl.) refers to those who are adversaries of the Lord, whether it includes Assyria, Israel, or humanity in general is an open question. In 1.10a 'they' appears to refer back to the adversaries and the note about one having gone out from 'you' assumes that it is one of those adversaries. In 1.12a there are references to 'they' and one may assume that it is the Assyrians, then spoken of as 'his' in 1.13, with a following reference to 'you' that one infers is Israel. 'She' in 3.10 refers back to the city of Thebes in 1.8. It is possible for the most part to guess as to whom the pronouns refer, but the Editor could have made each clearer, something that almost certainly would not have been necessary in the oral context in which each saying or speech originated.

11. Other rhetorical features such as <u>assonance and alliteration</u>, as in 1.2, 6, 10, and *b*, *q*, *q*, and *ts* in 2.3, <u>repeated verbs</u> as in 1.2, 8-9, wide use of <u>similes</u>, the use of *lo'... 'odh* patterns in 1.12-15; 2.13, negative phrases using *'ayin* throughout, especially *'ayn qetseh* ('no end')—with its *double-entendre* in 2.9 [10]), and the image of fire as 'devouring', will all be dealt with in the exegetical notes.
12. In 1.8-9 there is a <u>chiastic structure</u> that is important to identify and note (see exegesis below).
13. The nature of the material in the first two chapters is <u>personal testimony</u>, Nahum's reported understanding of God's nature and of the divine intention, along with vivid descriptions of foreign aggression that echo similar descriptions in Joel and Habakkuk, for example.
14. An intriguing feature of the editing of this book is the decision to leave any <u>reference to Nineveh to the end of relevant sections</u>. The first half of the book, 1.2–2.10, delays mention of the name of the one being denounced to the closing note in 2.8-9; this is the first time that 'Nineveh' is identified apart from the initial title that is an Editor's late addition (1.1). Similarly, in the Woe-oracle, it is not until the final verse, 3.7, that Nineveh is again mentioned. Furthermore, 'Assyria' is a name that does not appear at all until the final statement in 3.18-19 to conclude the material in 3.8-19. Whether this <u>delay-feature</u> is purely coincidental, or deliberate, is something to ponder, but as a distinctive aspect of the book as a whole, one must attribute it to the Editor's deliberate plan.
15. In terms of the order of books within the Scroll of the Twelve, Nahum follows Micah, and an <u>editorial link between Micah and Nah. 1.4</u> can be seen in the mention of Bashan (and Gilead) in Mic. 7.14. In the LXX, the order differs, with Nahum following Jonah, no doubt based on similarity of subject.
16. Since the literary evidence argues against any prophetic connection for Nahum, there remains a question as to why the report was included in the Scroll of the Twelve rather than being placed elsewhere.

Assyria in the Old Testament

Nahum represents one of several OT references to the Assyrians, not all of which reflect the same attitude towards Assyria; in fact, views with respect to Assyria differ considerably.

Beginning with Isaiah in the eighth century, Assyria is clearly an enemy that threatens Israel, likened to a bee in Isa. 7.18, and a despoiler of Samaria in Isa. 8.4. However, Assyria was not simply the enemy—in YHWH's hand it became a tool for the punishment of God's own people, the 'rod of God's anger' towards Jerusalem (Isa. 10.5). A similar attitude is found in Ezekiel—in 23.5, 11.

The Deuteronomistic History expressed antipathy towards the arrogant Assyrians who had captured the fortified cities of Judah (2 Kgs 18.13–19.36). Such a view is only to be expected of a Deuteronomic theology and worldview in which Israel was God's chosen one—Assyria was one of the many 'unchosen'.

Hosea mocks Ephraim or the northern kingdom as a 'wild ass' for seeking an alliance with Assyria (Hos. 8.8-9). Zephaniah 2.13-15 threatens desolation and humiliation on Assyria, as does Zech. 10.11.

On the other hand, Jonah the anti-prophet who refuses to accept the call to speak to Nineveh, finally relents when confronted by the God whose compassion knows no such nationalistic limitations, a compassion that embraces even Nineveh's animals (Jon. 4.9-11). The story of Jonah is best read as a tract against the narrow nationalistic views of the Deuteronomic cohort and as opposing the views expressed by Nahum.

Nineveh the City

One of the world's oldest known cities, and dating from the seventh millennium BCE, Nineveh sat at the confluence of the Tigris and Khosr rivers in what is today northern Iraq. Israel's oral tradition has its founder as Nimrod, a grandson of Noah, according to the genealogy in Gen. 10.11. Though archaeologists have explored the site since the mid-nineteenth century, not a great deal of information is available about its early occupation, and modern excavation is now hindered by its having become a religious shrine.

Nineveh became the capital of the Assyrian Empire under Sennacherib (704–681) who established a marvelous palace, its walls decorated with carved relief work that illustrated his victory over Lachish. It boasted of gardens and orchards, 80 km. of irrigation that brought water from the mountains to the city. He fortified it with double walls. Sennacherib was murdered by his sons in 681 but the dynasty continued to develop the city. Its palace contained a large library of cuneiform tablets, including one account of the Gilgamesh epic, the Babylonian Flood story.

Nineveh was captured and sacked by the combined forces of the Babylonians and Medes in 612 BCE, marking the end of the Assyrian Empire.

Foreign Nation Oracles

Israel's prophetic canon contains a number of oracles directed against foreign nations: Isaiah 13–23; Ezekiel 25–32; Amos 1–2 are the most well-known collections. Editors of each of these books have gathered into a single collection the oracles attributed to the prophet concerned as part of their editing process. The specific details as to an individual oracle's actual location and its time-setting in each prophetic mission is not always now identifiable. There are, however, several facts observable:

A. The OT oracles that identify their target as Israel's foreign enemies or challengers are, of course, not going to be heard by those nations unless the prophets traveled across borders to deliver their threats personally, a rather risky undertaking. Oral delivery being the form of communication, there is little evidence that any of Israel's prophets actually traveled to foreign lands for the purpose of delivering their message directly to the enemy. Of course, the one notable exception is in the delightful tale of the anti-prophet Jonah who, according to the narrative, did go to Nineveh, but his five-word threat (Jon. 3.4) was then overshadowed by the real preacher of the day, namely the 'king of Nineveh' who called for the people and their animals to repent.

B. The Foreign Nation oracles' intended audience was always Israel itself or Judah, never the foreigner, meaning that, whatever the content, the message's aim was to bring comfort or assurance to God's people, claiming that the enemy would be dealt with, that God's action involving that foreign nation was for Israel's ultimate benefit. To oppose Israel/Judah was to oppose its God, YHWH, so God must act to defend his name. Obviously, no foreign nation would take such a message as a serious threat to itself, even if somehow it was to hear of it. But then there is the question of whether a prophet's message was taken seriously by anyone, even Judaeans, as there is plenty of evidence that prophets were generally without respect—see Jer. 7.21-28; 11.18-20; 18.18—and their messages disregarded within Israel. Was Nahum's message widely known and appreciated? At least it has been preserved by an interested party!

C. The rhetoric used in Foreign Nation oracles is usually hyperbole, with promises of the complete devastation of the enemy and an assured safe future for God's people, as here in Nah. 1.15, whether actually realised or not. In other words, although levelled against Nineveh and the Assyrians, the book of Nahum is actually intended as a message of encouragement for Judah in this moment of crisis.

Nahum's Theological Ideas

It is very difficult to miss Nahum's opening statement and what he asserts of his God YHWH. God, in Nahum's view, is a powerful avenger of any who would oppose; all who oppose are 'enemies'. It is a particularly strong, and many would say, unacceptable, characterization of God. There is nothing in the opening statement of a loving and compassionate God until 1.7 where another and balancing aspect of the divine one is presented, namely the goodness of the Lord, a place of calm and protection despite the clamour of the world around. However, that goodness is, for Nahum, reserved for God's people, a rather nationalistic sentiment.

It is also in the opening statement 1.2a that the three references to God appear—*'el*, *YHWH* and *ba'al*. This is an important feature of the book's theological perspective for it first acknowledges the ancient and general Semitic term *'el*, the chief God of the divine pantheon that underpins Israel's pre-Mosaic religion—the epithets used of God in the most ancient traditions are names such as El-shaddai, El-elyon, El-elohe-yisrael, and El-berith. Then there is the 'name' revealed to Moses at Sinai, i.e., YHWH or Yahweh, the covenanting God. The third name used is the noun *ba'al*, literally 'master/lord', but also the name of the Canaanite god, Baal. It is tempting to speculate about the deliberate use of all three names that span the ages of Israelite religion, but that might prove to be too subjective. However, it is also to be noted that the use of 'Lord of hosts' in 3.5 does fit with the preferred title found in many of the late prophetic works—see Haggai, Zechariah, and Malachi.

For Nahum, the divine power is also portrayed poetically in God's relationship with the natural world—God is carried on wind and storm, his voice dries rivers and seas, mountains wither and rocks explode. God also overthrows the armies of his and his people's enemies—he is 'against' the armies of the world who oppose his people. YHWH is the God with sovereign power over the nations; he will humiliate those who contend against him, so the overall perspective is outward-looking rather than inward.

In 1.3 there are words that echo those found also in Exod. 34.6 and the covenant promise that is rooted in the Exodus tradition, rather than that of Deuteronomy.

Of great significance is the fact that Nahum does not speak of Sin or Rebellion, as traditional prophets did—see Isa. 1.2-4; the word 'Sin' (Heb. *chatah*) is never used here, nor does Nahum seek to explain the current crisis facing Judah as divine punishment—his focus is upon the 'adversaries' and the 'enemy'. Judah is not depicted as a failing and sinful state.

The numerically central verse of the collection is 2.10 (11) and it simply speaks of the current political situation as 'devastation, desolation', and deep fear in face of Assyrian aggression.

Reading Strategy

This reading aims to set the book in its literary, historical and cultural context, to the extent that those settings can be established. It approaches the book as the work of an Editor(s) who has collated numerous elements of Nahum's message that circulated orally within the Israelite community of the late seventh century BCE. It assumes that the message in its current 'frozen' form is the distillation of a number of those oral messages that give witness to the concerns and hopes of the man Nahum as his community faced the threat from the great military might of the Assyrian Empire.

Since Nahum the book does not exhibit the most basic of literary forms associated with prophetic literature, it will not be read as 'prophetic'; it is to be read as a report of the personal vision of the man Nahum, as the Title designates it. To do otherwise would be to distort its purpose and intent, as well as to project onto its verbal forms a predictive mode rather than a volitional one.

While many in church and synagogue have regarded Nahum as having little value and questioned its inclusion in sacred Scripture because of its alleged presentation of God as vengeful and angry (see chapter 1), this reader admits to the reality of human fear and dread in face of overwhelming foreign power that threatens individual and collective life. There is little to choose between Nahum and Obadiah or Psalm 137 when it comes to expressing a deep-seated fear and wish for revenge when confronting the threat to one's very existence. Nahum, to this reader, offers one very personal response to the situation faced by Judah in the late seventh century BCE (see notes on 1.6 below), as did the later Habakkuk (Hab. 1.3). To deny this reality and wish for some more pious document that depicts God as pure Love and Compassion, is to impose an alien set of values on this text. God as universally compassionate may be the overwhelming message of the book of Jonah (Jon. 4.9-11), but that is an alternative perspective to the one found in Nahum.

The reading being offered here takes the view that the opening section of the book, 1.2-6, is a report of Nahum's personal beliefs, his concept of the character of YHWH. As such, it is a valid view rooted in his personal experience, and it is a view to be placed alongside other views such as the Deuteronomic, in order to present readers with fuller access to the variety of theological perspectives found throughout the OT. One may choose not to agree with Nahum's theology, but it must not be denied him.

As a text from a particular ancient historical, cultural and theological setting, its integrity is to be honoured for what it is. The reading being offered wishes to acknowledge that, and suggests that to read this book through the prism of the New Testament or of any other ideology is inappropriate.

EXEGESIS

1.1 Title

A massa' of Nineveh: the book of Nahum the Elkoshite's Vision

The superscription contains important information about the work that is being presented in written form; it is both a *massa'* and a 'book'. While it has been customary to link the term *massa'* to the noun 'burden', derived from the root *ns'*, 'raise, lift', and found in narrative materials with this sense, this reader takes the view that when used in book titles, it is a *homograph*, that it identifies a particular literary type, one that can be applied to both later prophetic materials and wisdom materials, as in Proverbs 30, 31. It identifies an anthology or analect, a collection of documented speeches from the late exilic and postexilic period.

This superscription provided by the editor is vital as it provides immediate information as to the aim and purpose of the book. Without this information a reader would not know who or what its intention was until reaching 2.9 (10), the first mention of Nineveh. Up to that point the generalized language masks the direction in which the book is moving.

Identifying the collection as a 'book' (Heb. *sepher*) is unique, with some suggesting that the book-form was that in which the material originally appeared, but this would imply that few people had access to Nahum's message, given the very low level of literacy. Public readings of the 'book' would have been possible, but there is no evidence for that.

The book is then said to be a report of the 'vision' (Heb. *chazon*) of Nahum, i.e., everything in the book is a report concerning Nahum as a 'Visionary', his perception of the Ninevites, their deeds, and the fate that he longs to see overtake them. Importantly, Nahum is not identified as a Prophet.

The name *Nahum*, deriving from the root *nchm* that speaks of compassion and comfort (see Isa. 40.1), contrasts sharply with the tone of the opening speech in 1.2-6 about God's power and his vengeful character. On the other hand, the purpose of the book or of the visionary's message, was to bring comfort to its primary audience, Judah, in face of Assyrian aggression.

Nahum is linked with what is assumed to be the town or village of *Elkosh*, a site now unfortunately unidentifiable. This means that we cannot determine whether Nahum was from the northern kingdom of Israel or the southern kingdom, Judah, though it is assumed that his primary audience was those in the south. Nahum was presumably a Judaean addressing his own Judaean community, yet surprisingly perhaps there is no mention of Jerusalem, the Temple, priests or any other readily identifiable Judaean connection, apart from 1.15 and the vague mention of 'festivals'.

1.2-6 The Character of YHWH

> 2. A God jealous and avenging is YHWH, avenging is YHWH and master of anger; avenging is YHWH towards his adversaries, and one who rages against his enemies.
>
> 3. YHWH is slow to anger but great in power, in no way will YHWH acquit. His way is in the whirlwind, and storm and the clouds are the dust of his feet.
>
> 4. He rebukes the sea (Yam) and so dries it up, and all the rivers he makes dry, Bashan and Carmel have become weak and the buds of Lebanon wither.
>
> 5. The mountains quake afore him and the heights melt, the land/earth rises up before him, the world and everything living in it.
>
> 6. In face of his indignation who can stand? Who can arise in the heat of his anger? His anger is poured out like fire, and by him the rocks are smashed.

It has been common to suggest that these opening verses are an abbreviated or 'broken' acrostic, claiming the initial letter of successive vv. 1-8 to be consecutive letters of the Hebrew alphabet—from *aleph* to *kaph*. There is little question that what we have in this final written form is not an acrostic as defined, and it will become clear that rhetorical elements in the text will show that it never was. Furthermore, if it had been an acrostic, it must have included v. 8, which in this reading is not possible given that the rhetorical feature of *kalah 'asah*, repeated in v. 8b and v. 9, belong in the chiasm of 1.7-11 (see below re. v. 8). What purpose an acrostic might have served as an introduction to the book is never clearly argued, other than it being a neat or clever poetic device. An acrostic could have been an *aide-memoire* in an original oral context, but in this written text it does not appear.

Exegesis

The section is marked by a number of rhetorical features:

a. Three distinct 'names' for God—*'el, yhwh, ba'al*—in v. 2.
b. Assonance and repetition in v. 2—the participles *qn'*, *nqm* (3×), *ntr*,—and Niphal verbs *ntk, ntts* (v. 6b), together with the phrase *za'mo mi ya'ᵃmod* in v. 6a.
c. God in Nature—wind, cloud, sea, river, mountains, hills, earth, the world.
d. Divine anger (*chemah*) is an inclusion (v. 2a, 6b) defining the unit.
e. Geographical references to Bashan, Carmel and Lebanon (v. 4b).

The poem that is 1.2-6 has within it identifiable smaller units—1.2-3a focus on divine vengefulness; 1.3b-5 uses natural phenomena to depict the divine presence; 1.6 uses two rhetorical questions to emphasize God's irresistible power.

These all combine to build the picture of a powerful divine being whose main characteristic is anger and revenge, creating fear in all who might oppose Israel. It is a nationalistic statement brimming with Israelite confidence in their creator God. As a personal testimony it gives insight into the inner workings of Nahum's mind and that of many in his community.

1.2-3a As noted above, this verse contains a very special reference to God in that it uses three separate terms each of which carries significant theological weight. The first is *'el*, a general Semitic word for the god who was head of the divine pantheon, and a name that usually required epithets to fill out the sense or quality attributed. According to a note such as Exod. 6.3, the pre-Mosaic community, or Abraham and his descendants, knew of God as *'el-shaddai*, a name or concept that was enhanced once they were introduced to YHWH—or more accurately *'ehyeh-asher-ehyeh'*—at Sinai. Hence Israel's covenant God, YHWH, superceded the understanding of the more general *'el*. The notion of 'lordship' lies with the noun *ba'al*, a generic term for one who is master, but in Canaan and Canaanite religion, it was the name or title of the main Canaanite god, Baal. Language around this name was adopted in descriptions of Yahweh once the Israelites were resident in the Canaan context. It seems reasonable to think that the Editor of this text has carefully chosen to present God in this three-fold manner, though a modern reader may not fully appreciate what the intention might have been.

The statement refers initially to God as 'jealous' (Heb. *qanno'*), an adjective that is argued as being distinct from 'jealous' in the human context, lacking the negative connotations. It is then described as a desire on God's part that his covenant people owe sole allegiance to him, which in turn means that God will jealously guard the exclusive relationship Israel believed he has entered with it (see Num. 25.11; Deut. 6.15). It is an important concept in Israel's self-understanding, its view of itself. This characteristic is followed by three uses of the participle *noqed*, to refer to the divine one as an 'avenger/taking vengeance' on his, and Israel's, enemies or adversaries. The description further speaks of God's 'anger' (Heb. *chemah*). This latter term then serves as an inclusion for the section 1.2-6. It is an inescapable fact that the picture built up here is of Nahum's God as one who 'rages' against any who oppose him or his people. Revenge, anger, jealously guarding his people, these define Nahum's concept of the national God. In literary terms, the verse is strengthened by repetition and assonance—*qanno'*, *noqem*, *noqem*, *noqem*, *noter*—all directed against *tsaraw*, 'his adversaries' and *'oy'baw*, 'his enemies'.

There is a slight relenting in v. 3 as Nahum's testimony suggests that the divine anger is shown with due patience, not impulsively—literally, 'long of nostrils/face'—before eventually giving vent to rage. God is also acknowledged as great-of-power. A further characteristic of YHWH is that he will '*in no way clear (those who are guilty)*'. The Hebrew construction here is found in Exod. 34.7 and Num. 14.18 as well, and is a particularly strong expression, literally '*acquit he will not acquit*'. Together with v. 2 it indicates that YHWH will avenge all enemies of his people, but he will do so justly and in a considered manner. The fact that the form occurs elsewhere in the record suggests that it has become part of a learned communal confession that may well have links to a regular religious ritual familiar to Nahum and the Editor.

1.3b-5 With v. 3b the poem turns the testimony to begin a series of nature references as an alternative poetic way of asserting God's sovereignty over the whole of creation.

God's 'way' (Heb. *derek*) is to be seen in whirlwind and storm. The noun 'way' carries both material—a road or path—and metaphorical senses—divine laws, instructions, counsel. Here the metaphorical sense is a reference to natural phenomena as demonstrating or embodying the divine presence; they are signs of God's raw power (v. 3a). The *wind* and *storm*—destructive wind and gale—are both used frequently as agents or indicators of a divine presence (see e.g., Exod. 19.16; Isa. 28.2; Ps. 18.10-15). The *clouds* above are thus the dust raised as the Lord walks or hurries by.

Whether this is simply poetic language, a colourful way of speaking about God, or whether there was a strong cultural belief that these natural phenomena were actual physical signs of God's presence, i.e., a theophany, is an issue that exercises some commentators. However, the use of phrases such as YHWH *'the rider of the clouds'* (Ps. 68.5, 34), as was Baal in Canaanite mythology, suggests that it was more than just poetic language; the natural phenomena themselves seemingly were regarded as unambiguous signs in the heavens of the divine presence, and that it was a shared cultural worldview throughout the ancient Near East.

Verse 4 continues the testimonial using further cultural notions of God as engaged in a battle with *Yam*, the sea god, and *Judge Nahar*, the river, in common with Canaanite mythology. Both sea and river were regarded as in conflict with the creator. In the Canaanite myth, Baal is taken captive by Yam and River, but Baal eventually overcomes both to rise to be king of the gods. That religio-cultural worldview informs the use of the metaphors here. Nahum makes use of the imagery to claim his God as the one who has power over the chaos of creation, the one who brings order by his word (Gen. 1). The divine rebuke of sea and river asserts divine power over both and carries an echo of the Exodus tradition of crossing the Reed Sea.

The second half of v. 4 turns for illustrations to geographical locations, *Bashan*, *Carmel* and *Lebanon* (see also Isa. 33.9; Mic. 7.14) and draws attention to the change by repeating the unusual Hebrew verb *'umlal*, 'it withers', at the beginning and end of the line. Bashan was a fertile region in northern Jordan, east of the Sea of Galilee, and southwest of Damascus, part of what today is called the Golan Heights. It was known for its oak trees apparently (Isa. 2.12-13). Carmel likewise was an elevated area or mountain range extending from Esdraelon to the Mediterranean coast, north of the Shephelah and Philistine territory to its south. It too was a fertile area as the name Carmel, or 'orchard', indicates. The third location was Lebanon, presumably also a reference to the mountain range that runs parallel to the coast, west of Damascus, and famous for its cedar trees. Nahum asserts divine control over these well-known fertile regions and their products, YHWH being accredited as the one who can or does bring disaster to the vegetation for which each was famous.

In v. 5 mountains and hills are targeted in an allusion to an earthquake and its impact. Mountains shake and hills melt—when YHWH appears these are the ancient landscape forms that result. Similarly, the earth or ground heaves up as tectonic plates move and pressure the rock strata when God arrives—these events take place 'before him' or perhaps better, 'because of him'. The pronominal suffix attached here is probably personal rather than the impersonal 'it'. Yet it is not only the material universe that is jolted and reactive when YHWH appears—it also involves all who live in the region. The 'world' (Heb. *tebel*) usually is a parallel to 'earth' in poetry, and also includes its inhabitants. In a region of the world where earth tremors and quakes are well known, where the ancient mountains regularly shake, and the landscape changes—think of the Jordan rift valley—these natural phenomena are taken as clear signs of the divine in action.

Thus, 1.2-5 overall proclaims YHWH as sovereign over the natural world. In the context of the opening of the report, these verses are a significant statement of what Nahum believed his God to be—an all-powerful presence in the world, alive in the phenomena that were part of human experience in the region.

1.6 The opening section closes with two parallel rhetorical questions that make strong negative statements consequent on the preceding testimony. The first question, '*before his indignation who may stand?*' denies the possibility that any can stand against YHWH when the Lord is indignant (see also Ps. 76.8). The question-form itself is also expressed in an alliteration, *lipne-za'amo mi ya'amod* to heighten its impact. The second question-form, '*who can arise in (against) the heat of his anger?*' also denies the possibility of resisting divine anger. Both questions serve to emphasize human impotence when confronted by the avenging and wrathful YHWH.

That 'wrath', first spoken of in 1.2, now encloses the section rhetorically as God's anger pours forth. Two Hebrew verbs, *ntk* and *ntts*, also provide further emphasis as alliteration. The violence inherent in this imagery is at one with the opening testimony of divine vengeance.

While some commentators are uncomfortable with this picture of God's character and his partisan support for Israel against its enemies, it is important to recognise that the content of these verses presents one individual's dramatic testimony. To Nahum and/or his Editor, this picture or understanding of God is clear. Such an understanding may not fit with the testimony of another; it may be unacceptable and offensive to some readers, but it cannot be denied that this is what the text states, and states unequivocally. These are deeply-held <u>human words about God</u>, not God's word to a human audience. Failure to recognize that Nahum was not a traditional prophet, that he here expresses his personal view of one aspect of the divine character, robs the text of its power and reality.

1.7-11 Plot Against YHWH?

7. YHWH is good, a stronghold in the day of <u>the adversary</u>, and knows those who seek refuge in him.

8. And in the overflowing flood <u>he brings to an end</u> one who <u>rises</u> against him. And his enemies he pursues into darkness

9. *Whatever you <u>plot against</u> YHWH*

> *He will <u>bring (it) to an end</u>. He will <u>not rise</u> a second time, <u>the adversary</u>*

10. Indeed, as thorns they are entangled, like drunkards they are drunk, like dry straw they are completely eaten up.

11. One has gone out from you <u>plotting evil against</u> YHWH, he counsels wickedness.

Nahum's testimony continues, this component balancing divine goodness towards those who seek refuge against the wrath directed at those who would oppose YHWH. The report continues as a general statement, and no specific adversary is mentioned. The problem, if it is real, is that without the superscription readers have to wait until 2.9 (10) to discover that Nahum's concern was divine anger with the adversary, Nineveh.

The section presents as a chiastic pattern revolving around a central rhetorical question in verse 9a, literally *'what would you plot against YHWH?'* It is, like the previous section, general, so embraces all and any who would think to act against God. In v. 8b and v. 9b, bracketing the question-form is a phrase *kalah 'asah*, 'to bring to an end', the fate awaiting any who seek to rise (Heb. *qum*) against this wrathful God. Recognition of the chiastic form is important, as it is key to resolving the issue of the critical *m'qomah* in v. 8 (see below).

The general nature of the statement carries through to the pronouns used in vv. 10-11. Three similes are used to characterize the enemies as 'they' in v. 10, of which one in particular, the 'you' of v. 11, is described as the plotter with evil intent. Nahum's message in this section then is that although YHWH is good to those seeking refuge, YHWH destroys those who would plot against him.

As noted above, many scholars subscribe to the theory that 1.2-10 shows elements of once having been a partial acrostic. This has led to attempts to reconstruct that acrostic, requiring much emendation of the extant text. There is little to be gained from such an attempt that is also highly subjective. This reader finds that the rhetorical elements suggest that 1.2-6 and 7-11 are two related but distinct units, meaning that 1.2-10 is not, nor ever was, a single and cohesive unit within which lies a lost acrostic.

1.7 A simple statement opens the section—*YHWH is good*! The following *le* preposition, usually 'to/for', is difficult syntactically, but has been read as providing the example of divine goodness, namely '*as a fortress*' for the time of adversity, or 'in the day of adversity'. The latter phrase is found elsewhere (see Pss. 50.15; 77.3; Isa. 33.2) where it refers to problematic situations of oppression. Again, we note that the language is general and non-specific.

The verse 7c continues with the verb *yada'*, 'know'; rather than indicating an intellectual knowledge or awareness, the verb can also speak of deeper 'knowing', of close intimacy (as Gen. 4.1), that seems to be the intention here. YHWH knows '*those who seek refuge in him*'.

1.8 The first decision one has to make here is whether to read the initial phrase, '*And in the overflowing flood*', as a second object of the verb '*seek refuge*' in the preceding v. 7, or as related to '*bringing an end*' to something in v. 8b.

The final phrase in v. 7c began with the preposition *be*, 'in, with, by means of', and v. 8a opens with the connecting particle 'and', plus the preposition *be*, suggesting that the reference to the overwhelming flood is a second object of the verb in v. 7c. If the decision is that v. 8a continues v. 7, then we can read it as, '*[he knows those who seek refuge in him] when the flood overflows*'. The alternative is to understand v. 8a as introducing the clause that follows, so the flood or torrent that overtakes one is the condition under which '*he will bring an end*' to *m'qomah*. Arguments can be mounted in support of both positions, and neither is without numerous problems.

Verse 8b begins with the verb phrase, *kalah ya'aseh*, 'an end he will make'—the imperfect verb has frequentative value—with *m'qomah*, that on the surface appears to mean 'her place', as its object. Nothing in the immediate context helps identify 'her place', so we have here an issue created by a feminine pronoun suffix that seems without context. Most commentators accept the MT and interpret 'her place' as a clear reference to Nineveh, as cities are grammatically feminine. However, to adopt such a view is far too hasty an assumption, given that Nineveh has yet to be mentioned in the text. It also fails to recognize the significance of the chiastic structure of the section in which v. 8b *m'qomah* and v. 9b *taqum* are aligned, along with the *kalah 'asah* phrase. The LXX translators obviously had before them a slightly different Hebrew text than the present MT—it reads v. 8b as '*those who rise against him*', not as MT, 'her place'. The LXX evidences a participle derived from the verb *qum*, meaning that the MT of v. 8b should appear as *m'qwmm*, the final *he* (ה) of *m'qomah* written for final *mem* (ם). The two letters are quite similar and can be easily mistaken, especially when copied from an older MS that is worn. The LXX reading is therefore to be preferred as the chiasm requires, so the better translation of v. 8b is '*he brings to an end the one who rises against him*'.

It then offers a thought similar to the final clause—'*and his (YHWH's) enemies he pursues into the darkness*'. In terms of syntax, the final clause places an emphasis on 'his enemies' by setting it ahead of the verb 'pursues'. It is 'his enemies' that YHWH drives into the darkness, thus bringing them to an end. The metaphor of darkness is commonly used to portray something negative, so speaks of distress, of terror and destruction.

The material in this verse continues the general statement about God, with the actual Assyrian context not yet revealed.

1.9 The central element in the chiasm, it speaks of plotting against (Heb. *'el*) the Lord. The initial *mah* can be an interrogative 'what?', or 'why?' (as NRSV), but it can also be the more indefinite 'whatever'. As the core of the chiasm, v. 9a '*whatever you plot against the Lord*', provides a focus for both statements about God 'bringing (it) to an end' (Heb. *kalah 'asah*) in v. 8b and v. 9b. It provides a challenge in that whatever one plots or plans concerning the Lord, it cannot stand or 'rise up' against the Lord; it is doomed to fail. It will not 'arise' even if the adversary or trouble were to make the attempt a second time. The noun *pa'amayim* is a dual form, literally 'two times' or 'two steps'.

The verb 'you plot/plan' (Heb. *t'chashsh'bun*) is second-person plural, but there is no clearly identified subject, as is typical of a general statement. The verb itself can have both positive and negative connotations, but when followed by *'el* or *'al* it carries a negative sense, and is so used in Job 13.24; 19.11; 33.10.

1.10 The verse begins with the particle *ki* that appears to be an asseverative, 'Truly' or 'Indeed', but it is followed by the adverb *'ad* that clearly does not have its basic meaning of 'up to' or 'until' and many commentators seek a solution by emendation. Others regard it as functioning as a simile, 'like', given the context in which it is used here, but that application is also highly questionable. On the other hand, it may be possible to understand it here as 'to the extent that' or similar, referring to the 'end'

(Heb *kalah*) to which God will reduce those who work against him in vv. 8-9.

The statement here is more interesting for its use of alliteration in the examples in v. 10a, b. Those who would oppose the Lord are likened to tangled thorns (Heb. *sirim s'bukim*) and drunkards (Heb. *sab'am s'bu'im*). A third negative example is of such opposition being consumed 'like dried straw' (Heb. *k'qash yabesh*). The addition of the participle *male'* emphasizes how completely the straw will be consumed. Each simile characterizes the adversary in the most negative terms.

1.11 The statement alleges that he (undefined) has already '*gone out from you* (sg.)' also undefined, then described as '*one plotting evil against the Lord*'. The pronoun references here are general, as in the rest of the section, but many commentators are convinced that, despite the silence, it must refer to Nineveh, even to the point of identifying Sennacherib as the one exiting Nineveh to plot against the Lord. Of course, such a view might even be correct, but it is not justifiable from the text as it now exists.

The one who is plotting is further described as '*one who offers counsel of Belial*'. The term *b'liyya'al* refers to one who is regarded as useless, 'a good-for-nothing, a base fellow' according to BDB—see Judg. 19.22; 20.13 for examples. Some have suggested that the term is more in the nature of a proper noun, the name of a demon. It is clear that there is a mythological background to the term—see 2 Sam. 22.5-6 where it occurs in parallel with Mot, death, and Sheol—with some suggestion that it is the name of an Assyrian goddess, a view based entirely on the report being aimed at Assyria.

Any reader of the text of Nah. 1.2-11 has to wonder about the vague or generalized nature of that text and the role of Nahum. If Nahum was a genuine prophet, it would appear that readers are asked to assume that those audiences knew essentially what his vague speeches meant or intended. If Nahum was truly a prophet in the traditional sense and had had revealed to him what he was to say to his contemporaries, then why speak so vaguely about what God wanted them to hear? Why leave all mention of Nineveh for much later (2.8)? Without the editor's adding the Title to his report, none would know its purpose! Reading back into the report what is now known as its intention, inevitably urges modern readers to guess references to specific identities and situations and apply them to the text in a very subjective manner. Such should be avoided when clearer evidence is lacking.

1.12-15 (2.1) Relief for Judah

12. *Thus says the Lord*: 'Although (they are) complete, the more numerous they become, the more they will be cut down and pass over; I have oppressed you, <u>May I never again</u> oppress you'.

13. '<u>And now</u> I would break his yoke from upon you, and your bonds remove'.

14. 'The Lord has commanded concerning you, may there <u>never again</u> be seed/posterity from your name'.

'From the house of your gods I would cut off the graven and molten images; I would dig your grave because you are worthless'.

15. '<u>Behold</u> upon the mountains the feet of one bringing good news, one proclaiming peace'.

'Keep your feasts, O Judah, and pay your vows, <u>Truly,</u> may Belial <u>never again</u> overcome you. He has been completely cut off'.

This new section, one very difficult to decipher, is marked by several rhetorical elements that define its boundaries. It begins with the messenger form '*Thus says the Lord*' as do many prophetic speeches, but the corresponding ending phrase '*...says the Lord*' is missing. It then features three *lo'... 'odh* phrases in vv. 12, 14, 15 (2.1) any of which can be translated variously as '...no more', '...no longer', and '...never again'. These emphatic phrases provide both the sound and meaning components of the section. Unfortunately, there is no clear indication as to the object or people to whom, or about whom, these *lo'... 'odh* phrases refer, though it probably is Judah. However, v. 12b appears to target the enemies while v. 12c points to Judah(?). Lack of clarity throughout makes it unclear who is being spoken of in each verse or part-verse.

In addition, other markers are used to note progress through the unit—'*and now*' (v. 13), and '*behold*' (v. 15a), and '*for/because*' (v. 15e) introducing its climax. The root *shlm* in v. 12 and v. 15 serves as a keyword and inclusion, as does '*abar*, 'overcome/pass over' in vv. 12b and 15c. It is not until the final verse that the reader learns to whom at least <u>some</u> of these words are directed, Judah being identified specifically as the recipient of an exaggerated promise of future safety now that the crisis has passed! In other words, Nahum is not anticipating an invasion, but offers a message of comfort AFTER an invasion has been either avoided or defeated.

As with other sections of this report, pronoun use is confusing—singular and plural third-person verbs in v. 12, along with second-person singular pronouns that are not identified, raising questions about the identity of the 'you' in vv. 13-14. The identity of the one who brings good news is likewise unclear—was it Nahum himself or some other? And is the one who calls Judah to observe the feast and the one who expresses the wish in v. 15, God or Nahum? These are questions that remain without clear answers. The pronoun use is confusing but probably comes about as the inevitable result of the Editor collating oral material from his various sources.

1.12 The section opens with Nahum's sole use of the normal prophetic marker of a divine word being announced—'*Thus says the Lord...*'. Strictly speaking, the Hebrew text simply states, '*Thus has the Lord spoken*'. While it is customary to understand this as a prophet citing divine authority for what he is about to say, it can also be a more general statement of established fact, i.e., something the community already knows to be a divine order, law or command. What that statement refers to here comes as a problematic conditional clause in v. 12b beginning with *'im* 'though/ if'. There follows the adjectival form *sh'lemim* the meaning of which is contested; it has been seen as 'completeness', 'fulness', 'strength', 'quietness'. However, in Gen. 34.21 it describes people as 'friendly'; in Deut. 25.15 it describes a measure as 'accurate/honest', and in 27.5 it refers to stones that are naturally whole/complete, i.e., they need no further manual re-shaping before being used. These examples make it very difficult to be dogmatic about any suggested meaning here in Nahum. The wider context would point to a community of people who have grown and increased and overtaken another. It does not appear to describe the Judaeans, so perhaps it refers to the Assyrians—but caution is advised.

The question then is, how far does this report of God's 'speech' extend? It would seem that it consists of only vv. 12-14 with a question hanging over v. 12b. Despite this being a word allegedly from God, there are serious problems in deciphering it; its meaning is far from clear textually, and syntactically, as well as in terms of pronoun use.

There are two phrases *w'ken rabbim w'ken nagozzu...*, that in the protasis of the condition stated can express a developing result, i.e., 'the more..., the more...'. However, most commentators follow the view that the 'adverb of degree' (see BDB) suggests a meaning such as 'they are complete, moreover (*w'ken...*), they are many'. This, however, does not explain the repeated adverb *w'ken nagozzu*. This reader suggests a possible translation: 'Though (they are) a well-formed unit, the more they increase (*rabbi'm*), the more may they be cut off and passed over; I have afflicted you (*'innitik*), (but) I would do so no longer'. There is, in this opening statement, a distinct echo of a similar construction in Exod. 1.12 where, in a situation of increased affliction (*'anah*), the Israelites actually increased in number (*rabab*).

If this were the sense, then it would appear that Assyria is the one being described in the first half verse, and Judah in the second half. On the other hand, what exactly is meant by the description of the Assyrian army is far from certain.

The final line that appears directed at Judah, notes that '*I (YHWH) have afflicted you (Judah)*' a past but undefined action. Presumably this refers to the Assyrian threat or pressure that has been applied to Judah, interpreted as a divine action, though one without explanation or justification. It should not be assumed automatically that it is a punishment for Sin, as Sin is never spoken of in this book as a cause of divine action against Judah! The statement follows: *Let me afflict you no more*'. With this we have the first of three *lo'... 'odh* forms that mark this unit.

1.13 '*But now...*' begins this verse to indicate what concrete steps YHWH will take to implement the promise. The Lord is presented as speaking, pronouncing his intention to smash '*his yoke* (Heb. *mattehu*) *from upon you*'. The context would suggest that the yoke, here a metaphor rather than an actual wooden yoke, is that of an oppressing enemy. It is further emphasized with '*and your bonds let me tear off*—a very forceful verb-form (Piel) is used. Given that there is a measure of doubt about the precise circumstances being addressed here, it is not possible to know whether Judah has been attacked already, or whether it has been under great pressure from an as-yet undisclosed enemy.

1.14 From first-person speech to third-person, the editor notes that the Lord '*has commanded concerning you...*', but without identifying to whom the 'you' pronoun refers. This report of a command at some point in the past, presumably in *torah*, is followed by the second *lo'... 'odh* phrase that is cryptic and seemingly negative: literally, 'let it no longer be sown from your name'. The phrase seems therefore to announce an end to the posterity of some person or group, with the noun *shem*, 'name', indicating reputation and posterity. But to whom does it refer? Most regard it as the enemy who is here said to be at an end. On the other hand, this clause in v. 14b does not have the air of a proper command; it is more an indirect statement that should be read as a <u>negative jussive</u>—'*may there be no longer any seed from your name!*'

The verse then continues with a threat in jussive form, as a volitional: '*I would cut from the house of your gods (or God) (every) carved image and (every) cast image*'. This challenge could be applied to Assyria, as well as to Judah under certain circumstances, but the text does not permit any final decision as to which community is being addressed. Commentators are divided as to which community is in view, but in reality, any determination is dependent on one's subjective opinion, and thus none is convincing,

The threat ends then with another jussive, '*Let me prepare your grave, for you are worthless*', tying in with the threat of loss of posterity. (See Job 40.4 for Job's self-reflection as worthless [Heb. *qalloth*, 'light'].) The threat to bury sounds like a challenge to a person or persons. If it referred to burying the images themselves, though they be 'worthless', it would be less of a threat.

1.15 (2.1) This verse begins chapter two in the Hebrew text, so verse numbering now varies—the Hebrew numbering in brackets.

Our section closes with a note similar in thought and imagery to Isa. 52.7. It begins with a marker, '*Behold*!' addressed to an audience and calling them to take notice of an important messenger. At this point in the report, those addressed are identified as 'Judah', meaning all its inhabitants, with a message that speaks of *shalom*, peace, security and well-being. The messenger, however, is not identified—could it be Nahum? In light of the promise now made, the assurance given, it could be Nahum as spokesperson, but the promise itself could not be realised unless it implied that it was God who had made such a commitment (v. 15c).

The initial note in v. 15a that echoes Isa. 52.7, suggests that both Nahum and the Editor of the second part of the Isaiah scroll were fully conversant with the imagery as circulating within the oral world. The imagery of 'feet' and 'mountains' representing the progress of a messenger (Heb. *m'basser*) striding across the region is dynamic (as in Isa. 40.9; 41.27 etc.), and the use here of a participle suggests his imminent arrival. A watchman whose designated task was to keep watch on the heights for signs of persons approaching, calls to the city (or nation) alerting it to the imminent arrival of one who '*brings good news*'—the verb always has a positive sense. That news is then further qualified as a message of 'peace' (Heb. *shalom*). The language and imagery are traditional, so it is pointless to seek an identification with any one individual.

A second line moves to an imperative tone, a watchman's command or call for the people of Judah to celebrate by feasting (Heb. *chag*), and fulfilling any vows made. No specific festival is mentioned, whether domestic or communal. The people are urged to celebrate the arrival of the friendly messenger and await the good news contained in the message he carried. However, there is no explanation offered as to the significance of fulfilling vows in preparation for the messenger's arrival. All that can be ascertained from this very general call is that religious and communal life should continue to be observed—life as normal?

The content of the message, the good tidings, is supported by a hyperbolic statement in the third *lo'... 'odh* phrase—'*May Belial <u>never again</u> overtake you*'. And to emphasize that hope, the concluding words are '*he/it is completely cut off*'. On 'Belial', see notes on 1.11—it is a general term, perhaps with mythical and demonic connotations, but overall, a synonym for evil. It is tempting to identify this with Assyria, given that Judah is identified as the recipient of good news, but there is still the nagging question as to why the Editor refuses to be specific about the identity of those called 'the wicked'.

One thing is clear, and that is that the 'good news' about 'the wicked' never again invading, means that <u>the crisis has already passed</u>, that the enemy has been 'cut off' (Heb. *krt*). This is a theme that recurs in 2.13 (14) along with a fourth *lo'... 'odh* form, though applied there to the enemy rather than to Judah.

2.1-13 (2.2-14) Against Assyria

2.1. A scatterer has arisen against you, Guard the fortification, keep watch on the road, empower the knees, build up your strength.

2.2. (For the Lord is restoring Jacob's glory as/like the glory of Israel;

For ravagers have ravaged them and destroyed their branches.)

2.3. The swords of its heroes are bloodied, the strong men clothed in scarlet, the chariot flashes with fire when he prepares them and the spear-shafts shake.

2.4. The chariots race about through the streets, rushing about in the squares, they appear like torches, like lightning flashes they crush??

2.5. He recalls his leaders, they stumble as they move forward, they hasten to the wall and the protection is set up.

2.6. The gates of the rivers are opened, and the palace/temple trembles.

2.7. Huzzab is stripped, she is carried off, her slave women led away, like the sound of a dove they beat their breasts.

2.8. **Nineveh** is like a pool, its waters draining away. Stop! Stop! And none turn back.

2.9. Plunder the silver! Plunder the gold! There is no end to its treasure, its precious vessels outweigh everything!

2.10. Devastation, desolation, and destruction! The heart faints, the knees tremble. The legs shake, the faces of all glow???

This section can be further divided into 2.1-9 (2-10) and 2.11-13 (12-14), with 2.10 (11) as a bridge between the two. The latter is the numerically central verse in the book and serves as a pivot between the description of the imminent threat to Nineveh in vv. 1, 3-9, and the mocking words as Nahum pronounces its end in vv. 11-13.

One additional factor here is that 2.2 (3) appears to be out of order. Based on content, it should follow 1.15 (2.1) as part of the 'good news' to the Judaeans; God is about to restore Jacob's 'glory'. This is one example where there is little dispute over a copyist's mistake being acknowledged.

The section begins with an announcement that God has raised up one described as *'one who shatters'* or *'one who scatters'* (see notes below for discussion), implying that the Assyrians are facing an imminent threat brought about by Israel's God. It describes in moving poetic manner the advance of an army that is about to invade, and with the mention of Nineveh (2.8 [9]) readers finally know who the object of this pronouncement is. Leaving the identification of the target of this speech to the end of the first half (numerically) of the book is a clever device designed by the Editor, though its precise purpose is unclear to the modern reader. See also 3.7, 18 for 'delayed' identifications.

2.1-9 (2-10) Assyria under Threat

Assyria, without being named, is called to prepare to meet an invasion force, described as 'one who scatters' or 'one who disperses'. Again, one notes the very general nature of the language suggesting that this typifies all military encounters.

Verses 3-9 (4-10) offer a description of the battle to be anticipated, with the sounds of battle embedded in the poetry. Shields are blood-stained, as are the army's uniforms, swords flash and chariots career around the streets and squares of the city. The army is in haste to attack the walls and sack the treasury. The Ninevites are mocked as they try to flee like floodwaters from a dam, while the invaders call for the vast store of gold, silver and other treasures to be taken as booty.

2.1 Although there is no mention in the text that this is God at work, it is implied. The scene is simply set: one merely described as 'the scatterer' (*mepits*), though unspecified, has already arisen and is about to drive the Ninevites out, to disperse like the water escaping from a burst dam (v. 8 [9]).

The people are called, in mocking tones, to do three things—'*Guard the fortress*'—the root *ntsr* forms a compound expression *natzor m'tsurah*—then '*keep watch/spy out*' (Heb. *tsph*) the approach road(s), and '*gather all their strength*' (Heb. *'amats*) in preparation. The Hebrew dual noun *mothnayim*, 'loins' refers to a girdle to which weapons could be attached—usually 'gird up your loins' is to have weapons ready. The Editor, envisioning the impending overthrow of Nineveh, has chosen to use a series of four short imperatives to present Nahum's message of comfort for Judah. Alliteration using the *ts*-sound adds urgency to the tone of the call.

2.2 (3) As noted, this verse is clearly out of sequence as it relates directly to the content of 1.15 (2.1) and its message to Judah, providing justification for the message in that verse. How this misplacement has come about is unclear but certainly implies a copyist's error. The verse does add two more *ki*-clauses to that with which 1.15 (2.1) ends. In the first of these two *ki*-clauses the particle is most likely the asseverative *ki*, 'Indeed', while the other provides the reason for God restoring their glory, i.e., it was because they had been 'ravaged'.

Verse 2a speaks of YHWH in the process of 'restoring' (Heb. *shab*) the pride or glory/majesty of Jacob, that is to say, of Israel. The two names are, of course, essentially synonymous, so we have parallel phrases. Given that the Jacob/Israel name could encompass both northern and southern kingdoms of the Israelites, there is a hint of the community being restored to its glory days during the Davidic-Solomonic period. If so, then the hyperbole is obvious, but it does heighten the contrast to the description of Judah having been 'ravaged'.

The second line of the verse uses alliteration *bqq* in a duplicated phrase *b'qaqum boq'qim*, 'ravagers have ravaged'. It is in v. 2b that there is some confusion—literally, '*their branches they have destroyed*'. The olive branches here referred to may be metaphorical, i.e., future generations, or actual; there is little consensus as to which use is intended. Regardless, it paints a picture of devastation consistent with the definition of being 'ravaged'.

2.3 (4) Beginning here and extending to v. 9 (10) is a graphic account of an army's advance and plunder, in the context implying an enemy advancing upon the Assyrians (v. 8 [9]). Whether that enemy is the Babylon-Mede alliance or YHWH as the warrior, the point is the same. See also 3.1-3 below.

It begins with a description of the shields carried by '*his warriors*' where the pronoun 'his' can really only refer to the one mentioned in v. 1, the 'scatterer'. The round leather shields carried by the foot-soldiers were 'reddened', whether blood-spattered or simply painted a red colour. It is a dynamic picture meant to instill fear in Nineveh. In parallel is a phrase, '*men of valour*', who are '*clothed in scarlet*'. That theme of redness continues as the chariots are said to be '*flashing with fire*', whether with a red flag flying, or as themselves with metal parts flashing in the sunshine.

A slightly problematic phrase, *b'yom h'kiyno* literally 'on the day of his/its establishing', seems extraneous, especially when followed in 2.4 (5) by what clearly continues to describe the advancing chariots. The Hebrew *habb'roshim*, 'cypresses', is thought to refer to wooden arrows or spears made from that source, with the verb *hor'alu* referring to their being tipped with poison. The LXX has a different reading that relates to horses—a reading followed by NRSV—but the verb there does not appear to relate to anything in the context. The text is obviously uncertain, making the meaning unclear, other than being one other element that relates to an attack.

2.4 (5) The chariots race hither and thither (*yithhol'lu*, 'run amok') in the streets, and in the city squares they charge about (*yishtaqsh'qun*). The two verbal forms carry the idea of constant frenetic activity.

The overall impression the chariots give is that they are like 'torches', like 'lightning flashes', as they dash about, the sun reflecting off each one.

2.5 (6) The initial verb in this verse is problematic as a singular form without a defined subject other than the third-person 'he', together with the difficulty of explaining what is to be 'remembered' (Heb. *zkr*)— NRSV renders it as 'calls', others suggest a passive 'called out'. Scholars have many suggestions for emendation in an attempt to deal with the verb concerned but there is little consensus. The semantic range of the verb *zkr* is broad, much broader than simply recalling the past. Here it is not a looking back but keeping something in mind, it refers to a cognitive function, one that involves acting in another's best interests. Those who are 'his officers' are not identified as the direct object of the verb *zkr* syntactically, so another possibility is that the verb is a jussive and its singular form is a collective, suggesting 'May his officers act…'. Each attempt at a solution is problematic, so the wisest move is to admit that we do not know precisely what the Editor intended. Given that Nineveh is having to prepare to defend itself, it seems probable that the Assyrian army is being mocked as they 'stumble' in their rush to defend the city.

What they 'set up'—repeating the verb *kun* from v. 3 (4)—is a *sokek*, a movable siege shelter that protects a soldier from incoming arrows or other military objects. In the case of those trying to force entry into a city, missiles from the defendants on top of the wall could do great damage to the attackers. For those manning the battering ram that tried to drive open the city gates, some similar protection was also required.

2.6 (7) '*The gates of the rivers are opened*' depicts the attackers opening floodgates on a dam or aqueduct that brought water into the city, with the result that the city would flood. A secondary result was that the palace/ temple 'melts away', or is washed away. Since most of the building in the city was of mudbrick, it was always at the risk of crumbling after flooding. That seems to be the image portrayed here.

2.7 (8) The opening of this verse is another problematic text with a series of verbs, one of which is a *hapax*. The first verb means 'to take a stand' (*hutstsab*), however, according to a Targum tradition it appears that it could also be the name of a woman, Huzzab. Whether this was the name of an actual queen in Nineveh, or a local name for Nineveh itself, is uncertain. She is to be stripped bare and taken away—that is to be her fate. This is the reported vision that Nahum shared with his people in Judah; again, one notes that it is never identified as a word from God.

'Her maidens', or the women of the city, are seen to mourn at what happens to them and to their city, their pathetic cries sounding '*like the voice of doves*' as they beat upon their breasts. While the dove may often signal quiet and peaceful situations, their call is here seen as moaning.

2.8-9 (9-10) At long last, Nineveh, the enemy, is identified! It is compared to a pool from which the water has flowed out, presumably leaving a muddy mess. It relates to the previous v. 6 (7) that has seen the city flooded. Mockery is intended as there are calls for the people not to run away. The Hebrew expression '*imdu ʿamodu*, literally 'Stand! Stand!', mocks the Ninevites who flee from the invaders, but their plea falls on deaf ears. '*There is no turning back*' describes the situation—none resist the chance to flee. Rather, what happens next is that the wealth of the city is stolen. Whether this is the call of those fleeing Nineveh or those who are invading, all call for the treasures, the silver and gold, to be plundered. The imperative *bozu* 'plunder', is repeated to add force to the call.

The wealth of the city, its treasure, is said to be without limit—*'en qetseh*, 'there is no end', a cry with a double meaning. It is an exultant cry from those who plunder the enormous wealth, but what is at an end is the empire! Everything precious is lost. Hyperbole again dominates the description.

It is this final editorial climax that brings the report to its numerical mid-point, 2.10 (11).

2.10 (11) This mid-point verse is a pivot for the report—see this function also in Obadiah v. 11. The identification of a numerically central verse is a well-known Masoretic device that has relevance not just for copyists to check the completeness and accuracy of their copying, but also has significance for the content arrangements in the document. In the case of Nahum, 2.10 (11) is an independent statement that depicts destruction and fear, and is so general that it could be applied to both the Ninevites nervously facing their end, as well as Judah anticipating a violent Assyrian attack.

Physical terms—heart, knees, loins, faces—are used to internalize or personalize the situational response to the devastation. While 'loins' appears in 2.1 as well, perhaps as a kind of inclusion, the other terms are not used in the rest of the book with such a physical sense.

The alliteration *buqah um'buqah um'bullaqah* is a powerful description, using synonyms, of the destruction and devastation wrought by war. Hearts fainting and knees knocking speak of the human response to and in the conflict. The description of the effects of war are summarized as 'anguish' (*chalchalah*) in all loins, and faces that grow pale, literally 'they gather paleness'.

2.11-13 (12-14) Against Assyria

> 2.11. Where is the lions' den, the hunting ground of the young lions? Wherever the lion walks, there too goes the lion cub, none disturb.
>
> 2.12. The lion tears enough for its cubs, and strangled prey for his lionesses, he fills with prey his caves and with torn flesh his dens.
>
> 2.13. Behold, I am against you, says the Lord of hosts. I would burn your chariots in smoke, and may the sword devour your young lions. I would cut off from the earth your prey, and may the voice of your envoys never again be heard.

The second half of the book begins with a focus on the 'lion', a metaphor for the aggressive Assyria, and its prey. Keywords are 'lion' (Heb. *'aryeh*) and 'tear' (Heb. *trp*). It opens with a rhetorical question that simply dismisses the power of the 'lion' and concludes with a statement of divine opposition that has a unique form—'*Behold! I am against you, says the Lord of hosts..., ...and never again be heard...*'. See further on v. 13 below.

The verses that conclude the report mock the Assyrian army as the lion that has stalked and captured prey, filling his cave with 'torn prey' with which to feed its family. But, the lion and its family will be no more.

The reason for the coming demise of the Assyrians is that the Lord is '*against you*'. This is a statement of Nahum's belief, a long-standing state of affairs, for YHWH is Judah's God who jealously guards his own (1.2) and is *against* those who oppose his people (see also 3.5).

What follows is a narrative form that in four verbal clauses announces precisely what Nahum envisages the Lord doing—he will burn their chariots, kill ('devour') young soldiers with the sword, cut off their 'prey' from the earth, and silence their 'messengers'. The verbs are read as volitional. There is also a vocabulary link to the Woe-oracle that is added, namely in the notion of 'prey' as plunder (*trp*) in 3.1 and the references to the sword (*chereb*) in 3.3, 15.

2.11-12 (12-13) The rhetorical question is actually a negative statement to the effect that the 'lion's den' is no more. The lion was a symbol of the Assyrian king and thus of the empire, while here the 'den/hideout' (Heb. *m''on*) represents Nineveh its capital. A parallel phrase, '*and the pasture for the young lions*', is also part of the question. Some commentators want to interpret 'pasture' (Heb. *mir'eh*) as 'cave' to parallel the 'den', but the imagery is much more realistic, namely a reference to the hunting ground over which the lion ranges in search of prey, as in the following relative clause.

The lion is pictured on the hunt for prey to feed its cubs as well as other members of the pride. With a final phrase *w'en macharidh*, that suggests the lion 'unhindered' or 'unchallenged', the question has noted the Assyrian army and its once-undisputed sway over its empire (Heb. *w'en macharid*, 'none to frighten them'), capturing territory, slaves and treasures, as coming to an end.

The root *trp*, 'tear', is used three times in v. 12, as an active participle and as a nominal form. It refers to one that tears, or that which is torn, i.e., captured and butchered prey. There is also a note about the supply being sufficient (*b'de gorothaw*), emphasizing that the lion has been very successful in its campaign and filled its food supply now stored in its den. This references the success of the empire's military agenda. However, that is about to end.

2.13 (14) I have referred to the opening words of v. 13 (14) as a unique expression, certainly one of significance in this report of Nahum's work. The statement is '*Behold, I am against you, says the Lord of hosts*', one of two uses of the form in this report (also 3.5), especially in its ending format of '*...says the Lord of hosts*' (*n'um yhwh ts'ba'oth*). In other words, it is one of the few references provided by the Editor that draws on a traditional 'prophetic' form that normally concludes a divine speech, that here does not in fact conclude any preceding saying; rather it introduces one. Its application here and in 3.5 conforms to that same use and function as in Haggai where it provides emphasis and is clearly not a concluding device (see Hag. 2.4, 9,17). Also important is to note that it occurs in association with the phrase *lo'... 'odh* (see 1.12-15 [2.1]) giving the clear signal that the following verbs are all of a volitional cast. The verse draws on the imagery of the 'lion' and 'prey' notions in vv. 12-13 (13-14), translating them into realistic threats against the Assyrian army. This reader understands the threat here to portray Nahum's longing in cohortative and jussive voice—'I would burn..., may the sword devour..., I would cut off..., may it not be heard...'.

The verse threatens divine action not against 'lions' but against military hardware, against chariots, made mostly of wood and leather for lightness, and swords, its supply of materiel (its prey), and its 'messengers'. This is a clever application from metaphor to reality. The final statement is *'may the voice of your messengers no longer be heard'*. Who are these 'messengers' (Heb. *mal'akekah*) but Assyrian envoys such as are exemplified in 2 Kgs 18.17? They were military agents like 'the Tartan, the Rab-saris and the Rabshakeh', deputies of Sennacherib who brought messages from the Assyrian king and made demands of those about to be attacked. In this somewhat indirect manner, the Editor speaks of the end of the Assyrian empire.

From this we move to the Woe-oracle in chapter 3 that outlines the shame to which Nahum longs to see Assyria subject.

3.1-7 Woe to Nineveh

1. 'Woe is the city of bloodshed, completely deceitful and full of robbery; it never lacks plunder/prey.

2. The crack of a whip and the sound of a rumbling wheel; a horse galloping and a jolting chariot.

3. Horsemen charge, and sword flashes, a spear glints, a mass of wounded and a heap of corpses; there is no end to the dead bodies, over the dead bodies they stumble.

4. From the multiplicity of their harlotries, the good favour of the mistress of sorceries, she who acquires nations by harlotries and families with her sorceries.

5. "Behold, I am against you," says the Lord of hosts, and I would lift your skirts over your face; and show your nakedness to the nations, and your shame to the kingdoms.

6. And I would throw filth at you, and make a fool of you, and make you a spectacle.

7. And when everyone sees you, may they abandon you and say, "Nineveh has been devastated". Let none grieve over her. There is nowhere I might search for one who feels compassion for you?'

The initial 'Woe!' is a commonly used interjection expressing pain, sadness, as well as disgust at the behaviour of another, or at having to meet a difficult situation. It is found in numerous prophetic texts when announcing disaster or judgment upon persons or nations considered deserving of punishment. But its use is certainly not confined to prophetic texts, nor does it mean that by using it one is claiming to be a prophet. Its usual form is *'Woe to those who…'* using nouns and participles to identify the one(s) at fault. Here in vv. 1-4 the oracle describes a fearsome military advance that leaves countless dead, so a translation like 'Wow!' would not be out of place—*Wow, a bloody city*!. The army is also likened to a prostitute and sorcerer, deeply unflattering descriptors of the enemy. Nahum is then said to have announced in 3.5-7 that shame would be brought upon this army, on a nation whose military exploits have caused havoc in the region. It is at this point in the presentation that the Editor has used what appears to be more traditional prophetic language to report action against the foreign army, and that the nations will rejoice at its destruction. The first-person singular verbs are volitional—'I may/would…', rather than strict imperfectives indicating 'promises', for they are part of his vision, what he hopes to see happen. It is not until the final verse that the object of Nahum's tirade is identified as Nineveh. The decision to delay any reference to the object of the oracle is surely the Editor's—see *Literary Features* in Introduction.

These words, though seemingly directed at Nineveh, would not have been heard by the Assyrians unless Nahum had risked his life and ventured to Nineveh to denounce it. There is no evidence of any kind that oracles directed against foreign nations were ever heard by them; rather, the real audience for these words was Judah itself, words designed to offer comfort in face of Assyrian threats.

The oracle consists of short poetic lines in vv. 1-4, often two-word descriptions (dyads), linked together with the *waw*, 'and', particle. These short, terse statements create a rhetorical impression of the speed with which Nineveh's military overwhelmed the region. In vv. 5-7, YHWH is quoted as speaking, announcing opposition to 'you', actions that bring universal shame upon Nineveh—the verbs are, as mentioned, volitional. The final two question forms are rhetorical, denying the possibility that any would feel regret for what might happen to Assyria, or seek to comfort Nineveh.

There is a question as to the extent of the Woe-oracle—for most commentators it runs to the end of the chapter. The reading being offered here takes the view that the oracle proper consists of 3.1-7 only. What follows in 3.8-19 is a collection of word-pictures that pour scorn on Assyria via challenges that mock its potential to resist the divine one—3.8-9, 10-13, 14-15a, 15b-18, 19. Such a reading depends more on content than on specific literary markers, though the use of imperative verb-forms is to be noted, together with the final verse's rhetorical question (3.19c) that mimics the ending of Jonah (Jon. 4.9-11).

3.1 'Woe' (Heb. *hoy*) is a significant marker used when denouncing persons or groups whose conduct caused pain or opposition; it is not confined to prophetic speech-forms, though obviously frequent there—see e.g., Hab. 2.6, 9, 12, 15. In our example here the object of the pronouncement is a city described as '*a city of bloodshed*'. The words are directed against the city as representing the whole Assyrian nation, and characterized as an empire whose ruthlessness and terrorizing had shed so much blood. Nahum had witnessed this as part of his vision of and for Nineveh.

Further descriptors are added: '*completely deceitful and full of robbery*'. Both seem to be standard accusations against an enemy rather than particular charges. A third charge is that '*it never lacks plunder/prey*', which in the circumstances appears to mean that while ever there was land to capture, people to conquer, treasure to be taken, Nahum saw Nineveh as continuing its expansion and occupation. The keyword *terep* (see 2.12 [13]) refers to anything that can be taken as spoils of war.

3.2-3 Short dyads or two-word phrases this time conjure up an image of the battlefield with staccato sound-effects—the crack of the whip to speed the horses pulling the chariots whose wheels rumble across the ground; metal weapons flash in the sun as those riders on horseback charge forward leaving a scene of death and destruction; unnumbered corpses litter the ground causing the foot-soldiers to fall over them in their haste to move forward. The description is similar to that in 2.2-4 (3-5). This is a word-and-sound picture of Assyrian troops advancing, enough to put deep fear into the listening Judaean audience. (If the Ninevites were listening to this reporter they would surely be feeling pride in his description of their amazing military success!)

3.4 An initial *min*, 'from', may here serve as a particle, '*Because of...*', to be followed by '*Look, I am against you*' in v. 5, thus giving the reason for the Lord's action as anticipated. The battlefield success of the Ninevites is likened to the seductive words and alluring moves of a prostitute (Heb. *zonah*). The double expression *z'nuney zonah* adds emphasis to the charge. She is further described as *tobah chen*, literally 'good of grace', where 'good' means excelling at some activity. Nations and tribes are seen to have fallen for Assyrian seduction only to find that it was what Nahum labelled as 'sorcery', implying that there was something almost supernatural about the Ninevites' approach that had drawn tribes and people into its embrace. The repetition of the noun 'sorceries' in both lines seems deliberate as characterizing Assyrian behaviour.

In the second line, the editor has used the verb *mkr*, 'to sell' or 'to trade' (as a harlot) to speak of capturing other nations and peoples. I suggest that the phrase means that Nineveh is, *she who acquires nations by harlotries, and families with her sorceries*. Some commentators question the use of the verb *mkr*, 'sell/trade', as Nineveh was not 'selling' other nations. The prostitute sells her favours in order to seduce and draw men to her, so the idea of selling herself to entice others into her sphere of influence does appear to be a possible sense intended. However, if the verb is used with this sense, it is unique.

The patron goddess of the city of Nineveh was Ishtar, who was also associated in their tradition with sex and war, and her violent acts and sensuality were widely celebrated in the region. Here that imagery is availed of to depict the empire as a prostitute reveling in sex and warfare, inviting gullible peoples into its embrace.

The language is hyperbole, of course, but demonstrates a high degree of literary sophistication on the Editor's part.

3.5 The verse begins with the same phrase as was used in 2.13 (14)—'*I am against you, says the Lord of hosts*'. This is a bald statement made from the point of view of an Israelite follower of YHWH, the national God. Because of all that has been outlined in vv. 1-4, Nahum claims divine opposition to the perpetrators, identified simply as 'you', but the 'you' in question is ambiguous. Some see it as possibly pointing to Judah, but the wider context would point to Nineveh whose identity is being delayed until the end of the oracle (3.7). The note, '...*says the Lord of hosts*', is the traditional form with which many prophetic pronouncements conclude. Here, however, it is atypical and does not conclude an oracle; rather, it moves the oracle from descriptive mode about the blood-thirsty enemy to the report of a speech by Nahum—all main verbs in vv. 5-6 are first-person, supposing the Lord as speaker. See comments on the phrase in 2.13 (14).

The first demonstration of opposition is, '*I lift (or, I would lift) your skirts over your face*'. This idiomatic expression is based on the shame of a woman's private parts being put on public display (see also Isa. 47.3). The traditional punishment for prostitution was to strip the woman and expose her entire body for the purpose of shaming her. Given that the prostitute model is being applied, this method of punishment is appropriate. No doubt invading armies took advantage of vulnerable women and girls, so the point here is that the way they literally treated captives is now applied metaphorically to Nineveh, to her shame. Other nations (Heb. *goyim*) may witness Nineveh's fall.

It is at this point that, similar to 2.13 (14), the Editor's report takes on a slight 'prophetic' cast with imperfective verb forms having volitional meaning. To presume that the people of Nineveh heard this pronouncement should never be entertained, for the audience for whom this message was intended was Judah.

3.6 The threat to '*throw filth at you*' echoes a sentiment in Mal. 2.3, though using slightly different vocabulary. The noun *shiqquts*, 'detestable things', perhaps 'excrement', has a cultic background, referring to that which makes one ritually unclean and unfit to participate in worship of YHWH. Such a possibility would have little meaning to the Ninevites! The threat to make one 'like a fool' (Heb. *nabal*) is added, along with making one the object of contempt, though the expression appears to be simply 'like one seen' (*k'ro'iy*), perhaps with a connotative sense of one being looked down upon. The three phrases in this verse all intend to demean the enemy, who remains unnamed.

3.7 The climax of the oracle finally reveals who is being denounced in Nahum's verbal attack: it is Nineveh. Nahum pictures 'everyone who sees you' (Heb. *kol-ro'ayik*) shrinking back. There seems to be a slight confusion in this rendering in the sense that those 'who see you' appears to be a general statement meaning 'those who see you, the enemy, humiliated' in the previous verse 6. Witnessing Nineveh's demise would not cause people to flee or get out of their way, as some suggest, but rather be reason to stand around cheering. The verb Hebrew used here is *ndd*, and although it does have the meaning 'retreat from' or similar, the more appropriate nuance in the context is to envisage people *abandoning* Nineveh, turning from it, no longer in thrall to its sorceries.

The singular form '*and he says*' (Heb. *'amar*) can be regarded as a collective—'let everyone say...'. Their response would be to rejoice that '*Nineveh has been devastated*'. The verb *shadad*, despoiled or ruined, is a strong statement implying the end of the city and empire.

What follows is in interrogative mode, but whether it is meant to continue what the people say (Heb. *'amar*), is to this reader doubtful. Rather the question-form *mi yanud lak* is rhetorical, and actually means that nobody should grieve (*Let none grieve...*) over what has become of Nineveh. Likewise, the question *me'ayin ʾabaqqesh* is a statement to the effect that *'There is nowhere that I might search (for ones who have compassion for you)'*. None should feel the least pang of conscience or regret over the demise of Nineveh.

There is surely a great deal of irony in the editor's conclusion here—the verb central to this final clause is *nacham*, 'to have compassion'; it is also the name of the visionary *Nachum*, Nahum. He has no compassion on Nineveh and its people.

3.8-13 Nineveh Will be Devastated

3.8. Are you better off than No-Amon, that sits by the Nile? Water surrounds her whose rampart is the sea, the sea her wall.

3.9 Cush was her strength, and Egypt, it was endless; Put and Libya they were among your associates.

3.10. Also/even she (went) into exile, she went into captivity; also/even her young ones were smashed at the top of every street, and for her noble ones lots were cast, and all her great ones bound in chains.

3.11. May you also become drunk, may you lose consciousness, may you also seek refuge from your enemy.

3.12. All your fortresses are fig trees with ripe figs, if they are shaken they will fall into the mouth of the eater...

3.13. Behold, your people are like women in your midst, to your enemies the gates of your land are wide open, may fire eat the bars (of) your gate.

This section is the first of four that follow the Woe-oracle—3.8-13, 14-15a, 15b-18, 19. Each section uses images that relate to the end of the Assyrians, a nation mentioned only once, and at the tail-end of the book in 3.18. The opening verses, 3.8-10, refer to an event that has taken place on the international scene and about which the Judaeans were obviously aware, since the Assyrian troops would have passed by on their way south to Egypt and on their return.

The unit begins with a rhetorical question—*'Do you think you are better (stronger) than No-Amon?'* The words here are theoretically addressed to Nineveh, a challenge that denies such a possibility. It then continues with facts related to the ancient Egyptian city's defensive situation, surrounded by water—*'the sea her wall'*. Despite what it regarded as its secure and safe environment, it fell; from nobles to children, all were lost. Any thought that Nineveh might escape the same fate is illusory, is Nahum's warning. There is no claim that this is a word from God; rather, these concluding comments, 3.11-13, are Nahum's private and considered thoughts and hopes for Assyria's end, an integral part of his 'vision'.

3.8 Beginning with a rhetorical question, Nahum challenges Nineveh's thinking, implying that despite its obvious power, it is no 'better' than No-Amon, the city otherwise known as Thebes, in Egypt. The use of a verb-form rather than an adjective 'good' has slightly stronger emphasis on its doing good rather than just being good, or perhaps even as BDB suggests, 'be in a better situation' than No-Amon. The rhetorical question denies that possibility—the enemy is stupid to think it can escape its fate. (In Jon. 4.4 the verb is used to upbraid Jonah for thinking that his anger was justified—'Does it makes sense for you to be so angry?')

No-Amon means 'city of Amon', the sun god; it is now identified with Thebes—its Greek name—an ancient city about 500 km. south of Cairo, on the Nile. It was the Egyptian capital during the Middle Kingdom period and was the second most important city in Egypt after Memphis. It covered a vast area of more than 40 square kilometers and is now known by more familiar names—Karnak and Luxor. Thebes was captured by the Assyrians in 663 BCE.

The city is described as *'the one who sits by the Nile, surrounded by water'*. Not only straddling the Nile, but also set within a series of canals that feed into it, Thebes was 'protected' by its watery surrounds. The poetic language used in this description, involving *yam*, 'sea' and *mayim*, 'waters', needs to be recognized as metaphor rather than read literally—the 'ramparts' (Heb. *cheyl*) and *chomah*, 'wall', are figurative for the protection that the river and canals afforded it; they are not literal earth and stone walls. Some commentators have queried the description in the text because the mention of *yam*, 'sea', was understood to locate it somewhere close to the Mediterranean, but the suggestion fails to appreciate the poetic dimension of the reference. Expecting the reference to be geographically precise and exact displays lack of awareness of the nature of the text. Nahum and his editor would have known of Thebes and its reputation from traders passing through Canaan, and known of it being attacked as the Assyrian army made its way south to Egypt, whether via the King's Highway inland or by the coastal route.

3.9 The name *cush* is generally thought to refer to Ethiopia, here described as *'otsmah*, 'her (Thebes') strength', i.e., powerful supporter. Cush's identity is not without its problems because ancient Cush is not the same as modern Ethiopia—not to mention the same name found in Mesopotamia; rather *cush* corresponds to the territory now known as the Sudan. 'Egypt', seeming to refer to a separate entity, is also classified as being a source of strength, that together with Cush provided Thebes with unending, or perhaps unconditional (Heb. *'eyn qetseh*), support.

Additional assistance was given to Thebes by *'Put and the Libyans'* who were her allies (Heb. *'ezrah*). 'Put' in this context is most probably Libya or a Libyan tribe, to Egypt's west, so the two names are a hendiadys. Regional support for Thebes was extensive, meaning that its fall to the Assyrians was a momentous event regionally, witnessing to the enormity of Assyrian power. Using what was known of this within Judah, Nahum heightens the power in the rhetorical question of 3.8. Despite the support given to Thebes by her allies, it fell to the Assyrians. Despite Nineveh believing itself invincible, Nahum implies it is no better, nor better off, than Thebes.

3.10-11 Following the rhetorical question of 3.8-9, this verse turns to remind Nineveh that despite the help Thebes was given, it nevertheless fell (3.10), and the same could happen to Nineveh (3.11). The Hebrew text in *BHS* sets out this argument in two lines beginning with the particle *gam*, 'also', followed by another fourth line beginning with *w'kol*, 'and all...'. In 3.11 the same pattern of a double line starting with particle *gam* is used, and 3.12 beginning with *w'kol*. Whether this scribal pattern represents an original Editor's draft in accordance with an original MT is uncertain, but it does draw attention to the care given to the presentation by the Editor. (Readers depend on this and similar rhetorical details in order to respond sensitively to a text). Verse 13 then begins with *hinneh*, 'behold' introducing the reason Nahum provides for Nineveh to fail.

The issue for readers is the function or meaning of the particle *gam* in each of these clauses. Syntactically, it is mostly used as an emphatic, 'this too...' or 'nevertheless'. This would suggest that the use in v. 10a, *gam hi'*, is 'Nevertheless, she...' or 'Despite this situation, she...' to bring to attention the fact that Thebes was in fact taken and people exiled, the feminine pronoun referring to the city. In the second case, v. 10b, *gam* functions as the adverb 'even' and emphasizes the extent of the defeat, with infants and nobles all succumbing to cruel treatment and exile. The use in v. 10c of *kol* serves to encompass everyone in the humiliation of being bound and exiled.

The heads of children being 'dashed in pieces' sounds gruesome, but echoes the sentiments of Ps. 137.9 and the actual treatment of captured children, treatment that was designed to cower enemies. Casting of lots was a common cultural practice that helped decision-making by a random choice of one of two alternatives. In the case of the loot taken from captured cities and people, casting lots would have been an accepted way of apportioning the bounty.

In 3.11 there is contrast in the use of *gam*, in the sense that the application is made to Nineveh —instead of 'her', i.e., Thebes, now it is 'you', Nineveh. The fate of Thebes can be repeated in Nineveh, so 'also' seems a sensible understanding of the particle in this instance.

Three possible approaches for Ninevites are noted—drunkenness, hiding, and seeking refuge—each presented as a potential, yet cowardly, way to escape the fate that Nahum claimed was what it had inflicted on Thebes. Each of the desperate responses of the population of Thebes were the only ones now available to Nineveh. Nineveh was mocked with an additional image drawn of it being nothing more than a fig tree laden with fruit ripe for the picking, and where even 'shaking the tree' i.e., minimal threat, would cause the fruit to fall into mouths open and waiting. The imagery of fruit being devoured applied to the inevitable consequence for Nineveh, is quite dramatic. Who would devour the Ninevite 'figs'? That was not Nahum's concern; he does not indicate a potential attacker, but speaks to his own people of his hope to see it realized.

3.12 The reason Nahum believes Nineveh is about to fall is made plain in another mocking statement—'*Look at your people (troops)! They are women, in your midst (they become) your enemy!*' While the first clause is quite clear, the second Hebrew clause is ambiguous—NRSV suggests '*they are women in your midst*'. The tone is still one of mockery, but the preposition *le* before 'your enemy' (*le'oy'bayik*) seems to this reader to imply that Nineveh's troops are their own enemy; they are alleged to be in no condition to win on the battlefield. It would be like having an army of untrained and less powerful women, so they would be more a liability than the actual danger of facing the real enemy.

A second liability was that '*the gates of your land*', or the gates of cities throughout Assyria, are wide open, meaning every city was indefensible, allowing invaders easy access—hyperbole again, to make the point about Nineveh's precarious situation. Fire devours '*your bars*', the wooden beams used to lock a city's wooden gates, meaning they are now unable to keep the invader from entering the cities that then fall to them. The imperfective verbs may imply a current and continuing situation that would have consequences for the empire as a whole.

Both these statements picture the current situation from Nahum's point of view; they are his vision of the present and of what he expects to see happen.

3.14-19 Assyria's End

3.14 Draw water for the siege, strengthen your defenses. Fetch mud and tread the clay, strengthen the brick-kiln.

3.15 There may the fire devour you, and may the sword cut you off,

may it devour you like the locust, make yourself heavy/glorious like the locust, like the winged-locust.

3.16 May your merchants increase more than the stars of the heavens. A young locust sheds its shell and may fly away.

3.17 Your leaders are like winged locusts, and your scribes/marshals? like a swarm of locusts. They settle on the walls when the day is cold, and when the sun warms (it) they fly away, to a place unknown. Where are they?

3.18 (Woe) your shepherds are asleep, O king of Assyria and your nobles slumber, your people are scattered upon the mountains and there is none to gather (them).

3.19 There is no remedy for your hurt. your wound is indeed incurable; let all who hear news of you clap their hands over you; for none has escaped your endless cruelty.

3.14-15a A series of five imperatives urges the Ninevites to prepare for an attack, a siege. Of course, the Ninevites would not have heard this message, so Nahum is seeking to comfort Judah with a picture of an enemy about to end its domination. Nahum urges Ninevites to prepare supplies (water) to last through a period of siege, for city walls to be strengthened, more bricks to be made and fired—yet all will be in vain. *Fire*, instead of firing the bricks will burn the city down, devouring it. A second metaphor is that of the *sword*, the enemy's weapons that will *cut off*, or bring to an end Assyrian power. The imperative forms have *volitional* force, expressing Nahum's personal longing, the point being to mock Assyria while bringing hope to his people. Hence the translation above uses 'May you be...' 'May there be...' There is no sense that Nahum is predicting the fall, but rather expressing his deepest longing.

The metaphor of fire devouring leads to a third metaphor, that of the locust. *Locusts* were a constant problem throughout the region and were notorious for their destructive effect on crops and vegetation generally—see also Amos 7.1-3; Joel 1.2-7. 'Locust' (Heb. *yeleq*) is also a metaphor for both destructive impact as well as vast numbers. Here the noun represents one stage of the locust life-cycle, that prior to shedding its carapace or shell.

The insertion of the adverb 'there' (Heb. *sham*) at the beginning of 3.15 has been seen as locative 'there', as well as temporal 'then', but its primary function appears to be as a connector to link with v. 14, emphasizing the preparations Nahum urges with their inevitable failure—'even there, the fire will devour…'.

3.15b-18 The volitional mode continues in 3.15b with the imperatives translated here as, 'multiply yourself like the locust' and 'multiply yourself like the grasshopper'. This double use of the root *kbd* is challenging for the interpreter, and commentators have a variety of views as to its meaning. The basic root can refer to 'glory/magnificence' or 'heaviness'. In this reflexive mode, 'make oneself heavy' is meaningless, though there is a use in Prov. 12.9 that may suggest 'honour yourself', a self-aggrandizing call. Taking these basic ideas into consideration, it would seem that Nahum challenges the Ninevites to do everything in their power to bulk themselves up, increase their troops, to arm themselves to the hilt, to make every effort to demonstrate their military might—but, in the end, it will all be in vain! It is another means by which Nahum mocks the Assyrian.

In 3.16 Nahum suggests that the number of their traders and merchants have, like the stars in the heavens, become impossible to count—an assumed reference to the way Nineveh's trading power was overwhelming. It is, of course, hyperbole. On the other hand, like the locust that emerges from its shell (3.16c) only to fly off somewhere, anywhere, in search of food, Nahum envisages the countless merchants, its commercial power, as flying away, only then to take wing and disappear.

This is followed in v. 17 by a further application of the locust metaphor. Those who guard the city, and the city 'elders', are compared to the locusts and grasshoppers, who, though countless, disperse and fly off to 'unknown' places, meaning that they go wherever their needs drive them rather than that they cannot be found (that would be good news!). The noun *tipsar* here translated 'elders' is a loan-word from Assyrian—it can mean 'scribe', one who writes on clay tablets, or some other high official in the Assyrian community. It represents those with power in the empire. They are likened to locusts and insects that gather in swarms, dispersing when the day warms up for they are self-driven. The illustration is demeaning of Assyrian leadership and implies that the entire empire is, in Nahum's mind, about to scatter and be brought to an end. It will be as though they never were. The verse in MT ends with a term *'ayyam* that can mean 'Where are they?' Others attach it to the opening word of v. 18 and read it as another 'Woe'. This reader prefers to retain the MT and so the verse ends with the question-form that emphasizes the hope that they cannot be found.

Other metaphors are used to depict the Assyrian leadership in v. 18—shepherds, its king and its nobles, together with 'your people'. All levels of society are swept up in this verse with leaders said to be slumbering, unaware of what is happening, perhaps even uncaring or overconfident of their own invincible power. Meanwhile the people are left leaderless, without a shepherd, scattered 'on the mountains' (see the contrast in 1.15 [2.1]). We have noted elsewhere that it is only in the final verse or portion of sections of the report that Nineveh or Assyria is identified—this was clearly an editorial strategy. Here in v. 18 we have the sole mention of 'Assyria' as the empire whose end Nahum longed to see.

3.19 This reader sees 3.19 as the climax, beginning with another *'eyn* phrase (Heb. *'eyn-kehah*) '*no lessening of your breaking/smashing*'. There is no chance that Nineveh will see a decrease in its suffering, Nahum says, for what he longs to have happen he regards as a mortal blow. And when everyone hears the news (Heb. *shom'ey shim'aka*) as to what has happened to Assyria, they will celebrate. Given that Nahum's message, his vision, is intended for Judah to hear, it is the Judaeans whom he has in mind now—they will rejoice over what happens to Nineveh, as will every tribe and nation who has suffered under Assyrian tyranny.

The final note is, '*For over whom has not passed your evil/disaster (Heb. ra'ah) continually?*' The rhetorical question is an assertion that there is none, no one, upon whom the cruel power and might of Assyria has not trampled. Yet that may be about to end.

At the literary level, it is intriguing to note that this anti-Nineveh challenge concludes as did the book of Jonah, with a rhetorical question, and one that focused on the theme of compassion. What Jonah had to learn of God's compassion for Nineveh, its people and animals, Nahum rejected in favour of his view of God as vengeful and angry, a view that was made abundantly clear in his opening statement (1.2-3).

In this final chapter readers are presented with Nahum's vision for the end of Nineveh and the Assyrian empire and his desire to give hope to his people.

Habakkuk: A Commentary

Introduction

Habakkuk is the eighth book in the Hebrew Bible's Scroll of the Twelve, also known as the Minor Prophets. It consists of 56 verses only. Its placement between Nahum and Zephaniah has been read by some as indicating that Habakkuk was contemporary with those two men, but supporting evidence is lacking. Apart from one reference to the Chaldeans, a Neo-Babylonian empire that rose at the end of the seventh century BCE, there is nothing in the text to indicate a specific date for an event, an individual mission, or for the contents of the book to be brought together in this written form.

The short book attached to the name of Habakkuk, a shadowy figure of whom nothing other than his name and potential 'prophetic' assignment are known, is an intriguing document that represents social and religious issues that were prominent in the period from the late seventh to early sixth century BCE, leading to the end of the southern kingdom of Judah in 587 BCE and its aftermath. The book appears to be a report of a debate or discussion between Habakkuk and God in chapters 1–2, with an attached psalm in chapter 3—but see below on Structure. It contains echoes of issues found also in Joel, Haggai and Malachi, in Proverbs, Qoheleth and Job. Furthermore, it does not contain any of the traditional 'prophetic' literary or rhetorical tropes other than a collection of five 'Woe....!' statements in 2.6-19. It begins with a Lament form in 1.2-4 that raises the question of divine concern for justice as noted in other contemporary reports.

Habakkuk the book is an unusual document, described in the Title or Superscription as both a *Massa'* (see discussion in Postscript) and a Vision seen by or given to a man nominated as a Prophet. One of our tasks in respect of this oft-neglected book is to offer a commentary that unpacks that opening description, and to perhaps gain some further insight into Habakkuk's importance for the Judaean community at the beginning of the sixth century BCE. A similar Title has been given to the book of Nahum by its editor, though that is not to say that he was editor of both documents.

The Qumran Community of the first century BCE gave some prominence to their *pesher* or commentary on Habakkuk (1QpHab), but their text contained only chapters 1 and 2. The community there interpreted or 'domesticated' the text in light of their communal concerns and needs—e.g., the Chaldeans become the *Kittim*, or Greeks—and so is of little value to a modern reader wanting to know what the Hebrew text actually says in its original setting.

Outline of Contents

1.1 Superscription
1.2-4 Habakkuk's Lament (part A)
       Address to God, and Habakkuk's Complaint
1.5–2.20 Habakkuk and God in Dialogue
       1.5-11 God's Response?
       1.12-17 Habakkuk Challenges God
       2.1   Habakkuk Awaits God's Reply
       2.2-5   God's Reply
2.6-20 'Woe to you who…'
3.1   Editor's Second Note
3.2-19 Habakkuk's Lament (Part B)
       3.2-15 Confession of Trust
       3.16   Petition
       3.17-19 Song of Praise
3.20   Final editorial note

Structure

This reading will proceed on the basis that the book of Habakkuk consists of two major parts: (1) the Individual Lament in 1.2-4 and 3.2-19, and (2) an inserted Discussion in dialogue form in 1.5–2.5, plus 2.6-20. A single traditional Individual Lament-form has been chosen and broken apart to serve as the framework into which the Habakkuk-God dialogue created by the Editor has been placed.

Introductory notes at 1.1 and 3.1 and a concluding note in 3.20 are the work of the Editor. The note in 1.1 introduces the book as a whole, while those in 3.1 and 3.20 wrap around the closing elements of the Lament, presented in the current text as a separate psalm with 'musical' suggestion. It will be argued that 3.1, 20 were the Superscript of the original Lament, replaced by 1.1 as a new Title because the Lament has been modified and become part of a *Massa'*. (See note 1.1)

The book is structured, therefore, as a Superscript (1.1), introducing the Lament that has been editorially divided into two separate parts—**part A** (1.2-4) consisting of the first two components of the traditional Lament-form, i.e., the Address to God, and the Complaint, and **part B** (3.2-19) consisting of the remaining components of the form, i.e., the Confession of Trust, the Petition, and the Song of Praise. Inserted into this Lament and beginning at 1.5 is a Dialogue between Habakkuk and God (1.5-11; 1.12-17; 2.1; 2.2-5) followed by a collection of Woe-oracles in 2.6-20. The Editor has broken open the Lament in order to discuss the matter of Violence and Justice in the context of divine agency. The uniqueness of the dialogue would suggest that it is to be regarded as the core of the book theologically, while the traditional Lament-form plays more of a supporting role as the framework and context for that discussion.

The Lament itself is similar in every way to the Individual Laments found principally, but not exclusively, in the book of Psalms. It has the same structure and uses the same rhetorical features as those preserved in the Psalms collection. A timeless Lament has been chosen, whether by Habakkuk himself or by the Editor, into which to insert material attributed to Habakkuk in his dialogue with God on the very difficult subject of Violence and Divine Justice. Habakkuk, though nominated as a Prophet by the Editor, shared a common quest with the Sages in seeking some resolution of the problem of injustice and evil in the human experience of life, and of God's possible role in that.

The current Hebrew text that separates 3.1-19 from the first two chapters gives the impression that chapter 3 is an after-thought or add-on that may even have had a separate existence, but that would be to misread or to overlook the fact that the structural form overall is the Lament, and the Dialogue a later Editor's insertion. The fact that the Qumran commentary on Habakkuk, *1QpHab*, is missing the final chapter is of no consequence for our investigation of the MT text.

A Reading Strategy

The Dangers

When reading an ancient document originating in an alien cultural community it is vital to recognize that a modern reader was not its intended recipient—we are reading someone else's mail. It began its life in the mind of an individual who was a member of a community with its own identity, its own worldview, its own religious experience and perspective, and within that frame found expression.

As things stand at present, the Editor invites the reader to imagine Habakkuk, concerned with the problem of Violence and Injustice, expressing his concerns via a Lament, and God answering him. Habakkuk's concern is assumed to be known in the community and its general details known to many. It probably was the subject of numerous tellings as the issue was discussed throughout the community, perhaps in formal but also informal social and religious settings. Habakkuk was almost certainly illiterate, as was the vast majority of the population, and depended on his oral skills to share what moved him to speak out. Whether as encouragement, offering hope, criticism or condemnation, the words and issues were kept alive within that community until such time that a literate member wrote down some of what was circulating orally. Different versions of the 'prophetic' message were no doubt available, given that the speaker had undoubtedly spoken more than once on the theme(s) that demanded his attention. These were available to the Editor who collated and edited them into the Dialogue form in which we access them today.

A modern reader of Habakkuk always has to bear in mind that he or she may, and probably will, read into the document ideas and draw conclusions that are completely unwarranted. The Danger is that one comes to believe that one's conclusions about the text are 'correct'. A deep knowledge of the original language, of the setting and the cultural world from which it sprang, hopefully will provide one way to limit the preconceptions one might have, and lead to a more than superficial reading. Not all enthusiastic readers of Habakkuk will have those skills or knowledge, and even those who have them may allow themselves consciously or unconsciously to yield to other pressures or needs that may then distort what the text intended. Theological preconceptions or commitments such as a denominational priority, or a thoroughly Christianized perspective on the OT that imports and imposes NT ideas onto a text—e.g., the text of 2.4 as its core text—will inevitably predetermine what one sees and how one interprets it.

The Dilemma

The Dilemma facing one who seeks to understand what Habakkuk the book is about, is that we have so little information about this person called Habakkuk, other than his name. The historical setting of the book is to some extent unclear, Habakkuk's personality, background, beliefs, nothing other than the Editor's title in 1.1 that speaks of him as a Prophet (Heb. *nabi'*), is known. With such little information, a reader will be influenced in his or her reading by a certain understanding, a preconception, of what a traditional Prophet was and did. In the case of this book, that initial understanding of what a Prophet was will need to be abandoned because there is virtually nothing in the book that supports the view that Habakkuk was a Prophet, certainly not a prophet in the same mode as other major personalities such as Isaiah and Jeremiah, or in the narratives of even earlier prophets such as Elijah and Elisha. Why the book has been included in the Scroll of the Twelve and not somewhere else is one issue that must be addressed. All the traditional literary forms and other markers one might expect of a prophetic book, such as '*Thus says the Lord*' and '*the day of the Lord*', all are missing from this document, so why has it been regarded as a prophetic work? Allowing the text as it is to inform or re-orient one's perception of what the noun 'prophet' means in this book is required.

Another challenging element is attempting to determine whether Habakkuk the man actually used the Lament chosen, or whether the Editor chose the Lament with some knowledge of Habakkuk's concerns. In the final analysis, the decision seems to this reader to be beyond ultimate proof either way, though the assumption is that it was Habakkuk himself who made that choice, as it quickly established the core issue that troubled him.

The Decision

The reading strategy being offered in this commentary is an attempt to limit any extraneous influences and preconceptions, to the extent that they are known, and to allow the text to offer its own evidence, with close attention to its literary and rhetorical features.

This reader approaches the book as consisting of two distinct component parts—a Lament (1.2-4 and 3.2-19) and an introduced Dialogue (1.5–2.20), as mentioned above. These represent two quite separate and identifiable literary forms, each with its specialized vocabulary and rhetorical features. The entire Lament, not just its opening verses, is one chosen from a wide range of available Laments such as found now assembled in the Book of Psalms. This Individual Lament serves as the overarching Framework, while the Dialogue has been created to discuss, in terse poetic form, the issue of Violence and Injustice that is raised within the Lament. It is assumed that in the Dialogue the Editor is reporting what he knew of Habakkuk's issue with his God. Perhaps unfortunately, this is the only access a reader has to the alleged concerns of Habakkuk.

This reader sees in Habakkuk a situation comparable with that of the book of Job in which a legendary story about a man called Job, 'the blameless and upright', has been taken and broken open in order to insert an imagined dialogue between 'Job' and three friends. That pattern and the issue being discussed there find many echoes in Habakkuk.

Although the book is designated as 'prophetic' by virtue of its inclusion in the Scroll of the Twelve, there is little question that its inclusion there calls for a broader definition of what 'prophetic' might mean, given that the book shows no interest in traditional prophetic literary forms, has only one possible reference to YHWH speaking (2.2), and overall presents a situation in which the prophet speaks to and about God, rather than being a channel for God to speak to the community as happens with other prophets. Believing that the book is following a traditional prophetic mode and presenting a message to a community based on its location in the Scroll of the Twelve lacks other textual support, and so is misguided. Habakkuk the book purports to report a private discussion that a man named Habakkuk was believed to have had with God, and which an Editor, who was clearly a literate poet, preserved for a wider audience.

This reading begins from the perspective that Habakkuk the book is an Editor's report about a man confronting God with this ever so basic question about justice and violence. Furthermore, it is a concern that undergirds much of the Wisdom material in, for example, Qoheleth and Job. Even the 'Woe!' forms in 2.6-19 are not prophetic in any traditional sense, but are simply warning statements of a completely general kind based on one's or the community's past experiences of life. Habakkuk the book shows how prophetic demands and wisdom's advice coalesce in the period in question from the fifth century BCE onward in what were formerly distinctive roles assigned Israel's 'prophet' and 'sage' (see Jer. 18.18).

Ultimately, one hopes to determine whether the book has achieved what it set out to resolve—did Habakkuk ever find his questions in 1.2-4 about the Violence and Injustice in his domestic situation answered to his satisfaction? How did he cope with the divine response in 1.5-11?

Authorship and Unity

The question of authorship of Habakkuk is not a simple one. It is clear that an Editor has provided a Title at 1.1 and 3.1 but there are few if any other indications of authorship. Many readers will assume that Habakkuk is the speaker, if not the author, of 1.2-4 and of the prayer (3.2-19) because of the headings provided by the Editor. So, the question is, How much is from the pen of the Editor and how much from Habakkuk himself? What is the evidence in the text?

Any solution to the authorship question depends on the Structure of the book. The reading that follows is based on the thesis that 1.2-4 and 3.2-19 is actually a complete Lament psalm, into which there has been inserted quite strategically a discussion created between God and Habakkuk of a topic of mutual concern. Habakkuk we assume was not the author of the Lament, but he is here presented as citing one through which to pour out his frustration about the situation he saw as current in Judah with regard to two religious and social issues. *Torah*, he said was being abused, a matter that concerned all the prophets, as well as there being a lack of justice, a further but related matter that concerned both Prophets and Sages. These were both issues that divided the community and were widely talked about and discussed. The Editor, perhaps in consultation with Habakkuk, or at least being familiar with the discussion, has set the issue in Dialogue. Habakkuk's inner struggles with the issue are here presented in the Q-and-A format, to bring before a wider audience what Habakkuk's 'solution' was. While there was clearly no final answer, there is a resolution as Habakkuk remained faithful to his God in the 'not yet', and affirmed in 3.2-19 his joy as he anticipated divine rescue.

The Editor has given the work its Title/Superscript and noted that it is his report of the Vision of one, Habakkuk. The first-person elements in the text are presented presumably as the words or thoughts of Habakkuk, but they derive from two different sources:

1. The Lament Psalm that provides the framework for the book, i.e., 1.2-4 and 3.2-19, presents the words of an original and unknown creator of that particular Lament, written in the first-person so that one can consider using it as the means for expressing his or her own issue with God. According to the Editor's report, this is what Habakkuk has utilized to bring before God an issue that deeply troubled him.
2. In the case of 1.5–2.5, the Dialogue Habakkuk shares with the Lord, the first-person material is what the Editor has put into the mouth of Habakkuk—namely, 1.12–2.1 and 2.6-20. The remainder of the material, 1.5-11, 2.2-5 are reports of the Lord's responses to Habakkuk's two profound questions raised in the Lament (1.2-4). From this perspective, the book of Habakkuk follows a similar pattern to that of the Book of Job in which the Legend of Job in chapters 1.1–2.13 and 38.1–42.6 were broken open to insert a created dialogue between Job and three friends in 3.1–37.24 with a concluding note in 42.7-16.

With virtually no information about the man Habakkuk other than his name, it is not possible to speak of Habakkuk as the author; rather, it is an Editor's report of Habakkuk's encounter with his God. Whether that encounter was actual, or imagined, or simply a dialogue created by the Editor from Habakkuk's Lament to discuss a point of theology, remains to be explored.

As for the unity of the book, there is little question that it is a complete composition. There is a unity of purpose in the discussion of Violence and Injustice in the world and all is expressed in terse poetic language.

Historical Setting

There are few clues in the text to assist in locating Habakkuk and the book's contents within a particular historical context apart from the mention of the Chaldeans in 1.6. This neo-Babylonian Empire rose to prominence under its first ruler, Nabopolassar in 626 BCE. At the height of its power, it was ruled by Nebuchadrezzar (605–562 BCE). The Babylonian army and its advance is described in 1.6-11 as terrifying in speed and brutality as well as being comprehensive, 'covering the breadth of the earth'. Even allowing for some hyperbole, it is clear that the Empire was well established. In view of its advancing into Judaea some time around 597 BCE en route to capturing Jerusalem, it is conceivable that Habakkuk reflects Judaea's situation in the opening years of the sixth century BCE but before 587.

On the other hand, the issues of Injustice and Violence that so concerned Habakkuk are not confined to that or to any one moment; they are issues that are beyond time and place. In the moments before the Chaldeans swept into Judaea, Habakkuk's focus was on the way in which the tensions of the time impacted on the social fabric of a community living by *Torah*. And invasion by the enemy was not going to do anything positive towards solving that problem. The book contains no reference to the Chaldean advance as a punishment for Judaea's failure with regard to *Torah*, unlike the DH, yet so many commentators unjustifiably apply that motivation to this text. There is nothing in this book that points to sin and punishment as underlying the discussion.

Habakkuk's Place in the Scroll

Habakkuk is placed at #8 in the Scroll of the Twelve. Given the nature of the scroll, this means that at a certain moment in time, either additional sheets containing this new written material were stitched onto the end of the scroll that already contained Hosea to Nahum, or the long scroll had space enough to allow a scribe to add the Habakkuk material and a number of other written documents. We have no information about Habakkuk prior to its inclusion in the Scroll.

Does a book's location in the Scroll suggest anything with regard to its date? Are the various books on the Scroll arranged chronologically, or are there other principles at work? Why might it have been stitched into the Scroll or copied in this location rather than earlier or later in the order? Did it have an independent existence prior to gaining consent and entry into the list of authorized documents? Nahum's references to anger and violence (e.g., Nah. 1.2-3) as essential to the character of both YHWH and the Ninevites may have provided a connection to the issue Habakkuk wished to have answered. Does that account for their juxtaposition? Questions like these are fascinating to contemplate, but the chance of ever discovering what lay behind the process is elusive.

Relationship to Other Books

The theme taken up in the initial Lament (part A) is that of Violence and Injustice in Judaea and of God's non-response to the earlier pleas of Habakkuk for God to act. The result of this failure is that *torah* had lost its power; it had been abused and perverted, and as a result social harmony had been lost. In the case of Individual Laments, the worshiper looks for justice for himself—rescue—and for the perpetrator of injustice or oppression, punishment. Each of the Laments, therefore, has an affinity with the issues taken up by Habakkuk. Qoheleth and Job also, for example, sought to deal with the same problem of the relationship of material success with keeping *torah* (see also Mal. 3.13-15); 'sin', however defined, they argued does not always lead to punishment, nor faithfulness to blessing. This was and remains a human reality, and simple answers are not just misleading, they are damaging.

We see here the coming together of prophets and sages in seeking a resolution of the failed Deuteronomic perspective on God and community life. At the level of this fundamental socio-religious question, Habakkuk was at one with the Wisdom tradition in seeking an answer that made sense, only to find that it remained a mystery.

It is generally agreed that during the exilic period the Deuteronomistic History (Joshua–2 Kings) was brought together from the oral traditions and records of the time, retrofitting the theology of the book of Deuteronomy into the nation's story, beginning with the call and promises made to Abraham. What becomes clear is that within the life of Israel in the exilic period there were different cliques or circles, each with its own theological view. A major force in Israel was the Deuteronomic cohort; it represented a conservative and nationalistic understanding of the tribal identity. Its view of YHWH the national God was narrower than the more international view of the sages. Habakkuk needs to be seen in that general context with an implied questioning, if not outright rejection, of Deuteronomy's worldview and theses. Behind Habakkuk there lies a powerful Deuteronomic cohort whose views are being strongly contested and shown to be inadequate by other contemporary Judaean thinkers, and leaders such as Zerubbabel. See also Mal. 2.10-16.

At a literary level, there is a strong echo of Joel's description of the invading locust plague (Joel 2.4-9) in God's(?) account of the Chaldean army's advance (Hab. 2.6-11). At the level of Structure this reading argues for an outline similar to that of the Book of Job with the ancient Legend of Job providing a base for the insertion of a discussion of divine justice, sin and human suffering.

Literary Features of Habakkuk

Mention has already been made of the fact that despite Habakkuk being labelled a 'prophet' there is so very little literary evidence in the text of the book to support that call. Setting aside for the moment the Individual Lament (1.2-4; 3.2-19), we can focus on the inserted component of the book, namely the Dialogue that the Editor has created. This is the material that carries the theological perspective of Habakkuk as known to the Editor.

Habakkuk the book exhibits a number of well-established and general literary/rhetorical features, mostly brief poetic lines that, as a result, are often difficult to comprehend, passages that are obscure of meaning even when each word is known, along with several *hapax legomena* whose precise meaning is debated and uncertain. Since a document's literary/rhetorical elements are a reader's only evidence by which to grasp its meaning and judge its relevance, the following brief list of features is where this reader has focused.

- A. *The notion of 'seeing'* that the Editor used in the book Title (1.1) is featured in the several synonymous verbs (Hebrew *chazah, ra'ah, bit*) along with the exclamatory 'Behold!' The title refers to a visionary experience, so one expects to read of what was seen.
- B. *Similes* describing the advancing Chaldean army (1.8-9—like leopards, like wolves, like eagles, and in 1.14-16, like fish, like crawling things), along with *Metaphors* of hooks, nets and seines.
- C. *Couplets*, often in chiastic pattern (1.3, 7, 13; 2.13b) are an essential rhetorical device in most verses.

D. *Rhetorical Questions* using 'Are you not…?' (Heb. *h'lo'*) in 1.12; 2.6, 13.
E. *Repetition* of phrases—2.8 and 2.17.
F. *Contrast* in positive and negative phrases—e.g., 2.3 'it will surely come, it will not delay'—2.3-15, esp. 2.8.
G. *Double meaning*—Hebrew *nephesh* 'life, wine, wealth'? (2.3-5).
H. *Sarcasm and irony*—1.12-17 in Habakkuk's response.
I. *Quotations* from an outside, presumably shared, oral source—2.20 is also found in Zeph. 1.7 and Zech. 2.13.
J. *Hapax*—1.9 (*m'gammat*), 2.11 (*kapis*). Neither of these Hebrew terms are properly understood.
K. *Woe-oracles* are gathered and placed together in 2.6-20.
L. *Inclusio* the verb 'hear' in 3.2 and 3.16 (also 1.2 and 3.16 as contrasting)

Literary components of the Individual Lament derive from the unknown author of that work, so they have not been considered relevant to the defining of Habakkuk the book's rhetorical style.

Textual Issues

The Hebrew text of Habakkuk in the MT is generally readable, though there are a number of challenges with some passages obscure, the poetry extremely terse, and a number of *hapax* whose potential meaning is unclear. Unless there is incontrovertible evidence for an alternative reading and one that makes good sense, then this reader declines to follow an emended text. Suggestions for 'correcting' or 'improving' an ancient text by modern scholars with no lived experience of the language inevitably produce a text or reading that is highly subjective and arbitrary—the very thing that should be avoided if one hopes to understand an author's or editor's intentions. It is a fact of life that an ancient text such as Habakkuk, that arose and circulated in an oral context until being put into a written form and hand-copied over the years, will have within it many textual issues that no modern scholar can reasonably explain. These have to be noted, accepted and generally left.

Some commentators have sought to use comparisons with the Qumran text 1QpHab to resolve some as yet uncertain readings, but differences are generally minor, having to do with Qumran's alleged tendency to confuse the Hebrew letters 'y' and 'w' that, if not written carefully, can be misread.

Theological Basis of Habakkuk

It is important to distinguish between (a) the theology underpinning the anonymous Lament Psalm taken up by Habakkuk, and (b) that providing the foundation of the Dialogue. The Lament said to be quoted by Habakkuk, according to the Editor, evidences a theology typical of that of persons who are distressed about circumstances in which the individual or society is suffering, is being oppressed, or encountering injustice, and which God seems not to resolve to his worshipers' satisfaction. God, in this setting, is distant and possibly even seen as uncaring, so the worshiper uses the Lament-form as a liturgical means to pour out heartfelt dissatisfaction with his God. The fundamental questions are '*How much longer...?*' and '*Why...?*', implying that the worshiper's trust is being tested beyond comprehension. Israel's God is silent in the face of righteous suffering. The Lament form's confession of trust expresses the belief that the national God YHWH has a special and covenanted relationship with him or with them, such that he/they can appeal for special treatment and hope to be rescued from whatever the crisis that threatens. There is mention of God's past responses, consistent with the divine character, that give the worshiper confidence that God can be depended upon in this new context as well. In Habakkuk's case that clearly has not yet been forthcoming. So Habakkuk is questioning the covenant relationship and the divine character that he wants to believe is still in place.

The questions that Habakkuk has asked have to be seen against the background of a Deuteronomic theology in which faithfulness and obedience to *torah* will have beneficial and practical results in almost an automatic fashion (see Deut. 7.12-16; 28.1-14). The Deuteronomic cohort represent one of several different theological positions known at the time, and it is their hardline view that Habakkuk finds utterly inadequate. The notion that Obedience guarantees Blessing, while Disobedience brings Curses is clearly too extreme and simplistic, and Habakkuk is one example of those who question that basic assumption, along with Qoheleth the Sage and the editor of Job, for example. Habakkuk has been waiting for God to act, but thus far God has seemingly been unable to respond. While in the Lament there is no answer to Habakkuk's questions, there is a resolution; despite all that could happen, the psalmist remains faithful (3.17-19). This is the climax.

Then there is the Dialogue section, presumably the creation of the Editor, believing that it reflects the concerns that originated with Habakkuk. It is in this interaction that YHWH as the God of all the earth is most evident. While Habakkuk sees God as pure, holy and intolerant of evil and wrongdoing, nevertheless God is said to be about to release the terror of Chaldea's might against his own people. There is no justification or reason provided in this divine speech for God raising up the Chaldeans, so although Habakkuk's quote in 1.2-4 highlights the undermining of *torah* in Judaea, some wrongly assume that God's action in a Chaldean attack was designed to punish those in Judaea who are guilty of the violence—similar to Isaiah 10 and the call of Assyria as God's agent to punish Israel. This reader believes that such an assumption reads too much into the dialogue and appears to reflect an obsession with sin and punishment. While more traditional prophet-like denunciation of social evils, of unjust gain, of bloodshed and murder, even of sexual violence and idolatry that appear in the 'Woe' oracles, are presumed to be those of Habakkuk, they are not clearly articulated. They are general and could apply to any community, whether that of the Judaeans or Chaldeans. *Torah* as the basis for life, both individual and community, is rooted in the Sinaitic covenant theology to which Habakkuk adheres.

Exegesis

1.1 Superscription

The Massa' which Habakkuk the prophet envisioned.

The book of Habakkuk contains three editorial notes: the first is 1.1, and the second 3.1 with a final note in 3.20. The two final notes are here regarded as the original introduction to the Lament psalm quoted, as in Psalm 7, rather than introducing a separate 'prayer' (see below at 3.1)

The Superscription (1.1) contains three main elements other than the individual name 'Habakkuk': they are (1) the initial literary form, namely *Massa'*, that identifies the report as belonging to a form that exhibits both prophetic and wisdom characteristics. It has didactic purpose. See the Introduction to Nahum for discussion. The title also refers to (2) the report as something that Habakkuk 'saw', before adding a final note (3) that he was a prophet (Heb. *nabi'*). Apart from these three elements, we know nothing further about Habakkuk. His name is not mentioned again in the body of the text, nor is his title as 'prophet' ever repeated apart from the second editorial note (3.1). All first-person pronouns are assumed to refer to Habakkuk as speaker, but when he is addressed by God, no personal name is used—all speech addressed to him is in second person, in both singular and plural forms, suggesting an even wider audience.

It is the second element in the Superscription that is intriguing—the verb 'saw' (Heb. *chazah*) links with the noun-form *chazon*, 'vision' (2.2-3), though there is nothing in the text that approaches a description of an optical vision. His 'vision' is actually the situation he saw about him—violence! On the other hand, there is much in the book that has to do with seeing—apart from *chazah*, other Hebrew verbs, *ra'ah* and *bit*, as well as *tsapah* 'watch over', and the demonstrative *hinneh*, 'behold!' all belong to the semantic range of 'seeing', pointing to the notion of 'seeing' as clearly a metaphor, and a rhetorical theme for chapters 1–2.

The third element in the Superscription refers to Habakkuk as a *nabi'*, a traditional term for one who, among other things, is a 'spokesperson for God'. However, in this book Habakkuk begins with a complaint, a complaint addressed <u>to</u> God! There are a number of problems when the term 'prophet' is understood so narrowly as to limit it to speaking <u>for</u> God, but for the moment we should note that despite this title of 'prophet' being given Habakkuk, the text of the report does not use any of the expected formulae or rhetorical markers that frequent other so-called prophetic works—the closest one comes to the standard *'Thus says the Lord…, says the Lord'* formula is in 2.2 when we read *'The Lord answered me and said…'*.

Other than these three elements, the Superscription is silent with regard to Habakkuk the person. This is the only document in which the name *Habakkuk* appears; it is unique, and its etymology is uncertain and irrelevant. The book gives no indication of a time period or location to which the text can be attached. In fact, without the Superscription one could assume that Habakkuk the book was much more in the nature of an Individual Lament than identifying as a 'prophetic' text—see on Structure in the Introduction.

1.2-4 Habakkuk's Lament—Part A

2. <u>How much longer</u>, O Lord must I cry for help? But you do not listen!
   I call out to you (against the) violence, but you do not rescue.

3. <u>Why</u> do you make me witness evil, and make me see trouble?
   Destruction and violence are right in front of me, there is an upsurge
   in strife and contention.

4. <u>Therefore</u> Torah is ineffective, and justice never prevails; for the wicked
surround the just, and thereby justice is perverted.

One of the primary literary forms in the book of Psalms is the Lament; individual and collective forms are in fact the most common of all the forms represented there. This says a great deal about Israel's experience of life, as well as its freedom to openly complain to and challenge God when seeking divine help in confronting oppression or an attack of any kind, collective or individual.

1.2 The opening words—*How long, O Lord must I cry for help? But you do not listen!*—could be a quote from Ps. 22.2 if we could date each accurately; nevertheless, the words express in a profound way a person's frustration at the delay in receiving relief or help that the petitioner believes only God can give. See e.g., Ps. 13.1-2. The *How long...?* question is even better translated as *'How much longer...'*? It was and is a common experience, seeking divine help in a crisis and wondering if and when that help might come. When seemingly unanswered, it can lead to such black thoughts as here expressed, that God does not seem to be listening, and the help sought is not forthcoming. The appeal here would suggest that Habakkuk is in the midst of a crisis, and that he has already appealed to God for divine aid. Can we discover what that crisis was, and when might it have happened? Or is the appeal merely using a traditional form of words typical of all Laments and so flexible, usable in many different crises? In general terms, the crisis is one in which violence clearly is dominating life at the time, resulting in the overthrow or corruption of the justice system, for the violence is not being assuaged.

While the opening line of this appeal uses words similar to those in Ps. 22.2, the parallel second line, is reminiscent of Job's complaint in Job 19.7—'*I cry out "Violence", but you fail to answer!*' It is this second line in the appeal—*I call out to you (against the) violence, but you do not rescue*—that identifies the particular problem being addressed. However, the violent acts (Heb. *chamas*) and who is responsible for them is not mentioned. If we were able to identify the nature of the violence and the perpetrators, readers would be able to gain a clearer picture of the situation facing Habakkuk. However, such clarity is not possible, mostly because in Laments generally, only metaphors are used to speak indirectly of the problem faced—often they are simply identified as 'enemies', 'wild animals', 'dogs', 'bulls'—and, furthermore, the various metaphors can all be used together as descriptors of the one issue of the moment, further masking the specifics of the case (see e.g., Ps. 22.12-21). For this reason, the terms '*the wicked*' and '*the righteous*' found here as general terms cannot be identified in any more precise manner.

The violence envisaged in the Lament may be physical, emotional, political, economic, social or a combination of all forms. The important thing is that the reader is hereby drawn emotionally into a world that is real, and for which Habakkuk longs for divine rescue—but unfortunately thus far he has found no help.

1.3 The second appeal element in the Lament—*Why do you make me witness evil, and see trouble?*—asks the 'Why?' question, accusing God of forcing the complainant to continue to endure the violence and evil of his situation. Parallel verbs of 'seeing' emphasize what is in Habakkuk's line of sight; violence is all around him. His 'vision' (Heb. *chazon*) is what he can see—it is <u>not</u> a vision for the future! Habakkuk adopts hyperbole to stress the universality of the problem in society and to complain that God's inaction prevents its resolution. There is a high degree of emotion in these cries to God as Habakkuk pours out his frustration, even anger, blaming God for not acting to rescue him and the community from those who are inflicting the violence. The divine silence is deafening!

Structurally, the appeal in this verse is set out using the chiastic a-b-b-a format, focusing the appeal on the two central terms, *'awen*, 'trouble', and *'amal*, 'suffering'. Two further couplets, *Destruction and violence*, along with *strife and contention*, complete the description of the problem facing Habakkuk and his community. All are general terms providing a picture of an almost complete breakdown in society. Yet for all this we are no clearer as to those who are the cause of the problem, nor its specific form.

It is important to note that the verbs used in this appeal are imperfective, meaning that they imply a situation or action that is 'incomplete', and, in this case, point to a frequently occurring or constant state. This indicates that the threat to justice and the appeal for divine aid against that threat are both on-going.

1.4 The Lament part A ends with two clauses each beginning with the Hebrew phrase *'al-ken*, 'therefore', marking a consequence of the general violence. The first clause speaks of the *torah* 'becoming numb', that is, paralyzed and ineffective; it is powerless to deal with the situation that has arisen, presumably because *torah* is not being administered properly, i.e., justly. This is further clarified as *justice never prevails*. The Hebrew text is literally 'it does not go out for ever justice', clearly meaning that justice is never done. Perhaps this is exaggerated, but the point is strongly made—the administration of justice has failed and the consequences for the community are dire. This is further described as '*the wicked surrounding the righteous*'. Could we say, 'the wicked run rings around the just?'

The second *'al-ken* phrase speaks of the consequence of the situation for the righteous, noting that *justice is perverted*. What is done in the administration of justice is a deliberate perversion of what should happen, judgments are handed down that benefit those who do not deserve to be so served; injustice triumphs and *torah* is disempowered.

The Lament works toward this initial high point, indicating that the 'violence' (1.2) that affects the community is largely one of injustice, people who are refused the justice they deserve because the wicked have co-opted *torah* for their own ends. And while the righteous suffer, their prayers fall on an apparently deaf divine ear. From this reference to *torah* it would seem that the issue being discussed is also a failure of priestly instruction as well as a community failure to live out the demands of *torah*. In that case, Habakkuk's problem is not an international one but a domestic one.

In terms of the traditional Lament as a literary form, 1.2-4 represents only *two* initial elements, namely, the Address to God in the '*How long...?*' and '*Why have you...?*' components, plus the description of the trouble being encountered, i.e., the Complaint. Other component parts such as the Confession of Trust, a Petition, and a Song of Praise are now delayed. On this reading of the book, those remaining parts of the Lament-form are to be found in 3.2-19, the original Lament having been broken open to insert the Dialogue of 1.5–2.20.

1.5-11 God's Response?

> 5. *Look among the nations, and see (for yourselves)! Be astonished! Be astounded!*
> *Truly, a deed is being done in your days that you would not believe even if told!*
> 6. *For, Behold, I am raising up the Chaldeans, the nation (that is) fierce and determined,*
> *The one that marches through the whole world, occupying places that are not its own.*
> 7. *Terrifying and frightening are they, they administer their own justice and they air their superiority.*
> 8. *Swifter than leopards are their horses, more threatening are they than wolves in the evening,*
> *Their horses dash; their horsemen come from afar, they fly like the eagle swift to devour.*
> 9. *They all come to do violence, they set their face forward (?), taking captives (as one gathers) sand.*
> 10. *They ridicule kings and at rulers they laugh, they mock every fortress, mounding up earth(works) to capture it.*
> 11. *Then like the wind they sweep past, going on and causing offence; their strength is their god!*

This reading of Habakkuk sees the insertion of the Dialogue that begins here as strategically placed. That is to say, it begins to offer an 'answer' to the initial questions raised by Habakkuk, exploring the issue in 1.5–2.5, but in the end it is unable to satisfy. It is at that point that the Lament resumes at 3.2 with Habakkuk's only possible response—affirming faith in his God and awaiting God's rescue while living in the 'not yet'.

A change of speaker at v. 5 is not marked decisively, but the wider context suggests that God is now responding to Habakkuk's challenge. Although the Lament-form containing the complaint expressed personal disappointment, even anger, at the situation faced, 1.5-11 addresses 'you' plural, suggesting that the response is directed more widely, i.e., to the whole Judaean community. This shift in focus is more understandable if the dialogue component of the book is recognized as an editorial insert.

This 'small' change to *you* (plural) at the beginning of the inserted discourse may be significant as marking a matter of wider concern than the personal. In support of this is the fact that 1.5-11 is an independent unit that only appears to answer Habakkuk's questions in 1.2-4 because of its placement within the text. In actual fact, there is no answer in these verses to the two basic questions asked in the Lament opening. So 1.5-11 is an independent, virtually irrelevant pronouncement by Habakkuk's dialogue partner that creates a disconnect between them; God does not address the specific and domestic situation raised by Habakkuk in the Lament.

At the literary level, two themes, that of 'justice' (Heb. *mishpat*) and of 'violence' (Heb. *chamas*) in the initial address to God (1.2) are echoed in 1.7, 9, linking rhetorically or editorially the very moving poem about the Chaldean advance with the issue that is confronting Habakkuk. However, Habakkuk's initial complaint is about the undermining of *torah*, a purely domestic issue, when the so-called Response ignores that altogether, and makes a statement about the international scene, the rise of the Chaldeans. In real terms, what is here said to be God's response to Habakkuk's questions only adds fuel to the fire, because God introduces more violence into the situation by calling up the Chaldean army to attack Judaea (1.5-6).

The basic message of 1.5-11 is to indicate that the emergence of the Chaldeans as a threat to Judaea is being driven by God (1.6) without any explanation as to the reason for such; there is no justification offered for their attack, and certainly no mention of sin that many assume to be the reason. Such an assumption may well derive from a commentator's preconceived notion of what a prophet normally criticized. Nor does God attempt to challenge Habakkuk's assessment of the situation in Judaea; it is simply ignored.

When it comes to the specific questions Habakkuk asked of God, 1.5-11 does not provide any reasonable answer to the '*How long...?*' or the '*Why do you...?* questions, as we have noted, so one can begin to sympathize with Habakkuk being left with more questions than before, hence his negative reaction in 1.12-14. The clear disconnect between Habakkuk's questions and the contents of 1.5-11 makes it appear as though God actually ignored his two questions, questions that faith and wisdom struggle with unendingly.

There follows a vivid and dramatic description of the power and might of the Chaldeans and the speed with which they overwhelm their enemies whom they despise and belittle (1.7-11). Their own power is their god! There are clear echoes of the imagery and description of an advancing enemy found in Joel 2.1-9 with regard to an advance on Judah. This, together with the Lament setting of Joel, suggests that there was a general body of oral discussion, of shared rhetoric about the Babylonian attacks on Judah leading up to the Fall of Jerusalem in 587 BCE. Editors of both Joel and Habakkuk reflect this shared talk, along with the deeper questions that were raised over an extended period of time following that disaster.

At the structural level, we have to ask about the editorial purpose of breaking open the Lament-form in order to insert this created 'dialogue' between Habakkuk and God. What is the Editor attempting to do? It would seem that one purpose of the dialogue was to engage a discussion about the divine role in current events, in this case, the rise of the Babylonian Empire and its impact on God's people, Judah. In one sense, the Editor seeks to contextualize the issue of Violence and how Justice is managed; Habakkuk's complaint in this section is given an historical setting, but it does not answer his domestic questions.

1.5 The text calls the people to '*Look (among the nations) and see...*', inviting the community to be aware of what is happening on the international scene. How possible this was is doubtful, but the community at large would know to some degree what issues they were facing in terms of neighbouring nations impinging on Judah. The four imperatives—'*Look...see...be astonished...be astounded...*'—certainly provide a heavy emphasis on the call to be aware of what is or has been happening, and now to keep an eye on what amazing things are about to happen.

The initial *ki*, 'Indeed, ...' adds to the importance of the message to follow. These matters are described as '*a work/deed being done*', a participial phrase implying something about to happen or actually in current progress. The unprecedented nature of the action is further underlined by the statement '*you wouldn't believe it, even if it were explained*'.

The claim of divine action in 1.5b-6 is expressed using participles of the Hebrew verbs concerned. Recalling that Hebrew verbs depict states of being rather than times of an action, the participles here express matters currently in progress or imminent. This then has bearing on the moment in time that Habakkuk's Lament is editorially located vis-a-vis the 587 BCE destruction of Jerusalem.

At first glance it appears that the timeless Lament predates 587, but the Babylonian invasion of Judah was an incremental advance, and it is entirely possible that Habakkuk was witness to that and was dreading what the final outcome might be. On the other hand, there is no demonstrable relationship between the Lament quoted and the Babylonian invasion; the former is timeless and of unknown origin, while the latter is time-specific. The disconnect between the Lament and the dialogue in terms of a temporal relationship is most obvious at this point. Here, God announces that a Babylonian attack is about to happen and that he is the one who has arranged its irresistible advance. What the 'response' does not say is why the Babylonian invasion was necessary, nor what it has to do with Habakkuk's domestic concerns over *torah* being perverted.

1.6 The opening Hebrew particle *ki*, is the asseverative, 'Truly/Indeed'. Along with the *hinneni* + participle it speaks of the imminent or current divine activity of '*raising up the Chaldeans*'. The Hebrew verb *qum* that basically describes rising or raising, is frequently used to signal the first movement towards an action—one 'gets up' then to start an action.

The *Chaldeans*, an ethnic group centered on Ur, the city from which Abraham is said to have come (Gen 11.31), took over the marshy region of southeastern Mesopotamia and later infiltrated into the region of Babylon c. the tenth century BCE. They eventually ruled an empire known as Babylonia in southern Mesopotamia from c. 625 BCE to 538 BCE when they were defeated by the Persians. Two adjectives are used to describe the Chaldeans—Hebrew *mar*, usually descriptive of something bitter, is here more probably referring to a temperament, a fierce temper as in Judg. 18.25, since it is linked with a word *nimhar* that derives from 'haste/speed' that some regard as impetuous. Neither is exactly common, but the context assists our understanding.

They are then said to be '*going to all parts of the land/earth*' meaning that they are advancing on all the regions surrounding them. That is probably hyperbole to emphasize their drive to conquer, since the text then states a purpose, namely '*to possess/take over dwellings not their own*' or '*to occupy places that do not belong to it*'.

1.7 Another duality adds to the description—Hebrew *'ayom* describes something that is terrible or terrifying—a rare word, it is found only here and in Song 6.4, 10. Joining the description is the more common word *nora'*, 'fearful' *or* 'instilling fear'. This latter is often used in descriptions of YHWH and 'the day of the Lord'. The Chaldeans then administer their own form of justice (Heb *mishpat*) and demonstrate their arrogance

(Heb. *s'etho*). The former, justice, links rhetorically with the failure of justice in the Lament (1.3), and does so by emphasizing that justice is something that the Chaldeans will administer—it 'proceeds from them' (Heb. *mimmennu...yetse*). This should be seen as a positive step rather than negative, contrasting its failure in Judaea, where it 'did not proceed' (Heb. *lo'-yetse*). That the Babylonians administered their own justice is not something to complain about or wrongly interpret; the famous Babylonian Law Code of King Hammurabi of the eighteenth century BCE formed the basis of all Law throughout the ANE, even influencing that of the later Israelites.

1.8-9 A feature of v. 8 is the use of the leopard, wolf and eagle to represent the speed and destruction that are marks of the Chaldean army. Their horses are swifter than leopards, as dangerous as wolves, and their horse-borne attack as sudden and complete as the eagle swooping on its prey. Each image builds a picture of an army's relentless advance. Horses as military instruments may have originated in Anatolia and their use spread from there, being introduced into the Palestinian region during the early part of the second millennium BCE. Horses, whether ridden or as pulling chariots, were essentially used for military purposes. Speed was one of their major advantages over the asses and donkeys of daily life, so the point is made that even though this army comes from afar, its arrival is near. And they come intent on *Violence*! The reference to violence links editorially with the same term in 1.3

The advance of the horses and the riders is depicted in dramatic and compact form in v. 9b although the Hebrew text is problematic—singular and plural conflicts, gender conflicts, uncertain meanings, truncated colons. The initial Hebrew participle *m'gammath* is uncertain and despite emendations and varied opinions, there is no consensus as to its meaning or origin. Then *'their faces'* may refer to either the faces of the horses or their riders, or to both. The following term *qadimah* indicates a direction but whether it is 'forward' or the compass point 'to the east' is debated. There seems no reason to suggest that the Babylonian army will move east, so the better view is to read it as 'forwards'. The dramatic nature of the description suggests that the horses and the chariot riders both are straining forward as they race across the land. The second phrase in v. 9c pictures the army as '*gathering captives like sand*', a simile that expresses limitless numbers—see Gen. 22.17—rather than building sandcastles on the beach!

1.10 The arrogance of the Chaldean army is noted in the two Hebrew verbs, *qls* and *schq*, both of which speak of laughter and scoffing. The Chaldean army being raised by God shows personal contempt for all other rulers and kings. And when their fortified towns and cities are encountered these too are treated with contempt as siegeworks (?) are built against them and they are captured. However, there is no clarity in this verse as to whether what is captured is territory or people. Singular forms throughout the verse do not aid in clarifying meaning.

There is a wordplay in the second colon with the noun *mibtsar*, 'fortress', and the verb *tsbr*, 'heap up', having similar sounds. The latter verb is usually used in the context of accumulating vast amounts of things, but here is used with the noun *'apar*, 'dust', which most regard as meaning earth or earthworks, but obviously such a reading is incongruous. Some have seen 'dust' as a simile parallel to 'like sand' in v. 9b and so understand the illustration in v. 10b to refer to piling up captives 'like dust'.

A further issue in this verse is the final verb phrase '*he takes/captures it*' in which the singular form may be regarded as a collective reference to the Chaldean army as a whole, but the final pronoun is feminine and has no antecedent.

1.11 The verse opens with the Hebrew particle *'az*, 'Then...' usually indicating the next item in a list. It is possible to regard the particle as recording the capture of another city as the army moves on to the next obstacle in its way. Two verbs are used in v. 11a—'to sweep on' and 'to pass by/over'. The problem is that the subject is *ruach*, 'spirit, wind, breath'. Which of its senses is intended is unclear, but whatever sense is assigned will determine different interpretations. Does the army charge on from one city to another? Is the army traversing the region '*like the wind*?' Does the wind simply blow? And does the verb *'abar* denote passing by, or passing through, or crossing over? And what might the spirit/wind/breath 'pass over'? NRSV has seen it as a reference to the human spirit 'passing over' into sin and inviting divine judgment! This is done because the following term *'ashem*, usually carries the sense of one being 'guilty' of some cultic failing. But see 'A Final Note on Translation and Interpretation'.

The final phrase in the verse is a further challenge—literally, 'this his strength for his god' is meaningless as the particle has no antecedent. In light of the preceding description of the power and speed of the Chaldean army, 'its strength/power is its god' may be a possible interpretation, but suggestions for emendations to the Hebrew are arbitrary as there is no textual evidence for other than what we now see in the MT.

This entire section appears to begin with the promise of Chaldean emergence in the wider world, but before Judaea has been invaded. The primary focus then moves (vv. 7-11) to a description of the speed and devastation the army will bring. It does not attempt to answer Habakkuk's questions; it simply makes statements about the Chaldeans whose army God is about to launch upon Judaea.

1.12-17 Habakkuk Challenges God

A feature of the editorial insertion 1.5–2.20 is its lack of signage with regard to the speakers involved. The only reference to a speaker is in 2.2—'*the Lord answered and said...*' The entire book lacks the most basic markers of divine speech, and one can only assume that the first-person speech is that of Habakkuk and that the rest is reported speech put into God's mouth. Thus, this new section vv. 12-17 is assumed to report Habakkuk's reaction to God's monologue in vv. 5-11. Third-person singular references presumably are to the Chaldean army, as in v. 12c.

> *12. Are you not from the distant past, O Lord? My God, my sacred one, do not let us die!*
> *O Lord, you have appointed him/it for judgement, and as a rock for an accusation you have established him/it.*
>
> *13. Your eyes are too pure to look upon evil, and to watch wrongdoing you are not able*
> *Why then do you regard those who cheat, and remain silent when the wicked devour the one more righteous than himself?.*
>
> *14. And you have made humans like fish of the sea, like a thing that crawls, that has no leader.*
>
> *15. All with a hook he has lifted it up, dragged it out with his net*
> *And gathered it in his seine, therefore he is happy and rejoices.*
>
> *16. That is why he offers a sacrifice to his net and burns incense to his seine*
> *For by means of them his portion was abundant and his food was bountiful*
>
> *17. Will he therefore empty his net, and constantly kill foreigners without further thought?*

What is presented as Habakkuk's response to God's address makes it clear that Habakkuk is not at all satisfied with God's statement in 1.5-11. In fact, Habakkuk seems even more troubled by what God was alleged to have said, as he does not see the prospect of a brutal Chaldean invasion offering a solution to the domestic crisis of a weakened *torah* in Judaea (1.4). Translators and interpreters must consider Habakkuk's very human reaction to God's response if they are to re-present more than the surface words. Habakkuk's response is full of sarcasm, or at least it expresses his deepest disappointment at the divine indifference, that leads into the 'Why?' question in 1.13. To read Habakkuk's words as an expression of his profound faith, as some have done, shows a lack of sensitivity to the context—the response is full of irony!

Literarily, the response is set in terse poetic language that limits the use of the definite article and accusative marker so subjects and objects in these verses cannot always be clarified. The marker for the relative clause (*'asher*) is not used, so relationships within the verses are sometimes unclear. The temporal setting of the poem is also ambiguous, and translations make a choice between using all present tense verbs and using future tense. Add to this a number of actual Hebrew text issues, and the section challenges every translator and interpreter, though a general sense is definitely achievable. Habakkuk still asks 'Why?' (v. 13) his God seems unperturbed at witnessing the evil, the wrongdoing, the cheating, and the success of the wicked over the righteous whether it is within Judaea or on the international scene. It is beyond Habakkuk's comprehension that God fails to recognize the problem that Habakkuk 'sees'.

1.12 Habakkuk's reaction to God's speech begins with a rhetorical question in the negative: '*Are you not from of old, O Lord, my God, my sacred one?*' It is another way of saying 'You, Lord, my God, my sacred one, are from of old'. However, in its negative format the rhetorical question usually takes to task the one addressed—see also Isa. 40.21, 28; Ezek. 13.7. Here then is an abrupt beginning to Habakkuk's reaction to what God has announced, and it signals Habakkuk's deep frustration that God hasn't answered his questions in 1.2-4. The initial *h'lo'* from the outset tells the reader how to interpret Habakkuk's response—it expresses his doubt, his serious challenge arising from what he has just heard. To misread this is to misunderstand the very nature of Habakkuk's Response.

The section lists a number of abstract qualities of YHWH in the titles used—lordship, holiness, longevity, rock-like dependence. The disconnect between the original question about justice and violence and God's response, confirms the view that the dialogue is an inserted piece quite separate from the Lament that brackets the book.

The noun *qedem*, 'front, before, East' can apply to place as well as time; here it is a general or non-specific time reference to the past. As a form of address, the question expresses the state of the relationship that Habakkuk and his people share with YHWH. The dialogue can go in any direction from there!

The noun phrase '*my God my sacred/holy one*' presents Habakkuk as holding a traditional view of a personal relationship with YHWH, the holy one. By stressing YHWH's holiness or separateness, Habakkuk is subtly(?) reminding God that it is in the divine nature to be on the side of those who are mistreated, not in cahoots with the violent Chaldeans. There is a clear note of sarcasm in Habakkuk's reaction.

The line continues with a phrase that in MT is 'we shall not die', or 'do not let us die' if one reads the verb as jussive. The original text, according to the rabbinic reading, should be 'you will not die', and the LXX, followed by many translations, reads it as such. It is nevertheless a very strange pronouncement for a human to make about God, for gods were not subject to death.

The second half of the verse may also be under the influence of the opening question-form 'Are/Did you not...?' in which case the question continues as '*O Lord, (did you not) appoint him to/for judgment?*' It is a further challenge to God—something like, '*Have you forgotten that you determined...*'? that recalls God's long-standing commitment to Israel. The question itself is ambiguous, however: it could mean that the Chaldeans were (1) to be judged (passive), or (2) to act as judge (active), in line with the following verb *l'hokiach*, 'to rebuke'. Verse 12d reads as '*O Rock, to rebuke you have designed him*'; this would seem to imply an active interpretation as appropriate, but what would that mean? Israel's traditional attitude towards foreign powers would suggest that the passive, 'be judged', is the more likely interpretation but certainty is elusive.

1.13 The first half of this verse is very challenging. It continues the statement about aspects of the divine character and involves the use of the two Hebrew key verbs *ra'ah* and *bit*, both having to do with '(not) seeing' or '(not) looking'. Both verbs here are figurative, referring to God's <u>attitude</u> towards the evil that is being done in the world. Initially '*your eyes are pure beyond looking at evil*' meaning that God is of such purity that he cannot tolerate evil. The purity (Heb. *tahor*) here is that of ritual cleanliness, meaning that one can participate in the cultic life of the community. Normally this state or status is applicable to humans rather than to God.

The second half verse 1.13b is similar, literally '*to look on wrongdoing you are not able*'. Again, this is a traditional theological statement about the divine nature as understood—God is unable to tolerate wrongdoing. Habakkuk is making these <u>ironic</u> statements to remind God that these are the principles that should be operative, that are consistent with God's nature, but.... they aren't being implemented! They lead into the repeat of the 'Why?' question that God seems to be refusing to answer.

The 'Why?' question asks God, who <u>cannot</u> 'look on' evil, why he(?) <u>can</u> 'look on' those who cheat and deceive, and say nothing when the evildoer devours the one who is more righteous than himself (see e.g., Ps. 10.1, 13). The irony is that God fails to protect the righteous from the wicked. Habakkuk is more than just mystified at divine inaction on behalf of the righteous, he is positively angered and expresses that in this sarcastic response. The questions he raised in 1.2-4 remain unanswered.

The question of injustice in the human community and of God's role in resolving the difficulties it raises, lie at the heart of Habakkuk's Lament, as they do at the heart of every Lament. The issue was also central to the ponderings of the Sages—see Qoh. 3.16–4.3 and Job. The Editor's report of the Habakkuk-God dialogue indicates that prophets and sages alike were troubled by their experiences and what they saw happening in society, while seeking some answer other than the narrow and inadequate thesis of the Deuteronomic cohort (e.g. Deut. 28.1-14).

1.14-15 Habakkuk turns to the past and speaks of God creating *'adam*, humanity, like *'the fish of the sea'*, while the second simile refers to *'things that crawl'*. The two references link humanity's numbers with the creation narrative in Gen. 1.21-24. Schools of fish and swarms of insects may appear to be leaderless, but is that the point being made here? Or, is it human insignificance? Perhaps it serves as nothing more than an introduction to the illustration of the net or seine with which fish and insects can be caught. In the present context, it would appear reasonable to see these similes as referring to the way in which the Chaldeans treated those whom they captured, literally using hooks and/or nets to ensnare and manacle those whom they made captives and took into exile (See Amos 4.2). The Hebrew noun *cherem* has two distinct meanings deriving from the same root letters—a *homograph*: (1) refers to devoted objects that are under the ban, that is 'taboo', and (2) a 'net' such as one thrown by a fisherman standing in or near the water. The latter is the sense here.

Having captured their prey, the Chaldeans customarily rejoice and celebrate—that is the nuance of the imperfect verb forms.

1.16-17 As a result (Heb. *'al-ken*) of this military success the Chaldeans regard their 'nets' and 'seines' as objects of devotion, and offer sacrifices to them as thank-offerings for their success. This statement mocks Babylonian religion; it is figurative and hyperbolic, expressing the view that the

Chaldeans are so committed to pillage and war that it resembles religious devotion, as in 1.11.

The second line of v. 16 is ambiguous. Literally it reads, *'for by them he grows fat his portion, and his food is rich'*. The problem term is 'his portion', a term that often applies to one's inherited land (Deut 3.13), but it can also refer to other rewards. Here the link to food suggests that the 'fish' are real fish and not simply a metaphor for captured peoples. Either way, the point is that the Chaldeans grow rich and 'fat' on their exploits as they capture enemy territory and peoples.

The rhetorical question in v. 17 about continuing to empty the nets is figurative for assuming an on-going policy of merciless rape and pillage. It is no wonder that Habakkuk refuses to accept the thought that his God is sending against his people the might of this brutal Chaldean army. Habakkuk's vision of YHWH may have been a traditional one, but that is now under enormous pressure given the unacceptable divine response of 1.5-11. God's integrity is at stake!

2.1 Habakkuk Awaits God's Reply

1. Let me take my stand upon the lookout, and take my place on the ramparts;

Let me keep watch to 'see' what he will say against me, and how I shall respond (to him), with regard to my dispute.

After his challenge to God in 1.12-17, Habakkuk retreats to his post to wait and see what God has to say to him regarding his on-going 'Why?' question. The text does not intend to describe Habakkuk's work site or his profession as some have suggested; it is simply the Editor's transitional marker in the dialogue as Habakkuk anticipates God's perhaps negative reaction to his challenge. He has no idea how God will react, so in that sense this transitional element heightens the tension in the dialogue report.

The first-person verbs in this statement can be read as simple imperfects, but in terms of syntax they are cohortatives—Habakkuk is presented as musing about the next stage in the dialogue. The final verb, Hebrew *'ashib*, literally 'I return'—here in the sense of 'retort'—is often emended to read as third-person, '...what he will answer...'. This follows the rabbis' suggested reading arising from their unease with the notion that one should not be so impudent as to argue with God, but such an emendation is based on notions unrelated to the text. The first-person form makes perfectly good sense in the context of the dialogue.

There is an echo of Job 13.3 and 23.4 in the use of the noun *tokachti* to describe Habakkuk's 'complaint' or argument. Job had no qualms about presenting his case (*tokeach*) before the Almighty, wanting to argue the matter as does Habakkuk here.

2.2-5 God's Reply

2. Then the Lord answered me and said:
  Write a vision plainly on the stones so that one running past can still read it.

3. Indeed, there is another vision for the appointed time; he witnesses to the end and <u>will not</u> deceive.
  If he delays, then wait for him, for he will certainly come and <u>will not</u> delay.

4. Behold, the arrogant whose spirit/soul is not straight within him, but the righteous person by his faithfulness endures.

  5. And yet indeed wine is a cheat, a man is arrogant and <u>will not</u> last,
  The one who opens his spirit (is) like Sheol, he/it is like death that will not be satisfied.
  Gathering to himself/itself every foreigner and collecting for himself/ itself every people.

Verse 2a is the only reference in the book that identifies YHWH as a speaker.

The Lord calls on Habakkuk to 'write a vision'. Despite the use of several Hebrew verbs for 'see', including *chazah*, there is no description of or reference to the content of a 'vision' (Heb. *chazon*) other than what Habakkuk could see around him (see 1.3). What then was Habakkuk to write, or draw? Was Habakkuk one of the tiny minority who were literate? The Editor has called the book 'a vision' here and at 1.1, but it would seem that what has been called a *chazon* was not related to a message concerning the future, as in some prophetic books, but simply the violence and injustice he witnessed in his community. Whatever the solution to the issue of the 'vision', these four verses are perhaps best regarded as an introduction to the collected oracles that follow in vv. 6-20.

Unfortunately, the text seems to have suffered some problems in transmission from oral to written form, and perhaps in the transmission of the written form again, because it presents numerous difficulties to translators and interpreters. Terseness of its poetics is one issue, along with the identification of the pronouns especially in 2.3 and 5, and the isolated clause that ends 2.4. Syntax in places is complex and unusual (see below).

Despite these limitations, it is possible to sense that something irrevocable is about to happen at a time of God's choosing, that the singular pronouns refer essentially to the Chaldeans, and that their arrogance will continue to push them to seek further territorial gains at the expense of other nations. If this be the sense, then these verses reaffirm what was spoken of in 1.5-11, meaning that Habakkuk's initial questions (1.2-4) are no further advanced.

One rhetorical feature of the speech is the balance of positive and negative clauses in 2.3, 5: *it longs for the end and* will not *lie; it will certainly come and* will not *delay; a man is arrogant and* will not *last; he is like death that* will not *be satisfied.*

2.2 The order to '*write a vision*' plainly begs the question of the 'vision' itself. As noted above, this is not some visual object that needs depicting in written form, but of what exactly the vision consists is unclear. Writing or drawing it '*on the stones*' would appear to refer to specific stones or tablets as though they have been provided for that purpose. As for the tablets (Heb. *luchoth*), they could be stone, requiring that they be engraved with some message, or clay tablets that would be imprinted using a stylus, then hardened. The more important point is that the message should be easily read, widely accessible—'*so that he who runs may read it*' while some suggest translating it as '*he who proclaims it may run*'. The verb (Heb. *qore' bo*) usually implies something read aloud and if the latter sense is correct, then it seems to imply a person running about shouting its message. There is some suggestion that the imagery of one running past the stones or tablets is idiomatic for a quick read—also implying very large letters or drawings. However, from what is known of such objects or obelisks, the calligraphy is generally so small that a person would need to stop and examine the text in order to appreciate what was written or drawn, and, if wholly written, then only the literate could access the 'vision'. The form that would be most widely understood would be illustrations or diagrams that were typical of the Chaldean armies and of its enemies, rather than anything consisting only of 'alphabetic' letters.

Attempts to link these tablets to the Ten Commandments in importance is a bow too long!

2.3 Why must Habakkuk wait for a vision if he has already been given one? The Hebrew adverb '*od* can mean, 'still, yet, again', so it is a very vague introduction to the fixed time (Heb. *mo'ed*) that God has set. The verbs attached to the description seem inappropriate, for visions do not hurry or become delayed, or be late; they are just visions one has and perhaps shares. The pronouns here that could be 'he' or 'it' therefore are best seen as referring to a person not a vision.

A verb (*yapeach*) that usually means 'to blow/breathe' is difficult to link with the vision and so its translation has been a guess, along with the verb *y'kazzeb*, 'lies'. Neither seems appropriate to the vision context but some commentators have 'squeezed' the meanings or emended the text to make them fit their purpose. That problem has been resolved in the sense that a Ugaritic root *ypch* that refers to 'witnessing' may offer a more suitable reading—see Prov. 19.5. It also supports the view that the third-person singular pronouns should be regarded as references to a person and not to the vision itself. The content of the vision may well be the several 'Woe…' clauses in 2.6-20.

2.4 The attention-getting *hinneh*, Behold! marks the description of *his spirit* (Heb. *naphsho*); it is said to be 'swollen'. The Hebrew noun *'upp'lah* is from a root that describes something as 'swollen' or 'tumor-like', and here is made to refer to a certain kind of person, one who contrasts with the parallel 'righteous one'. Proud and arrogant, *puffed up*, would describe such a one, and it also combines well with the other characteristic, he is '*not straight*', not upright or true. One may assume that they are the counterpart of the righteous ones, that is, 'the wicked'. The *nephesh* or 'spirit', more often than not refers to the real person, the 'soul', the essence of what it is to be human. It can also represent the emotions and desires one has. However, another meaning can be attributed to the Hebrew noun *nephesh*, namely 'throat'. The connection is hard to see for most readers, but it is applied to Sheol's desire to devour, its insatiable appetite, and so it has come to have the probable meaning 'throat' or 'mouth and throat' as in v. 5c. So, we have a suggested translation, '*Behold the arrogant whose spirit/soul is not true within him*'.

The initial *waw* in v. 4b is read as 'but' in order to make the contrast—'*but the righteous one lives by his faithfulness*'. The Hebrew noun *'emunah* refers to one's reliability or moral trustworthiness, one who maintains his integrity, not 'faith' as understood in modern parlance. The question remains as to whose faithfulness is intended; is it because of the *'emunah* of God that one can rely on whatever God says or does, or is it the individual's faithfulness and trustworthiness? At the human level it contrasts with the one who is not an 'upright' or reliable person, thus it connotes those who can be trusted, the righteous. The verb concerned is *chayah*, and it refers to a manner of living, that is, living with integrity.

Those spoken of as '*not straight*' here may imply the Chaldeans, while '*the righteous*' would imply those who lived by what is set out in the vision. However, many commentators prefer to see these terms as referring to the Judaeans. The problem is that the singular nouns are so general as to defy any specific identification.

Readers with a Christian background are probably more familiar with the version of these words as quoted in the NT, in Heb. 10.38, the basis of the later doctrine of justification by faith. (See the note on the 'core' of the book in the Conclusion). Despite the difficulties and uncertainties in the Hebrew text, many make the claim that 2.4b is the climax of Habakkuk the book. To take this position illustrates the preconceptions of the reader and removes the text from its proper context, imposing a preferred theology onto the OT text. The NT wording and interpretation tend to follow the LXX that renders the Hebrew as '*but the righteous from (my) faith shall live*'. (The possibility of misreading in LXX is dependent on the pronominal suffix 'y' or 'w', letters that are identical but for length, that can easily be mistaken in an old written MS) This LXX rendering is certainly ambiguous, more so than the original Hebrew, and could refer to the trustworthiness of the righteous person, or the trustworthiness of God. Most OT scholars recognize that MT '*...by his faith he will live*', i.e., the faithfulness of God is what gives life. This is a statement of fact—integrity and faithfulness are the mark of one who is righteous.

We note here that the Qumran *pesher* on this verse speaks of God delivering those who suffer because of their 'faith in the Teacher of Righteousness', i.e., their own leader. The community has domesticated the text to make it apply to their own situation in true *midrashic* style.

2.5 There appears to be a break in the flow of ideas at this point as v. 5 begins with '*And yet, indeed...*'. The connection, however, is uncertain, and some commentators suggest a new section begins here. The topic certainly is different, though it does take up the theme of insatiability and rapacious attacks on other peoples, the presumption being that it refers to the Chaldeans.

What does '*the wine*' have to do with deception? The sudden mention of wine has led some to consider an alternative reading, one found in the Qumran commentary or *pesher*, that suggests it is 'wealth' that deceives, and that is what is found adopted by NRSV—'*wealth is treacherous*'. This reader will retain the MT text while recognizing its difficulty.

Does '*the wine*' refer to those who drink it, who drink too much of it, for wine itself cannot deceive. It sits with another terse phrase, '*the proud/arrogant man*' (Heb. *geber yahir*) in which the noun *geber* implies a strong man, perhaps a male military figure. The adjective y*ahir* is rare, but see Prov. 21.24. The line then concludes with '*he will not endure*', suggesting that, whatever the first phrase means, the emphasis is on failing to persist in the course.

We encounter another problem with the second half of the verse as it begins with a relative that is not connected to a preceding noun, unless one regards *geber* as the antecedent. There is something consistent about this suggestion because there is a concern in God's speech with those who are proud and arrogant—as in v. 4. Perhaps the militaristic overtone of the *geber* noun makes the whole speech point to the Chaldean army as its object, and the rest of the verse adds to the nature of the army's advance.

On this reading, the army is said to '*open wide its throat/mouth like Sheol*'. This analogy links with the description in 1.13 of the way the wicked '*swallow*' the righteous. *Sheol*, the place to which the dead go, is the metaphor for an insatiable appetite, strengthened by the next phrase '*and who, like Death, is never satisfied*'. These thoughts are thoroughly consistent and perhaps influenced by the perception of Sheol and Death in Prov. 30.15. That appetite is further described as '*gathering to itself (foreign) nations, and collecting to itself all peoples*'. In this analogy, the language used for the appetite for conquering to expand the Empire is set out clearly.

2.6-20 'Woe to you who...'

The Editor, following the report of the Dialogue, has now gathered together a series of five stereotypical 'Woe' oracles—see vv. 6, 9, 12, 15 and 19. It is generally assumed that these are related to Habakkuk's vision, but that relationship is not obvious, or necessary, although the verbal and thematic links with what has preceded, especially in the opening Lament, can be identified. Each oracle begins with the marker or exclamatory *hoy*, 'Woe' or 'Alas". This is followed by a participial form that identifies the person(s) to whom the warning is issued, then there is added an announcement of the punishment that will be inflicted (except in #5), and some reason or justification given for the pronouncement, introduced by *ki*, 'because...'.

Assuming that these are Habakkuk's messages, we note that these five oracles are indeed directed at people or certain elements in the community; that is to say, this is 'prophetic' material in the more traditional sense. To that extent, they differ absolutely from the Lament and Dialogue where Habakkuk speaks only to God.

Apart from the general structure of the Woe-oracles, there is little unity between them in terms of content, so it would appear that the Editor has simply gathered together what he knew of Habakkuk's public warnings. What the original setting of each might have been in Habakkuk's presentation is now lost. Can we identify those who might have been addressed in each oracle? Only in a very general way, though plunder, bloodshed, violence and idolatry seem to be common issues being condemned. The perpetrators are not identified, so readers cannot be certain whether they are within Judaea itself, or on the wider scene. There is a possible hint that Edom might be one context (2.9), and the reference to Lebanon having been violated appears also to have some now unknown historical basis (2.17). Overall, however, the content is completely general, defying attempts to identify with any degree of confidence the persons, groups or foreign armies against whom the oracles were directed. Further, there is nothing in any of the oracles that provides a clue as to the possible time period envisaged for each. Habakkuk's question about domestic injustice now seems irrelevant, and remains unanswered in these oracles, whose context and purpose in the present collection are presumably very different from an original presentation.

The collection is introduced by v. 6a—*Are not these, all of them, against him/it, will they not raise a proverb and mocking tales about him?* Verse 6a serves as the transition from the concerns of 2.2-5 to the 'Woe' collection rather than being a component of the oracles themselves. Its transitional function is similar to the role of v. 2a, making it clear that the 'Woe' oracles have been gathered into a discrete unit consisting of well-known forms. This editorial action is especially obvious as it groups all five oracles under the rubric of *mashal*, a literary genre primarily associated, not with prophetic materials, but with proverbial wisdom (see Prov. 1.1; 10.1). The discrete collection is rounded off in 2.20 with another editorial quote—*The Lord is in his holy temple; may the whole earth keep silence before him!*—one that is found also in Zeph. 1.7 and Zech. 2.13, indicating that it was a common or shared call used by the later prophetic community of which Habakkuk was said to be a part.

2.6-8 First 'Woe' Oracle

6. Are not these, all of them, against him/it, will they not raise a proverb and mocking tales about him?
   and he will say: Woe to the one who has accumulated that which is not his—how much longer?—and who glorifies himself with pledges.

7. Will not creditors suddenly arise, and will they who violently shake you not wake up
   And you will become loot for them?

8. Because you have stolen from many nations, all the other peoples will steal from you.
   From the blood shed of people and violence in the land, the city and all who live in it.

Beginning with a rhetorical question, the oracle states what is about to happen: some wise saying that mocks him/it is going to become widely known. The saying has to do with stolen goods, things that were not his to possess. The introduction ends, as did 2.2, with the phrase '*and he will say*', so readers can expect what follows to be the content of what was said. Presumably this is what Habakkuk said to his audience either directly, or indirectly if it was referencing the Chaldean army. If the latter, the foreigners would not know of its content, so the real audience for these words was always the domestic one, as they were the ones who needed to know that God was on their side.

As for the content of the oracles, it has to do with ill-gotten gain and/or people becoming wealthy by taking 'pledges'. The latter seems unusual because things taken in pledge have to be returned to their rightful owner at some legislated point. It is clearly addressing an entity that has a reputation for invading other nations but who will now have to face similar reaction because of the bloodshed and violence they perpetrated. A keyword 'violence' (Heb. *chamas*) links directly with 1.2 and Habakkuk's complaint towards God.

2.6 The verse opens with a rhetorical question, literally '*Are these not, all of them upon/against him/it, a mashal they raise....?*' Who are those identified in such vague terms? The 'everyone' (Heb. *kullam*), and the subject of the verb 'raise', seems to refer to those nations and peoples who have been devoured by the 'arrogant ones' of v. 5. This 'everyone' will mock them by means of clever or wise sayings (Heb. *mash'lim*). This reader views each of the five sayings in the Woe-group that follows to have implied that it was the Chaldeans who were to be taunted and mocked.

The noun *mashal* has a general meaning 'simile, proverb, poem', but it is a term with wide application, not confined only to the two-line parallel form that dominates Prov. 10.1–22.16. In Job 27.1 and 29.1 *mashal* carries the sense of a well-argued discourse. A parallel term *chidah*, a riddle or enigmatic saying, helps fill out the meaning, a clever saying with mocking intent (*m'litsah*).

One has to ask about the purpose of an oracle such as this if the object was the Chaldean, because they would not hear about the threat from a small Judaean spokesperson, but if they did, they would simply laugh off such warnings as an empty threat from some foreign god. Loss of face or reputation was not something that would concern an empire such as Chaldea since it was so powerful and feared. No, any threat was for Habakkuk's domestic audience to hear, and from it to receive hopefully some comfort, knowing that YHWH, according to Habakkuk, would deal with the situation to their advantage.

'*Woe to the one who multiplies what is not his*' echoes the reference in 1.6 to the Chaldeans capturing dwellings 'not his' (Heb. *lo'lo*). However, the short phrase '*ad-mathay* 'how long?' or 'how much longer?' that follows seems completely out of place, despite it echoing the Lament's cry in 1.2. What the function of the question is, or is thought to be, is a mystery, but it suggests that there has been an issue with the oracle's written transmission.

Verse 6d then continues with a further characterization, namely '*the one who enriches himself with heavy debt*'. The verb in this clause derives from the root *kbd* that can mean 'heavy, glory', and in its unusual hiphil form with the following preposition means to 'make oneself more glorious/wealthy'. The slight problem relates to the rare noun—this is its only occurrence—that is thought to mean 'heavy debt', but it must refer to people being heavily indebted to the lender, who thereby becomes more wealthy. The translation as 'pledge' would be problematic as there were laws about objects taken in pledge; pledges were borrowed objects that had to be returned within a fixed period, so they were never a source of wealth for lenders or borrowers.

If these words were spoken of as applying to Chaldea in the pre-587 BCE context that seems to have been its more likely setting, then there is an issue to be faced—the invasion of Judah and the destruction of the Temple and subsequent exile of many Judaeans appears to question the worth of Habakkuk's warning.

2.7 Another rhetorical question opens this verse and warns that the one described in v. 6 will find himself, in addition, challenged all of a sudden by 'creditors'. They are those who figuratively 'bite' (Heb. *nshk*) or those with money who lend and who, against the rules, demand interest. In parallel is the clause '*will they who violently shake you not wake up?*' The introductory '*will they not...*' applies to this second clause to emphasize the threat implied in the 'Woe!'. The subject, namely *those who violently shake you*, is a rare participial form, and an example of one of several created poetic forms used in this book. Once the opposition is aroused, the Chaldeans—if they are the object here—will themselves become booty and be stripped.

Here the financial metaphor is used, analogically it seems, against the Chaldeans who have become materially very wealthy by virtue of their military exploits, capturing and looting other lands. The time of reckoning is fast approaching.

2.8 The threat being made in this oracle links the fate of the Chaldeans with the terrors they had brought upon the nations and upon peoples they had captured and oppressed, whose blood they had shed so violently. Two explanatory clauses claim that what they plundered will now be plundered by the 'peoples', applying the principle of an 'eye-for-an-eye'. Justice is promised, to be enforced by '*many nations*' and '*the rest*' of the peoples. This latter term 'the rest' (Heb. *yether*) refers to that which is left over, the excess, but what exactly it refers to in this context is unclear. Perhaps it means those who survived Chaldea's oppression and who will now seek revenge. The second explanatory clause refers to '*bloodshed*' and '*violence*' as the reason for a revenge attack for Chaldea's plunder directed against humanity (Heb. *'adam*) and against the earth/land (Heb. *'erets*), against the cities and their inhabitants. The phrase '*a city and all who dwell in it*' is repeated in the fourth Woe-oracle; the singular form, 'a city', has collective significance.

Once again one comes to realize that despite the threat in the oracle, there is no reference to the foundational issue Habakkuk is said to have raised, namely violence and injustice on the domestic front; the oracle, though expressed in very general terms, nevertheless appears to target Chaldea and its imperial programme. The question of its reality always looms.

2.9-11 Second 'Woe' Oracle

9. Woe to the one who *by violence makes ill-gotten gains for his family*
   To place his nest on the height, to make it safe from the hand/power of the evil person

10. *You have brought shame to your family by bringing an end to many peoples, and your whole being is corrupt.*

11. For *a stone from the wall will cry out, and a wooden beam respond.*

Translation and Interpretation of this oracle is beset with difficulties because of the terseness of the syntax, its grammatical issues, and an apparent lack of coherence throughout. Beginning with the basic notion that the oracle is a warning, or is roundly critical of certain violent behaviour, it can be assumed that the oracle condemns those who seek benefit for themselves and their family from such violence, yet who must then protect themselves from revenge attack. If directed against the Chaldeans, it is an indictment of their violence towards other nations and peoples, and of their attempt to protect themselves from being attacked by other powers. This attempt to elevate themselves will end in shame, warns the oracle, as their whole being, their *nephesh*, is corrupt. The final verse, a prophet's assessment of the alien, uses material imagery that may be intended as literal, suggesting that it looks forward to an end of the city and/or its empire. In that sense the warning is a general one, not specific nor imminent, although the Babylonian Empire did fall to the Persians in c. 559 BCE.

2.9 The second oracle directs its attention to any who seek unjust gain. The Hebrew phrase that forms a compound expression—a participle and a noun from the one root referring to getting '*evil gain*', by dishonest practices—emphatically denounces that person. It is followed by an odd phrase that is simply 'evil to/for his house'. Whether this means he brings evil to his house, or uses evil practices to benefit his family, is the issue, but the connection between the two phrases in line 1 is unclear, so it is difficult to link them so closely.

Line 2 consists of two phrases also, and each is introduced by an infinitive. The first is '<u>to place</u> on the height his nest'. The verb involved (Heb. *sim*, *sum*) can refer to establishing something, locating something in a specific place, or simply to appoint; its specific meaning depends on the context, and together with the location phrase '*on the height*' in which the noun can also refer to one's pride as well as physical elevation, interpretation is uncertain. The '*nest*' is often a metaphor for one's home, and for security, and recalls Edom's reliance on its mountainous location for its security (Obad 1.3). It is not possible to link the verse to an actual historical event or situation.

The second infinitive clause is, '<u>to escape</u> *from the hand of the evil person*'. It suggests an attempt to make oneself safe and secure from harm, for Hebrew *ra'* can refer to danger or threat as well as to moral evil. The question is whether these infinitive clauses express the <u>purpose</u> or goal of the initial dishonesty, the seeking for dishonest gain, or its <u>result</u>.

2.10 '*You counselled shame for your house*' does not seem to be a meaningful statement of some past error, but taking counsel '*for the shame (you have brought) to your house*' is a possible reading. An initial problem is that the verse moves from third-person to second-person so there is an implied change in audience. So, who are those addressed, and by whom? Is it the Chaldean leader's family, who, protected from revenge attack, are now secure but have 'lost face' in the process? Is the 'house' metaphor a reference to the dynasty and thus to the empire?

Along with this is the phrase '*cutting off of many peoples*', presumably decimating those whom they had defeated. This is followed by an even more enigmatic phrase '*and sin/corruption of your real self* (*nephesh*—see notes in vv. 4-5). I read this as critical of the Chaldeans whose very soul, according to Habakkuk, has become corrupted.

2.11 The verse opens with an asseverative *ki*, that emphasizes the point being made, but what exactly is that point? The imagery used in this verse seems not to relate to the preceding elements of the oracle in any way. What does it intend? References to stone and wood, such material objects, seem out of context here, although there is a reference to 'houses' in v. 9 to which the 'wall' and 'wood' may connect, despite that fact that 'houses' is a metaphor for family.

The use of singular forms—stone, wall, wood, and the hapax *kapis* (beam?)—are presumably collectives, but what do the verbs 'call out' and 'answer' signify? Is there sufficient evidence that they are calling for revenge, as some wish to read here? Do they point to the destruction of the 'houses' in v. 9? Are they implying that the intention to have the 'nest' and 'houses' safe from harm will be overthrown, that the Chaldeans will never be safe from attack? One can only ask questions of this oracle, but one can never be sure what is or was intended.

2.12-14 Third 'Woe' Oracle

12. <u>Woe to the one who</u> builds a town by bloodshed, and establishes a city by injustice.
13. Is it not from the Lord of hosts, the peoples grow weary merely for fire And the nations grow tired only for nothing?
14. <u>Indeed</u>, may the earth be filled with the knowledge of (lit. to know) the glory of the Lord,
    May it cover like water the sea.

What is emerging as typifying this collection of Woe oracles is the lack of cohesiveness in the contents of each, the difficult syntax and grammar, and especially of the question as to the relevance of the final line of each with the issue that precedes it. Just as 2.11 seemed unrelated to 2.9-10, so here 2.14 has little relationship to 2.12-13. It seems to be an extraneous verse from Isa 11.9.

2.12 Initially, the oracle condemns those who build a city, i.e., establish or expand their empire, by killing and taking over another's land and territory; it is not simply a matter of constructing a residential property. To do so by warfare that involves the shedding of much blood, capturing and enslaving others and all else that warfare involves, is condemned. The Hebrew term *damim*, literally 'bloods', refers to the shedding of blood, usually in a violent manner; its parallel here is *'awlah*, violent and unjust action. Together they paint a picture of the very worst of what national or tribal aggression involves. It is perhaps a fixed expression from the period given both its neat parallel structure in a-b-c format (build-town-bloodshed; establish-city-injustice), and a similar form in Mic. 3.10, where it is applied to those unjust leaders in Jerusalem.

2.13 The first line of this verse raises a textual as well as theological problem. The Hebrew text is literally, '*is it not behold from with the Lord of hosts*'? The introductory rhetorical question form '*is it not...*' is found several times in this book, so that isn't unusual, but to follow with *hinneh* (Behold!) does seem an unusual construction. For that reason some read it as *hennah*, 'they', but that becomes a grammatical problem as a feminine form without any grammatically feminine context.

The more serious question has to do with the phrase '*from with the Lord of hosts*'. In the first instance, we need to identify what it is that is 'from the Lord', and if it is a reference to the bloody warfare by which cities are established, as in v. 12, then attributing such condemned activity to God or to God's initiative creates a major theological issue, i.e., that the Lord has caused it or motivated the nations to so act, similar to the Isaiah 10 reference to God using the Assyrians as a means to punish Israel. For this reason, some regard the Woe oracles themselves as what has 'come from the Lord'. Less problematic but relevant is the use of the title, 'Lord of hosts' which, while common in the later prophets, is never used elsewhere in Habakkuk, so from that point of view, it is irregular and many regard the whole phrase as a gloss. It is quite possible that the text has been corrupted in the hand-copying process.

Verse 13b, using strict parallelism, makes the point that all human attempts to establish cities by violence come to nothing; they fail. The imperfective forms '*grow tired*' and '*grow weary*' are indicative of actions that are frequent, making the point that any who set about using violence to establish their empire always are going to be defeated. Here it is expressed as '*for the flames*' and working '*for nothing*', emphasizing the vanity of all such violent action.

2.14 Most commentators note the incongruous insertion of the verse at this point in a Woe-oracle. It does repeat what may be a common or shared celebratory call found also in Isa. 11.9, and if the verbs are read as jussive—'let (it) be filled' and 'may they cover...'—then it expresses a shared wish or longing for a new world order. It is not necessary to argue that Habakkuk has borrowed from the Isaiah text, nor to regard it is predictive; rather, it had become a common expression of hope for the future. However, there is no logical connection to its present textual context which is one of condemnation of those who depend on violence to establish and maintain power.

The clause '*to know the glory of the Lord*' is a reference to people acknowledging the power of YHWH, for Hebrew *kabod* carries a broad semantic meaning—'heavy, powerful, glorious'—not to be limited to any single sense. The infinitive form '*to know*' has to be appreciated as experiential knowledge, not just intellectual awareness. So, the verse is expressing a longing that there might be a time when YHWH's power and glory is universally experienced. The analogy of water 'covering' the sea is perhaps a widespread ANE form. For Judaea the sea (*yam*) was often regarded as alien and threatening, and even disdained as the name of a foreign god, Yam.

2.15-17 Fourth 'Woe' Oracle

15. Woe to one who makes his neighbour drink, pouring out his anger/wine and also making (him) drunk,
    in order to look upon their nakedness.

16. You sated yourself with shame rather than glory, may you drink also and expose your uncircumcised self
    May the cup in the Lord's right hand turn against you, and turn your glory into disgrace.

17. Indeed, may the violence done to Lebanon overcome you, and (may) the devastation of beasts terrify you,
    Because of the shedding of human blood and the violence done to the land, the city and all who live in it.

The fourth Woe oracle focuses on drunkenness and lewdness, on shame and lost glory, but whether it is a literal reference to one's corrupt personal life, or metaphorical regarding Chaldean warmongering is uncertain; that may depend on whether the reference in v. 17 is directly related to vv. 15-16, an issue that needs settling—especially given the tendency for the final verse in these oracles to appear unconnected to the preceding verses (see notes on 2.8, 11, 14). However, the contrast between the theme of exposing oneself in vv. 15-16 with that of 'covering' in v. 17 may suggest that here there is some kind of connection between all elements in the oracle.

2.15 This oracle condemns those who make their neighbour drink—the object of the verb is missing but the context implies drinking an intoxicating liquid. Why would one cause or force another to drink to the point of drunkenness unless there was some ulterior motive at play? The singular grammatical forms are presumably to be understood as collectives.

The Hebrew phrase *m'sappeach ch'math'ka* is rendered in NRSV and others as '*pouring out your anger*' which seems incongruous unless anger is the driving force behind the attempt to make someone drunk. This has led to a view that the noun rendered '*anger/wrath*' (Heb. *ch'math'ka*) is actually a liquid of some kind, perhaps wine?, though the second-person suffix is out of place. The root involved has to do with being overheated and thus inflamed, but it is not confined to emotions; it can also refer to the effects of alcohol. For this reason, a translation such as 'pouring out your wine (for him)' may be recommended. It does tie in with the notion of abuse that follows but may also refer to the Chaldean abuse of those whose land its armies have captured.

The purpose of getting the neighbours drunk is said to be '*in order to look upon their nakedness*', whether this refers to sexual activity, or, as some have suggested, taking away captives who are doubly humiliated because they are stripped and then forced to walk to their place of exile. We note the use of a keyword *bit* 'to see, look at'. The more likely view is that the neighbour is made drunk for sexual purposes.

2.16 Referring to the past, the oracle reminds that those addressed had '*sated themselves with shame rather than with glory*'. The shame here is often associated with revealing one's nakedness (e.g., Nah. 3.5). There is also a mocking tone to the expression for the one addressed is also an object of shame—'*also you show yourself as uncircumcised*'. If this be the sense, then being uncircumcised would suggest that the object in view is more than likely a non-Israelite, i.e., the Chaldean. From Israel's point of view circumcision was a significant sign of one's covenant identity (Gen. 17.9-14). Like the Philistines who were mocked as 'uncircumcised', so too here, that nationalistic view of others as outside the covenant was applied to the Babylonians.

The second line begins with what this reader considers a jussive with the verb *sbb* meaning to 'turn around' or 'encircle' but with the sense of something that turns against one. The subject is '*the cup in the Lord's right hand*', in which the metaphor of the 'cup' represents divine judgment (see Jer. 25.15-29). The jussive '*May the cup...turn against you*' is a wish or longing for the one shamed to be punished by the Lord. It is followed by a second element, namely that what one sees as glory be turned into shame. Some understand the noun *qiqalon* to have something to do with 'vomit' but its real derivation is unknown. However, one can note that it does represent an intensification of the noun *qalon* 'shame', used at the beginning of the verse. Overall, then, the verse highlights the shame that can come to those who indulge in certain sexual activities. Whether that is literally intended to condemn certain individuals in the society, or whether it is metaphorical and has to do with Chaldean empirical pursuits, one cannot be certain.

2.17 Basic questions are asked as to the meaning and contextual appropriateness of this verse.

The initial asseverative *ki*, 'Truly,...' emphasizes what follows, namely the wish that the Chaldeans(?) be overwhelmed—literally 'may it be covered'—by '*the violence of Lebanon*'. Whether this is a subjective genitive or objective genitive is the issue. Is this a reference to violence done by Lebanon, or violence brought upon Lebanon? Given that it appears to have some historical reference, commentators seek evidence from other sources to support one view or the other. A link is usually sought between the Chaldeans and an invasion of Lebanon. That points to the interpretation of the genitive construction as objective—violence done to Lebanon by the Chaldeans. If this be the case, then the point is to argue that Babylon may be 'covered' or overcome in the same manner or degree that they inflicted on Lebanon. Commentators have sought some possible historical event or situation to which to connect, such as Nebuchadrezzar plundering Lebanon's cedar trees (Isa. 14.8), but this seems far-fetched. The real problem with this verse is that there is no connection between Lebanon and the issue of drunkenness in vv. 15-16, meaning that it points to the independence of v. 17. Its real meaning and present location within the Woe-oracle may never be clear.

The issue is magnified in the second half of the line, rendered here as '*and (may) the devastation of beasts terrify you*'. The matter of the genitive construction remains, but context would suggest that it is the devastation caused by beasts, a subjective genitive. That clearly is not a literal devastation but an illustration of something that can terrify. As an analogy, it also bears no relationship to the theme of vv. 15-16.

The second half verse is a repeat of 2.8: '*Because of the shedding of human blood and the violence done to the land, the city and all who live in it*'. The inclusion of this text merely adds to the mystery of its relevance here, the more so when it is inserted as an explanation for the preceding.

2.18-20 Fifth 'Woe' Oracle

18. What benefit does an idol offer when the idol maker has created it? (it is) a metal image and an instructor of lies;
   For the maker trusts in what he has made, making worthless things unable to speak.

19. <u>*Woe to the one who*</u> *says to the wood 'Awake!' and to a dumb rock 'Get up!', (Woe to one who says) it can teach!*
   Behold, it may be covered with gold and silver, but there is no life/ spirit in it.

20. The Lord is in his holy temple; may the whole earth keep silence before him!

The fifth Woe oracle in vv. 18-19 mocks those who make and converse with idols (see also Isa. 44.9-20; 46.6-7; Jer. 10.2-16). Verse 20, in powerful contrast, calls the world to be silent in the presence of YHWH. It can be regarded as a conclusion not only to the fifth oracle but to all five, and resounds with Yahwistic zeal. Some regard it as the culmination of chapters 1–2, in which case silence in the divine presence is the only answer offered to Habakkuk's probing questions in 1.2-4.

Unlike the previous four 'Woe' oracles, this one first asks rhetorically about the usefulness or benefit of idols and clearly anticipates a negative answer. The 'Woe!' marker is introduced late following the mockery.

Polemic against idols is a frequent cause of prophetic attack, largely because the idols are made by humans, and even if aesthetically worked, they nevertheless are utterly dependent upon those who made them and worship them—they are useless. YHWH, by contrast, is for Judaeans, the Creator of all. The specific reason given for the verbal attack here is that idols are dumb and have no 'spirit' within them—they are lifeless, and cannot respond to any human command or prayer. The attack is expressed in such general language that readers cannot tell whether the 'Woe!' are directed against Judaeans or foreigners.

2.18 The verse begins with the interrogative in a rhetorical question that anticipates a negative answer—*'No, there is no value in...!'* The noun *pesel* describes something carved or shaped, of wood or stone; it may represent an animal or human—an idol—and *massekah* refers to anything cast in metal. Together these are characterized as *'a teacher of lies'* or one who is a teacher of falsehood. It's not that the idol is literally a teacher but a source of false ideas. The fact that the idol is dumb and unable to speak is stressed because, in contrast, for the Judaeans YHWH is the God who initiates communication. On the other hand, there is in this book only one vague reference to God speaking—in 2.2—and none of the formal features of prophetic messaging are used by the Editor to highlight the contrast.

From the idol itself, the thought moves to the one who makes or fashions the idol. He is said to foolishly 'trust' (Heb. *btch*) or rely on what he has made, despite the fact that he has made 'dumb false gods' that cannot communicate. There is a play on the word God/god (*'el*) in the word *'elilim* that describes these man-made gods.

2.19 Here begins the 'Woe'-form proper. It is directed against the one who speaks to the wood/tree, the wooden object, and demands that it '*Wake up!*' There is irony in this because in the Psalms the worshiper also calls on the Lord to '*wake up*' or '*Arise!*' and act (see e.g., Ps. 44.23). To say '*Rouse yourself!*' is also a common call to God to act. The mockery here is that to call wood and stone to act is foolish.

The first line then concludes with two words the significance of which is unclear. The Hebrew *hu' yoreh* is literally 'he teaches'. For some commentators this has significance as it raises the question of divine revelation, but since the reference is to idols that can't speak, they turn the statement into a question—'Can it teach?' (NRSV), even, 'Can it give revelation?' (TEV). This is unacceptable syntactically. Others suggest it is a gloss and disregard it, but such a move is unjustified without supporting evidence. In view of the use of the noun-form *moreh* in v. 18 where false teaching is attributed to the idol, here the text can be seen as a further warning against those who <u>say</u> certain things. Thus, '(Woe to those who say....that) it can teach!'. There is no necessary reason to question its presence in the text, even if awkward.

That idol is also the subject of the second line. '*Look, it may be overlaid with gold and silver, but it is lifeless*'; it literally has no spirit within it. The phrase '*but all spirit (ruach)*' is emphatic when followed by the negative '*there is not*', to make the point beyond doubt—it is completely lifeless. Enhancing a man-made god by clothing it with silver or gold does nothing but make it look to have value; it adds nothing to its supposed power to do anything, let alone instruct or benefit one who worships it. Alas for anyone who says it can!

2.20 To conclude the Woe-oracle collection, the Editor calls on the whole earth to be silent before YHWH. Whether this is to be regarded as the closure of the final and fifth oracle, or more likely of the oracle collection as a whole, it is ironic that he calls the world to silence when Habakkuk wants answers. What the dumb idols cannot provide by way of 'teaching',

YHWH offers in the silence. Awed silence in the presence of the holy God contrasts with the idol's inability to say anything. Calls for silence in the divine presence can be found in Deut. 27.9, Zeph. 1.7 and Zech. 2.13 (Eng.).

In sharp contrast to the idols and their makers who are mocked in vv. 18-19, the Editor adds a powerful confession regarding YHWH—*The Lord is in his holy temple*. The Judaean notion that their God was resident in his Temple in Jerusalem and thus present among his people was a cornerstone of Deuteronomic theology. That view finds expression here. The question then is whether this is merely a traditional saying, or whether it does in fact reflect an actual historical circumstance—the Temple prior to its destruction in 587 BCE, or following its rebuild in 516 BCE. The very general nature of the Woes that do not permit the identification of those addressed makes any decision about them problematic, but for this reader, the likelihood is that the call is a traditional Deuteronomic one, whether linked formally with the cult or not.

The imperative tone of the call for silence in the divine presence expresses the belief that YHWH, though 'resident' in the Jerusalem Temple, is, in the mind of the Judaean community, the God of the whole world, of '*all the earth*'. This confident theological claim does little to answer Habakkuk's most fundamental question about the divine response to Violence and Injustice (1.2-4). He longs for God's clear and positive answer, but none is forthcoming. So, what can Habakkuk or any reader do? Resumption of the Lament in 3.2 shows the only way forward—an abiding confidence in God in the 'not yet' interim.

3.1-19 Habakkuk's Lament—Part B

The thesis that this reader has sought to develop is that Habakkuk the book consists of an Individual Lament (1.2-4 and 3.2-19) drawn from an available Psalms collection, and a Dialogue that the Editor has created of Habakkuk's discussion with God (1.5–2.5) and the Woe-oracles of 2.6-20. The Editor has broken open the Psalm in order to insert that dialogue. Habakkuk's original quote (1.2-4) from the Lament psalm contained the first two component parts of an Individual Lament, namely the Address to God and the Complaint; the remaining components of the Lament are now to be found in 3.2-19. They are: the Confession of Trust (3.2-15), the Petition (3.16), and the Song of Praise (3.17-19). The theological core of the book lies within the Dialogue, while the Lament, an ancient poem given its affinity with other ancient OT poems such as Deuteronomy 33, Judges 5 and Psalm 68, provides its framework. Why this particular Lament was chosen as the frame is beyond further enquiry, apart from noting that its initial questions, similar to those in Psalm 22, are the key issues troubling all those of faith.

The Editor has included an Introduction at 3.1 that was part of the original Lament, displaced by his new Superscription at 1.1. The concluding note at 3.19d also would have been part of the original Lament Superscription. That these elements have become separated in the hands of the Editor can leave the superficial impression that Chapter 3 is simply an add-on, a completely independent prayer that Habakkuk once composed. It is a view perhaps enhanced by the fact that the Qumran commentary on Habakkuk, 1QpHab, is missing this final chapter. However, it is important to recognize the integrity of the Lament, a complaint addressed to God in generalized language typical of all Laments, a model for pouring out feelings to God as one encounters unexplained dilemmas, both personal and communal. Furthermore, the intruding Dialogue is strategically placed to follow the initial questions, after which at 3.2 the Lament resumes as Habakkuk offers the only response available to him, affirming his continuing faith in his God in the 'not yet' of his life.

What is important to note is that the Dialogue portion of the book was not able to provide any final solution to the questions Habakkuk had asked in the Lament's opening—'*How much longer...*'? and '*Why...*'? The Dialogue clearly was not satisfying. Despite that failure, it is in the resumption of the Lament—now at 3.2—that we see Habakkuk confirming his and God's relationship, living with the questions he has asked, but in hope of a final resolution.

In what follows, some attention must be paid to many difficulties in the Hebrew text, as can be expected of a poem that is ancient and that has been transmitted over the centuries in both oral and written forms. However, the reading offered here will seek to limit the notes to those issues critical to a meaningful translation.

3.1 Title

1. A Prayer of the Prophet Habakkuk; according to Shigionoth.

As noted above, this reader posits that this Heading was part of the original Introduction to the Lament itself, now placed by the Editor here where the Lament resumes, since the Editor provided a separate Title at 1.1 that he applied to the whole work. The meaning of *shigionoth* is a little uncertain, but in Psalm 7 it refers to a musical notation, the name of a popular(?) tune or of the accompanying instruments.

3.2-15 Confession of Trust

2. O Lord, I have heard the report about you, and I am in awe of your deeds, O Lord.
   Through the years may he (YHWH) live, through the years may you be known,
   In (my) trembling, remember mercy.
3. May God came from Teman, and the holy one from Mt. Paran. Selah
   His radiance covers the heavens and praise of him fills the earth.
4. His brightness is like the light, two horns/rays from his hands
   And there his strength is hidden.
5. Ahead of him there went a plague, and flames from his feet,
6. He stands and measures the earth, he looks and the nations tremble
   The ancient mountains shatter, the ancient heights melt.
   Ancient highways were ruined.
7. In place of iniquity I saw the tents of Cushan quake with the curtains of the land of Midian.
8. Was your anger against the rivers O Lord, or your wrath against the rivers, or against the sea your rage?
   When you rode victorious on your horses, your chariots
9. You took out your bow and seven staves were visible Selah
   You split open the streams of the land, the mountains saw you and shook
10. The wind passed by, the abyss shouted aloud, the sun high above raised its hands
11. The moon stood still, your arrows streaming to the light, your javelin to the bright one
12. In your anger you trampled the earth, in your rage you threshed the nations
13. You marched out to rescue your people, you came to deliver your messiah/anointed one
    You smashed the head of the wicked, you slashed them from back to neck Selah
14. You smashed their heads with your two clubs, (you scattered their hair to the wind and gloated over them like the oppressed feasting in secret)
15. You trampled the sea with your horses and churned up many waters.

The Lament resumes following the Dialogue that proved unsatisfactory for Habakkuk. Habakkuk had only one recourse, and that was to reaffirm his faith in YHWH his God and to await salvation; he must live with the tension of the 'not yet'. It is a feature of all or most of the Laments that they conclude with a similar affirmation of faith and trust.

The general theme in this section of the Lament is to acknowledge YHWH in conflict with and victorious over all other powers. Holy War imagery and the rhetoric of shaking the natural world provide the vocabulary, along with echoes of Exodus' theophanic language in 3.3-7.

In vv. 8-15 the imagery of God, riding in his chariot and equipped with weapons of war, makes use of the cosmic warrior notion, here to bring deliverance. The question asked as to divine anger and fury raised in v. 8, is answered in vv. 12-15. In this ode to YHWH, the psalmist has expressed his confidence and trust in YHWH to deliver his people from the wicked oppressor.

The variety of images and the general nature of the language used in this portion of the Lament (Part B) is thoroughly typical of the Lament-form. Lines do not have the same length. There is no specific reference to Habakkuk's basic concern with the loss of *torah's* power in Judaean society, nor is it to be expected—that is the nature of the formal language as the focus is on acknowledging divine power. As is typical of all Laments, there is a cornucopia of images used—sun's rays, plague and pestilence, catastrophic earthquakes, mountains shattering, horses and chariots, bows and arrows, floods, cosmic phenomena, whirlwinds. All are poetic images in the service of confirming divine power and glory which the worshiper acknowledges in confessing a trust in YHWH.

3.2 The Lament that was truncated at 1.4 is now resumed. It begins, as did Obadiah, with a note about what has been heard—*O Lord, I have heard your report*, i.e., the report about you. The Hebrew verb *shama'*, 'hear', carries the fuller sense of having heard and responded, or obeyed, which here opens up the Confessional element of the Lament-form. There is an implied encounter with YHWH, perhaps in a vision (1.1), a theophany.

Here the psalmist addresses YHWH, stressing humility in the face of the divine reputation of which he has been made aware. That is further explained as '*your work/achievements*' a reference that appears quite vague, but almost certainly within the tradition refers back to what God did in the Exodus and in the victory gained over the Egyptians, including perhaps the successful journey to Canaan.

In line 2 the phrase, literally, '*in the midst of the years…*' is an idiom thought to mean 'throughout the years…', with the following verb read as an imperative or jussive, '*may he live!*'. Then in strict parallel, '*throughout the years may you be known!*' Not only for the past, but into the future, the poet calls for God's deeds to be recalled.

The final line in this verse again is terse, calling for God to '*remember*', that is to say, look with favour on the worshiper. The phrase *b'rogez* features a root *rgz* often associated with anger/wrath, but when used twice again in v. 16, it is clear that its focus is on human 'trembling' or awe. Balancing this is the noun *rechem,* normally 'mercy', a divine attribute. The poem appeals for God's mercy towards the one who trembles before God, i.e., shows humility in the divine presence.

3.3 A change from second to third person and to narrative style marks the remainder of the section to v. 7. Such change is often to be noted in many OT texts; grammatical variations and inconsistency over the whole is simply a factor in ancient poems with such a long transmission history.

'*Eloah*', an ancient divine name used widely in Job, and '*Qadosh*', the Holy One (1.12), are two poetic references to God; they predate Israel's knowledge of and use of 'YHWH'. The verb '*came*' stands in mid-point of line 1 to serve both halves of the line, describing the divine one as coming '*from Tem*an' and '*from Mt Paran*'. Teman is a location associated with Edom (see Obad 9; Amos 1.12) and Mt Paran refers to the desert region around the Sinai. This may suggest the two ends of the traditional Exodus journey, so this kind of reference establishes YHWH's reputation within the Israelite story, that is, if the imperfective verb form *yabo'* is read (unusually) as a simple past tense. If it is read as a frequentative, it is difficult to see its intention. This reader prefers to see it as a jussive, expressing a wish or hope that YHWH will come (again?) as in the past.

The significance of God coming from (Heb. *min*) these two separate locations is unclear unless the preposition is used in the sense of 'belonging to a place'; that would suggest God as originating or operating in both locations, with indirect references to the traditions associated with each. What those traditions were is unspoken.

The marginal note *Selah* is thought to mark a division in the text, but in this case, there seems minimal logic in its insertion at this precise point.

Verse 3b pictures God as universally present, 'covering' (Heb. *ksh*) the heavens with his majesty, and filling the land with his praises. This is traditional hyperbole. The notion has probable connections with Egyptian sun worship as the divine glory is likened to the sun's rays bursting forth upon and lighting up the world (v. 4).

3.4 The divine brightness shines *ka'or*, 'like a light', in a simile representing the sun with its rays spanning out throughout the universe—it is expressed in literal terms as '*two horns from his hand/arm*'. Although 'horns' are more of a military image in ancient Israel, here it clearly suggests a burst of light, connected with glory. In other iconography, rays are depicted as bursting forth from the shoulders, but here the Israelite version prefers the divine arm as the source of light and power.

The verse concludes with what can be regarded as an exclamation—*'there (is) the hiding-place of his power!'* or 'That's where he hides his power!'

3.5 In imagery similar to that of Joel's description of the advancing plague or army (Joel 2.3), here the Lament uses the motif to emphasize the completeness and the awesomeness of the divine theophany. Using the 'plague' motif, echoing the leadup to the Exodus escape, it offers another description of the divine different from the preceding one of the sun's rays. The plague or pestilence is a general term, though the root *dbr* also can refer to pasture, so the metaphor of pestilence shifts the imagery to an impact on the agricultural world.

The Lament continues with its brief description of Israel's God with yet another image, literally *'there went out flames to/for his feet'*. The imagery of flames or sparks flashing out from one's feet does seem unusual, and some have seen this as meaning that beams of light or sparks left a trace behind him as he moved forward. The Hebrew *reshep* 'flame', also was the name of a Canaanite god. The reference to 'feet' is taken by some to be a rhetorical balance to the 'face' (Heb. *panayw*) used in the first half verse to give a 'before-after' contrast. Whatever the specifics of the text, the picture is of YHWH's spectacular destructive power.

3.6

He stood and measured the earth, he looked and the nations trembled
The ancient mountains shattered, the eternal heights melted.
Ancient highways were ruined

The verse has a number of peculiarities, not the least of which is its brevity—six words, four of which are verbs in line 1. The unnamed subject is obviously 'God' who is said to 'stand' and to 'measure', to 'see/look', and to 'leap/jump', here probably with a sense 'make to tremble', hence 'shaking'. The object of the first two verbs is the 'earth' and that of the second two verbs is 'nations'. There is a reasonable parallel between both half verses, the imagery being of YHWH standing to *'measure the earth'*, demonstrating control, though the specific purpose of this action is not further elucidated, unless it is shaking the earth to strike fear into the earth's people (see Job 37.1).

The second line contains a verb the root of which is uncertain, but linking it with the verb *ptsts*, 'to shatter/break apart', seems to co-ordinate well with the objects, 'mountains' and 'heights' (see also Job 16.12). This sits well with the second half line with the heights 'sinking down' or 'melting' permanently. The Hebrew noun *'olam*, meaning 'an age' or long period of time, is often regarded as an adjective describing the mountain heights as ancient, i.e., the noun refers to time past rather than future. Perhaps the sense is more of a permanent demise. But the point of it all is that this cumulatively describes how the divine presence impacts upon the created order.

The final words of the verse are commonly regarded as a gloss, or an out-of-context intrusion. A literal rendering illustrates its incongruity: '*pathways/tracks eternal to/for it/him*'. Was the Editor thinking of actual roads, or is the language purely figurative, reflecting an ancient theophany? Commentators are divided in their understanding and interpretation of these words, and so there are numerous solutions proposed, including some that require emendations to the text. Seeking to minimize preconceptions and acknowledging that these and other parts of the text are possibly corrupt and beyond a modern reader's full linguistic comprehension, it is important not to arbitrarily or forcedly reshape the text to conform to one's theological, cultural or linguistic 'insights'. The complex process of oral transmission, collecting and collating materials from various sources, scribal editing, then making hand-written copies, will inevitably make for occasional errors and confusion within the process. Commentators are best advised to admit the problems and move on in the hope that what is confused or problematic wasn't the crux of some central argument!

3.7 This verse notes two geographical references, Cushan and Midian, that tend to root the verse in an historical context, a reference to Israel's past, balancing the note about Teman and Paran (v. 3), as well as rounding out the *inclusio* in the sub-section vv. 2-7.

Cushan appears to be a reference to Cush as Ethiopia, if the LXX is correct, otherwise it may refer to a desert tribe in the Sinai, along with Midian, a tribe known as that to which Moses' father-in-law belonged (Exod. 2). It is interesting to observe that the place names in v. 3 are associated with Edom to the north(?) and those in v. 7 are both to the south. Israel's encounters with these people groups extended over a long period of time.

The prepositional phrase with which v. 7 begins—literally 'under iniquity' or even 'in place of iniquity' (Heb. *tachat 'awen*)—is followed by the verb phrase 'I saw'. Some commentators wish to exclude the opening words as a gloss. It seems that for some it is just another inexplicable text, although much ink has been spilled in attempts to offer an explanation. However, this reader suggests that the general sense of the verse is that something adverse (*'awen*) has happened to the tents of Cushan's army. This then fits well with the second half of the verse in which the 'curtains' of the tents of Midian 'trembled', so both phrases imply divine action taken against them.

It would appear that the Lament is recalling events in Israel's past in which God was said to act positively on Israel's behalf. While there is little concrete evidence here as to what those events might have been, it is a situation that fits well with the generalized language of the poet. Of more importance is the role of these reminders in the Lament; namely, that the individual is confidently confirming God's powerful and dramatic actions on behalf of Israel in its past, the only basis for its hope for the future.

3.8 The Lament moves in vv. 8-15 to a very different mode, this time focusing on God's victory over the natural world—the waters, the mountains, the heavens and the sea. It has some distinctive rhetorical features such as a preference for second-person address that, according to some scholars, point to it being an archaic piece, but in its present setting its focus is consistent with the overall theme of God's great cosmic power. God is presented as the driver of his war chariot, armed with weapons to smash, beat and crush, armed with his bow and arrows, javelins and spears with which to pierce the cosmic 'enemies' and powers. There is a mix of both historical and mythological elements that use Exodus and creation motifs.

Divine anger dominates the figurative language of this verse. A trilogy of terms—'wrath', 'anger' 'rage'—are set within a rhetorical question about divine action against the rivers and sea.—see also Nahum's view of God (Nah. 1.2-3). There is no background provided in terms of a reason for the divine anger, suggesting that this is a traditional poetic reference using mythological imagery to portray God's attitude to foreign enemies—the ancient gods, River (*Nahar*) and Sea (*Yam*). The response to the questions comes in vv. 12-15. YHWH is pictured in his chariots drawn by horses—horses were not ridden into battle in ancient times—leading his army into battle against the enemy.

The final word in the verse, Hebrew *y'shu'ah*, can be read as the purpose for this warrior attack, namely, to save or <u>rescue</u>. The worshiper is thereby reminding God that in the past he has come to the aid of his people, and he is trusting that the same divine intervention will benefit in the present.

3.9 Here we confront another challenge. The one word in the initial part of the verse that is clear is 'bow' (Heb. *qesheth*), while the rare word *'erya* that carries a sense of nakedness, along with the verb from the same root, presumably describes the bow as being uncovered, taken out of its sheath or cover in readiness for action. In the second half line there are three Hebrew terms each of which can be identified, but each is multivalent making the translation and interpretation fraught. If there is a parallel with the first half line then we can assume that other weapons, or other objects that can be used as weapons, are being identified. Beginning with the general sense that YHWH was riding into battle, his *bow* ready for use, it seems logical to understand the rest of the line to refer to '*arrows*' or '*spears*' and possibly to seven of them. The noun *mattoth* seems to refer to '*clubs*' or similar, while the final word, a participial form *'omer* is unclear. Further certainty is not possible; unfortunately, this is sometimes the reality when dealing with ancient documents that have a very long history of development and transmission.

The verse then changes direction following the *Selah* (see v. 3) and a third colon speaks of YHWH '*splitting the earth with rivers*'. The phrase here is close to the notions in Ps. 74.13-15 that speak of the underground waters that well up and divide the ground or land. Still, we are in the realm of mythological language and thought, not an actual or specific location such as Mesopotamia and the region of 'the two rivers'.

3.10-11 A series of cosmic reactions is given prominence here. Mountains, Waters, Sun and Moon, imagery very similar to that found in Ps. 77.16-19, respond to what they see of divine activity; they writhe, see and flee, melt and dissolve. (See also Judg. 5.4-5.) Each responds to YHWH's attack in its own way. This commonality of poetic expression reflects the oral transmission of ideas that use stock forms and vocabulary.

Mountains are personified and spoken of as witnessing God bringing about victory or rescue (v. 8); their response is described as 'writhing' or dancing about, as torrents of water as in a cloudburst (Heb. *zerem*) sweep past and inundate the land (see also Isa. 28.2). The deep (Heb. *t'hom*) gives voice or screams out, presumably in terror (see Ps. 93.3-4). This latter recalls the Noahic flood story (Gen. 7.11-12) in which the windows of the heavens opened, releasing a deluge, and the waters below the earth welled up to combine into a flood that covered the land.

The Sun raises its arms/rays in a salute to the power of the divine one (v. 4), while the Moon stands still high in its orbit (Heb. *z'bulah*). The two colons are similar to those in Josh. 10.12-13. (There seems to have been some copyist confusion here as to breaks between v. 10 and v. 11)

These cosmic reactions to God's actions are said to have been to his '*arrows streaming to the light*'. Then there is the parallel, '*your javelin to the bright one*' meaning that God's weapons flash in the light of sun and moon. The lightning flashes and other stunning heavenly phenomena in these metaphors give a bright poetic picture grounded in the mythology of the times.

3.12-13 The questions raised in v. 8 here find a response—God's cosmic adventure and its impact were expressions of divine anger, fury and wrath, but its ultimate goal or purpose was the rescue of his people. God's awesome activity, spelled out partly in the imagery of holy war—'trampling' is a military term—and partly in cosmic shakeup, spoke of the divine intention to save '*your people*' with a parallel phrase '*your messiah*' (singular). The latter is a description rarely used other than for the one anointed as king or high priest. Here, however the context would suggest that it has been applied to the people in general rather than to one specific individual. The later and Christian adoption of the term 'Messiah' as the unique divine agent is certainly not applicable here where it has a more generic sense. It is possible to posit that the application here of what was once a specific promise to David and his descendants, has been democratized, as seen in Isa. 61.8-9, extending beyond any narrow definition to embrace the community as a whole.

The references to '*treading the earth*' and '*trampling the nations*', as in all Laments, are generalized so that they have virtually a universal application. It is not possible, nor was it intended, that specific enemies be identified. Here the worshiper confesses to divine power intended for the rescue and benefit of God's people, saving them from '*the wicked*' who likewise are not specifically identified. The 'wicked' in the Psalms of Lament are often equated with 'the godless' and 'those who work evil', for all are enemies of God. The non-identification of these folk is deliberate, so that whatever the circumstance, the Lament remains usable.

The presentation continues with a description of more violence as '*You smashed the head of the wicked (house), you slashed them from back to neck*'. There are serious questions about the relevance of the MT phrase that is literally '*from the house of evil*'. The head is the point of the body being aimed at, according to the mythology, so what the metaphor of the 'house' might represent is far from clear. This means a rendering like NRSV's '*laying it bare from foundation to roof*' is far too dependent upon a literal reading about an actual house (or family). What may lie behind the imagery is rather the stripping or laying bare of the victim whose head has been smashed, even to disemboweling from base to neck, or 'from head to toe' in common language. Not only is the victim smashed over the head, but innards are completely laid bare. In the context of confessing trust, the worshiper is exalting divine violence in the pursuit of rescuing his people/messiah.

3.14 The 'wicked' are the subject of this affirmation as the worshiper acknowledges God's rescue, turning the wicked ones' weapons upon themselves. It adds a colourful description of the way the wicked came to attack only to be defeated by God's canny knack in turning the situation to his own advantage. However, there is much in the Hebrew of this verse that makes no sense, and although other texts support the Hebrew text as it is, this only witnesses to the fact that it has been garbled for a long time and corrupted in its earlier transmission. There is little value or reward in pursuing the matter any further—simply admit our present inability to make sense of the verse.

3.15 This verse returns to the thought of v. 8 and can be viewed as an *inclusion* for this sub-unit ending the Confessional component of the Lament.

The image is of God walking in/through the water with his horses, as in Ps. 77.19, echoing the language used to describe God's aid in the escape from Egypt. The second half of the verse is not quite so clear as the initial *chomer* is multivalent, referring either to the roar of the water, or the piling up of water as at the Reed Sea crossing. The root has a basic sense of ferment or foaming, as well as of objects forming a heap, or becoming red, so context is important in deciding its present meaning—a general consensus is that it is the piling up of water as in Exod. 14.22. The phrase *mayim rabbim* is literally 'many waters', not mighty waters as NRSV. The 'many waters' would include the water above the heavens and that below the earth, as well as the rivers and lakes and sea on the surface. The language throughout is mythological, not historical.

3.16 The Petition

> *I have listened and my insides tremble, my lips tingle at the sound, decay comes upon my bones, and under me my feet shake; I await the day of disaster to come to the people who attack us.*

The Lament form moves here to the anticipated divine help. Initially it speaks of the worshiper's reaction to the display, or reputed display, of divine power; it impacts his whole being and humbles him. It is a second physical response to the divine, the first being in 3.2 at the beginning of the Confession, and now here at the beginning of the Petition for help, the fourth component of the Lament. The second half verse expresses a longing for God to act and rescue by dealing with those who are the attackers. He calmly awaits—the Hebrew verb deriving from the root meaning 'to rest'—expecting God to bring down on the head of the enemy some disaster (Heb. *tsarah*) that will end the trouble, whatever form it might take, that he is experiencing—but still the cry is '*How much longer...?*'

The Hebrew phrase *yom-tsarah*, 'day of disaster', echoes other phrases using the 'day' concept such as 'day of the Lord'. The reference is to some moment in the future, but usually an imminent moment, as it is a time or period in which the divine one is expected to bring judgment, punishment or rescue/salvation depending on the situation. Casting it into the distant future, and into the NT, as some commentators are wont to do, fails to value its specific contextuality.

The language used in the Petition is full of emotion as the worshiper tells of the impact of the divine theophany—his insides/belly, his feet, bones, his lips/speech, all are affected deeply.

There is a minor issue with the Hebrew syntax of the second colon involving the use of the relative *ʾasher*, especially as it is the sole use in the Lament. However, this issue has no impact on the thought of the verse. The imperfective verbs are read here as frequentative, describing the worshiper's constant attitude.

3.17-19 Song of Praise

> *17. Even if the fig tree fails to blossom and there is no yield on the vines,*
>   *Even if the olive crop fails and the fields yield no food,*
>   *Even if the flock is cut off from the sheepfold, and there are no cattle in the yards,*
> *18. Yet I will rejoice in the Lord, I will exult in the God who rescues me.*
> *19. YHWH, my Lord is my strength*
>   *He has made my feet like those of a deer, and enabled me to walk on the heights.*
>   *For the conductor with/by my stringed instruments'*

The fifth component of the Lament form is the Promise or Vow to heap praise upon YHWH. These verses conform exactly to that purpose. No matter what the situation, the worshiper testifies to God's power to rescue. The six elements in this verse form a series of conditions; they are the protases, introduced by the particle *ki*, 'if', or 'even if...', with the apodosis following in v. 18. Six possible conditions are listed that are detrimental or hugely challenging, followed in vv. 18-19 by the psalmist's confident praise of his God who rescues him and gives strength.

Under normal circumstances the Praise component would be in anticipation of the rescue, and follow a possible priestly intervention that gave assurance to the worshiper that God would not only hear, but act to save. Here there is no priestly confirmation present.

It is immediately evident that the six conditions mentioned are all agricultural and pastoral, not having anything to do with an aggressor or the violence of invading armies. This in itself indicates that the Praise is not rooted in an actual historical event, but, as is typical of Laments, draws on normal experiences within the life of a community that was largely dependent upon its agriculture and pastoral pursuits, to spell out or illustrate its relationship with its God.

The Lament ends in Praise of YHWH that denies the Deuteronomic view that crop and harvest failure are linked to divine punishment for sin. That note is clear—even if there were to be a crop disaster, it does not equate to punishment because of a failure of faith/faithfulness on the worshiper's part. The psalmist here proclaims his faith in the face of any such challenge, thus bringing the psalm to its climax. The climax to the Book of Habakkuk resides here in the Song of Praise, not in 2.4 as some have proposed. (See notes on 2.4, and the Conclusion.)

3.17 These concluding verses are, for this reader, the true climax to the issues raised by Habakkuk, not the statement in 2.4, for they express the only solution that Habakkuk can see. Holding onto his faith in God's goodness, despite having to continue waiting in the 'not yet' of daily life.

As noted, the initial particle *ki* introduces the series of six potential situations in which natural phenomena fail, while the verbs that follow in v. 17a indicate them to be frequent possibilities. If the fig tree failed to blossom, it would never produce fruit. Likewise, the grapevines, if there was no *y'bul*, 'produce/increase' on them, there would be no grape harvest and no wine. Then there is the possible 'disappointment' (Heb. *kichesh)* of the poor olive harvest, and the crop failure from the fields. In both these latter examples the general verb *'asah*, 'do, make, create', is used to note the produce of the olive trees and fields as primary focus. The Lament has set out to picture a potential failure in the provision of the fundamental products that sustain life as the background to a declaration of confidence in God's rescue/salvation.

It should not be forgotten that Judah's physical location on the mountain spine that ran the length of Canaan, disappearing into the southern desert, was always on the edge of agricultural and pastoral disaster. Rainfall was always an issue, driving hot winds from the east a danger, and soils depleted in the central and southern regions, so to focus here on potential famine is deeply meaningful. No matter how often—not if—famine threatened, the Lament stands firm in its rejoicing in YHWH who can rescue and provide.

At the rhetorical level, chiastic structures in the Hebrew text are significant: fig, sprout: produce, vines; work, olive: fields, work; sheepfold, flock: herds, yards. Thus we have examples of N-V-V-N and V-N-N-V (noun and verb), along with A-B-B-A (noun only) sentences.

3.18 The apodosis opens with a forceful declaration—'*Nevertheless I...*' Even if conditions were to become so fraught, yet the worshiper proclaims his commitment to his God. '*...I will triumph in YHWH, I will exult in the God who rescues me!*' Yet another chiasm adds to the rhetorical strength of the confident assertion in the apodosis. The two verbs here can be read as cohortative, 'Let me triumph,....let me exult...'. The phrase '*God of my salvation*' is better rendered as 'the God who rescues me'. The significance of this phrase here is that it encloses the Lament, further supporting the contention that 1.2-4 and 3.2-19 are of one piece. In the opening complaint (1.2) the Lament stressed that God had not 'saved/ rescued' (Heb. *lo' toshi'a*) from the violence and injustice of the moment. Now that situation is reversed as the worshiper announces confidence in the divine power to rescue (Heb. *yish'i*).

3.19 The verse begins with another declaration—'*YHWH, my Lord is my strength*' or, '*...is the one who strengthens me*'—similar to the nominal form 'my salvation' in v. 18. Many of the Laments concluded with the worshiper's witness or testimony before others, in the presence of the congregation (see Pss. 13.5-6; 26.11-12; 31.23-24 etc.).

That strength is then expressed poetically as, '*He makes my feet like those of a deer, and enables me to walk on the heights*'. The imagery here is not unique, but found elsewhere as illustrating strength and agility—see also Ps. 18.33; 2 Sam. 22.34. God, says the worshiper, has established or placed my feet such that they are like the feet of a deer. The simile draws on the analogy of the mountain deer who are able to run up and down the rocky slopes without faltering; such is the one who draws strength from YHWH. The phrase '*on the heights*' presumably refers to the ease with which the deer navigate the slopes, though there are some commentators who see it as a 'trampling' on one's enemies in light of the use of the same verb in 3.15. The Hebrew verb *yadrikeni*, 'causes me to walk', is actually more sedate than the notion of trampling or stamping down on an object.

A final note from the Editor is, '*For the conductor with/by my stringed instruments*'. I have taken the view that this closing note, along with the note at 3.1, were part of the Superscript of the original Lament-form. In the editing process, both have become separated as the Editor provided his own new Superscript at 1.1 while preserving the psalm's original note. This would suggest that perhaps it was the Editor who chose the particular Lament-form to illustrate the issue Habakkuk raised rather than Habakkuk himself, but that can never be proved.

Conclusion

On the Reading Thesis

I leave it to readers to determine whether I have been able to demonstrate convincingly that the fundamental structure of the book of Habakkuk is of a complete Individual Lament-form into which has been inserted by the Editor a Discussion about the perversion of *Torah* and the justice implications thereof within Judaean society of the time. I do believe that the structure of the book as argued here offers a more complete view of the Editor's plan, and does not leave chapter three hanging. The suggestion that there is a similarity with the structure of the Book of Job remains.

What I have not been able to do, perhaps, is to define, to complete satisfaction, the actual or specific words of Habakkuk the so-called prophet, as distinct from those used by the Editor in compiling his report. Did Habakkuk choose and make use of this particular Lament, or was it the Editor's choice, knowing what troubled Habakkuk. Are the words recorded in 1.12-17 really those of Habakkuk, or are they the words, or a version of words, that reflected his concerns and that were in circulation in the oral world? Of course, the words attributed to God in the Dialogue are completely dependent upon Habakkuk's own claim as to what he heard, but in its present form they are the words of the Editor.

I believe that there may be sufficient evidence to credit Habakkuk with originating the Woe-oracles, in 2.6-20 even though they represent an edited version of what he is presumed to have said to various elements of his audience at various times and in multiple settings. The many steps between an original utterance by Habakkuk and the final written and 'frozen' record presented by the Editor mean that a modern reader is quite removed from the actual encounters that are claimed in this text.

What we do have in this book is an example of the fundamental human struggle to co-ordinate one's experience of daily life with faith in a God who is defined as loving and caring. Habakkuk does not solve the problem, but offers further evidence, along with the sages, that there are no simple answers and that one must live with the tension and doubt.

On Habakkuk 2.4 as the Core Text

A number of writers or commentators on Habakkuk have concluded that 2.4 is the 'climax of the book' (e.g., Taylor) or its 'core' (e.g., Robertson). Whatever the value of the claim or reading, it requires textual or rhetorical support. Yes, the statement about the righteous and faith/faithfulness does find expression in 2.4-5, but is there evidence that this is the major conclusion to be drawn from Habakkuk the book? Certainly, the verse contains a contrast—the proud against the righteous, the arrogant against the upright. Is it merely a matter of contrasting one lifestyle with another? And what does the word *'emunah* refer to—God's faithfulness or human integrity?

The Hebrew text of 2.4 reads as, '*the righteous one in his faithfulness shall live*' while the LXX renders as '*...from my faithfulness will live*', i.e., God's faithfulness. The ambiguity does not detract from the point being made that the righteous person is the one who lives in a manner that exemplifies faithfulness or integrity, whether that be one's own decision and nature, or that of God. It is a statement of recognizable fact—this is how the righteous operate—their integrity or faithfulness demonstrates that they are the righteous. This is not some kind of prophetic promise; it simply states a fact of life. While integrity is an important principle for living, is it the crux of God's argument in the dialogue with Habakkuk? The question raised by Habakkuk in 1.2-4 speaks of the wicked 'surrounding' the righteous to pervert justice, so here God affirms the principle that faithfulness and integrity are what define the righteous person. Furthermore, this applies generally, to religious and non-religious as well—'faith' or 'faithfulness' does not have the Christian content that the NT reference in Hebrews implies. Whatever the *midrash* of Heb. 10.38 intends in its Christian context, it cannot be imported to determine what Hab. 2.4-5 means or implies in its peculiar setting.

Along with the reference to 2.4, it is interesting to note that the text in Heb. 10.37 uses language that appears to echo Hab. 2.3 by quoting (?) the phrase '*...it will not delay*' applying it to one who is to come. Has the author of Hebrews borrowed some cliché's from Habakkuk to 'decorate' his text about suffering? The important thing to note about *midrash* is that it ignores the context and meaning of the original material, in order to support a later writer's present use, so its value to any specific OT exegesis is denied.

The reading proposed here would contest that 2.4 is the climax or core of Habakkuk. While it may be important to the dialogue in 1.5–2.5, the book's climax must be central to the Framework to qualify as its core. For that reason, it is the concluding element in the Lament that determines what the climax is—namely, the Song of Praise with which the Lament concludes, that is 3.17-19.

On Prophets and Sages

Although the Editor identifies Habakkuk as a prophet, there is, as we have seen, virtually nothing in the book of a rhetorical or literary nature that supports that attribution. The lack of traditional rhetorical and literary forms normally found in prophetic literature runs counter to its inclusion in the Scroll of the Twelve. Only the Woe-oracles survive as a hint of Habakkuk's prophetic connection, but even these are rebadged in 2.6 as *mashal*, a proverbial form within what is a new category of speech, the *massa'*.

While prophets had always been deeply involved in unmasking the social evils of their time, they were not alone in raising the issues of injustice, unfairness, oppression, evil gain, and the like. Sages had also long been active in educating the community as to what was best or ideal for living in community and under God. While prophets may have sounded more demanding, more certain because they had a 'word from the Lord', and called for an 'absolute' standard, grounded in *torah*, the Sages advocated the more conditional, what was 'better' or 'best', on the basis of lived experience. Habakkuk the book evidences the coalescing of these concerns as the 'prophetic' tradition and the 'wisdom' tradition are brought together. This points to a subtle change in the nature of Israelite prophecy, a phenomenon that does seem to point to it playing far less of a role in the postexilic period. What is clear is that within the Scroll of the Twelve there emerges a broader definition of a 'prophet' and of 'prophetic literature'.

In addition, Habakkuk is here noted as very familiar with the Lament tradition and its role as a medium for speaking to God. Whether this means that he was closely involved in the liturgical or cultic dimension of Judaean life is a question that has been raised, but familiarity with the psalms does not lead necessarily to that conclusion. Rather, Habakkuk is presented as a more complex but complete figure who stood somewhere between the prophet, sage and committed worshiper of his God.

On Violence and Theology

According to the Deuteronomistic History (DH) the demise of the southern kingdom of Judah was believed to be brought by Israel's God, YHWH, as punishment for the religious policies of Manasseh in particular

(2 Kgs 24.1-4). Violence perpetrated by Judah's enemy was an essential part of that enemy's imperial expansion and it resulted in a 'loss' or defeat for Israel's God YHWH. The problem was that not only did YHWH fail to stop the enemy advance, YHWH actually arranged for it to happen. The destruction and humiliation of Judah by the Chaldeans was thus a very confusing experience. For the Judaeans it was the Babylonian gods who triumphed over YHWH in the battle. Yet at the same time the prophets and the Deuteronomists interpreted the event as YHWH's means of punishing Judah, for it was YHWH who led the Babylonians to their victory, not their own foreign gods. It was an interpretation that was fraught—how could YHWH be both the agent of punishment and the loser in the power struggle between the competing gods? It is no wonder that in the Dialogue Habakkuk asks the most basic of questions—*How can you look on evil? Why are you silent when the wicked swallow the righteous?* (1.13).

What may concern readers is that Habakkuk the book offers no easy solution to the questions raised in the Lament. In fact, as the Dialogue begins, the problems raised by Habakkuk are exacerbated as God, according to the Editor (1.6), was about to call in the Chaldeans to inflict more violence into the situation. Although there is no clear explanation for this intended action, it does accord with the DH thesis that religious failure, such as Hab. 1.2-4 indicates present in Judah, brings about divine displeasure and punishment. Habakkuk could not comprehend how and why God permitted such violence, appearing to support the wicked against the righteous (1.13), and to use violence as a tool to encourage the wicked. Readers are right to be confused, as was Habakkuk.

Violence and Injustice are an unfortunate part of the human experience, and Habakkuk offers no solution, but does offer an approach—it is the one found in the closing part of the Lament (3.17-18), its climax. Whether it is an approach that will satisfy readers is something to ponder. Sin as offering an explanation for divine punishment is obviously not part of the scenario here, nor is it in Job where the righteous one suffers without explanation, so the Deuteronomic reading in terms of Blessings and Curses (Deut. 27–28) proves misleading, to say the least. So, what does Habakkuk offer? His approach was to affirm his trust, to hold to the belief, that despite all that is contrary, YHWH is truly loving and caring, and that in the 'not yet' his and the community's experiences of God in the past (3.2-16) will sustain and give hope for whatever was to come. As Habakkuk does not use the 'prophetic' promise mode and speak of the 'day of the Lord', the question and answer are left open. Perhaps Qoheleth had the last word (Qoh. 4.1-3)?

(I have deliberately avoided any reference to the NT and what later Christianity has suggested as a 'solution'. Habakkuk must be read and understood within its own timeframe and context)

Select Bibliography

Books

Anderson, F. I., *Habakkuk: A New Translation and Commentary* (AB, 25; New York: Doubleday, 2001).

Clark, D. J., and H. A. Hatton, *The Book of Habakkuk* (New York: United Bible Societies, 1989).

Mason, F., *Zephaniah, Habakkuk, Joel* (Sheffield: JSOT Press, 1994).

Roberts, J.J.M., *Nahum, Habakkuk and Zephaniah: A Commentary* (Louisville, KY: Westminster/John Knox Press, 1991).

Robertson, O.P., *The Books of Nahum, Habakkuk and Zephaniah* (Grand Rapids, MI: Eerdmans, 1990).

Smith, R.L., *Micah—Malachi* (WBC, 32; Dallas, TX: Word Books, 1998).

Taylor Jr., C.L., *The Book of Habakkuk* (IB, VI; New York: Abingdon Press, 1956).

Articles

Hiramatsu, K., 'The Structure and Structural Relationships of the Book of Habakkuk', *JBL* (2016), pp. 106-29.

Sweeney, M., 'Habakkuk and Mythological Depiction of YHWH', *SBL ejournal* (2018).

PREFACE

Over the past several years, preparing notes on the Minor Prophets for a Study Bible project, I have come to appreciate again something of the wealth of oral material that was circulating in Judaea's exilic and postexilic communities that provided the rich resources that numerous Editors subsequently collated and set in written form. In particular, there was a wide range of Judaean formal and informal responses to the tragedy of 587 BCE and the destruction of Jerusalem, along with the taking into exile of so many citizens to Babylonia. This vast oral bounty was kept very much alive, as is evidenced throughout the literature of the period. From the report in Jeremiah 49 through to Joel, Amos, Obadiah, Haggai and Malachi, and in Psalm 137, we see evidence of popular and prophetic responses to those events, expressing anger and calling for divine intervention upon the perpetrators, Babylon and especially Edom. Such was the depth of Judaean resentment at the deception by Edom, at the challenge to YHWH by Babylon and its gods, that for the better part of a century the community lamented, pleaded, ranted, and demanded that God wreak vengeance on these enemies. There may not have been another time in Israel's journey that gave rise to such a concentration of community anger and bewilderment at divine tardiness as seems to be true of the years post-587. Prophets made promises intending to give the community hope for a better future, using exaggerated language to shore up community spirit, but it seems they had little impact on the anger felt, nor did it reduce the calls for divine revenge that filled the period.

Forced isolation over the past two years due to the pandemic has had a 'silver lining' as it has freed up time to work on the text of this and other Minor Prophets and, one hopes, gain a deeper sense of what is reflected in their now extant documents. In particular, I have had a growing appreciation of the role of oral transmission in a cultural group's own story in an age when literacy levels were so low and access to any written materials incredibly limited, not just by illiteracy but even more so by the fact that hand-copied texts were so restricted in circulation. Unlike today when everyone wanting to read a Bible or other book has ready access and literacy levels are high, the ancient Israelite community was held together by its oral traditions. These traditions were kept alive and passed on by a band of reporters/editors. From oral forms, presumably in Aramaic, to translated literary works in higher-level Hebrew, the postexilic period was marked by a process of collecting, editing, and framing of the community's memory, its hopes and fears. This reader has sought to tap into this deep well of an ancient community's story and discover what has made it such a rich resource for any interested in the life of the spirit.

Malachi: A Commentary

The brief 55-verse 'book' that completes the Scroll of the Twelve, the so-called Minor Prophets, brings to an end that division of the Hebrew Bible known as The Prophets (*N'vi'im*), the second of its three major divisions—the Law, the Prophets and the Writings (*Tanak*). Malachi is not the final book in the Hebrew canon, for that traditionally lies with 2 Chronicles with which the third division, the Writings (*K'thuvim*), ends. In the Christian Bible, of course, Malachi is placed at the close of the entire OT canon, following the LXX tradition that placed The Prophets last.

The book is introduced by the Editor using a Hebrew term *massa'*. It is not a common term, but is one shared by the three books in this Commentary. The term is used in Malachi in a non-narrative context to signal that the book belongs to a special literary classification, one shared by both wisdom and prophetic material. This special term appears in Prov. 30.1 and 31.1 as well as in a number of prophetic books such as Isaiah 13–23, Nah. 1.1, Hab. 1.1, Zech. 9.1 and 12.1, suggesting that Malachi, like the other two books, stands somewhere between the prophetic and wisdom traditions. See further in the Introduction to Nahum.

Malachi is never referred to in the text as a 'prophet'. This is a significant fact that must be considered seriously before determining whether this book is truly prophetic, or whether it belongs only marginally to that category, a determination which will influence one's overall approach to reading. It raises the question as to why the book Malachi, along with Nahum and Habakkuk, was given a place in the Scroll of the Twelve; what was it about the content of the book that led to it being included there and not somewhere else? And why was it placed as the final 'prophetic' representative? Did it just happen to be the last written record available to those who determined the contents of the minor prophets' scroll? Was there some obvious reason to place it at No. 12? Clearly, Malachi is an interlocutor who, according to the title provided by the Editor, was an agent for the 'word of the Lord' to Israel in the postexilic period, so why did the Editor not nominate him as 'prophet' as was done with Haggai? This reading will seek to demonstrate that Malachi the book is not prophetic in any narrow sense, but sits in a place between the Prophets and Wisdom showing influence from both traditions.

Malachi as a whole cannot be regarded as one of the more significant OT documents though it generated much interest in both the Jewish and Christian worlds because of the closing promise that 'the prophet Elijah' would be sent. The prophet here named Elijah has often been interpreted by Jews as the Messiah or a messiah, and seen by Christians as realised in the role of John the Baptiser, the forerunner of Jesus. Of course, this is a text that does not actually state who that promised Elijah could be, whether it is the old Elijah *redivivus* as some later Jewish and early Christians surmised, or an altogether new prophet with the same name. The LXX rendering would support the former view as it adds '…the Tishbite' as the earlier Elijah was known (1 Kgs 17.1). Is this final note then the primary reason for whatever significance it has?

The term *malachi*, 'my messenger/angel', can be a personal name, but more likely it describes an office, similar to that of Obadiah ('servant of yah'). As 'my messenger' (the LXX has a reading 'his messenger') there is ample evidence to read *malachi* as a role rather than an individual's name with the clear implication that the message-sender is God. In 2.7 the word 'messenger' is applied to one aspect of the priestly role, while in 3.1 we find the 'messenger/angel of the covenant', the identity of which is uncertain. In other words, there seem to be a number of potential community members who can and will fulfil that somewhat general role of message-bearer. What this reading will seek to demonstrate is that the eponymous 'Malachi' is a *collective* term for several messengers—see below under Authorship.

The message being shared by 'my messenger' does relate in a small way to the impending future (3.1; 4.1), and to that extent has an overtone that is similar to that of the better-known prophets, but for the most part the question-response format created by the Editor addresses current situations and issues that were being faced in post-587 BCE Judaea. The common, but often mistaken, view that a prophet was concerned primarily with the future distorts the biblical application of the term 'prophet'. While there are several references in this book to 'the day', or 'day of the Lord', that look to some future moment, the focus in Malachi has to do with what are deemed to be six present but problematic situations within the community, to be highlighted and corrected. That future 'day' must have been imminent, otherwise for any intended audience it would have become largely irrelevant. If one determines that Malachi is 'prophetic', the term then requires a much broader definition than usually given it, as is also true of Jonah and Habakkuk.

Historical Situation

Malachi is built around material illustrative of Judaean responses to the trauma of 587 BCE. When Babylonian troops invaded the southern kingdom of Judah from the north and west, the Edomites from the south and east opportunistically joined them; Judah was attacked on all fronts, Jerusalem invaded, and the glorious Temple of Solomon destroyed. That blow was not only material; it was also a profound theological challenge with regard to Yahweh's power and commitment, and one that tore away all pretence of an ancient family relationship between Judah and Edom that tradition had upheld. As a result, Judah nursed a deep anger and resentment, lamenting what had happened, asking serious questions of its theologians, and screaming for revenge against its enemies—see Psalm 137. From the time of Jerusalem's destruction, the transport of numbers of exiles to Babylon, the reorientation of life and of language in exile, there was great tension between those who fought to keep alive their exclusive sense of self and those who adapted to life in a foreign world. Once Babylon was overrun by the Persian Cyrus, whose enlightened policy towards exiles allowed Judaeans to return home in 538 BCE, there to re-establish themselves, leaders sympathetic to Persian interests were appointed as civil (Sheshbazzar and Zerubbabel) and religious (Joshua) authorities in Jerusalem. Haggai the prophet served the community after the return in 538, encouraging them to restore the ruined Temple in 520 BCE and the task was finally completed in around 516 BCE. Cohorts of priests and ordinary citizens had made their way back to Judaea over the period, along with Ezra and Nehemiah, resuming life along with those who were not taken into exile. Judah and Jerusalem began to rebuild after 50 years of exile, no priestly activity in the devastated Temple, years of foreign rule and uncertainty while re-establishing themselves under Persian control. Over a period of 80 and more years the open sore of humiliation at the hands of enemies and a supposed 'brother' gnawed away at Judaean feelings.

Those feelings remained raw, as can be seen in the wide range of oral materials drawn upon by Jeremiah, Amos, Joel, a Psalmist, Obadiah, Malachi and others that cover the many intervening years. The depth of frustration and anger is evident in each period and in each expression throughout those exilic and postexilic years. No other trauma seems to have evoked such a sustained period of communal anguish as these appeals for God to do something, if not for the people, then for God's own name's sake, his reputation. The Malachi text makes much of God's reputation among the nations, but within Judaea it was being seriously questioned. The book of Malachi reflects the call for God to do something NOW, otherwise his reputation locally was in trouble.

Authorship

Who authored the book named Malachi is not a question that can be answered if one is thinking in terms of an individual writer; indeed it is a non-question because what we are dealing with is an anonymous third-person report of activity associated with an eponymous agent, Malachi, 'my messenger/angel'. How many have contributed to the handing-on and preservation of these materials is impossible to determine, and the time between any original oral presentation and incorporation into this final literary work is likewise unknowable.

The book is the work of an Editor(s) who has compiled a report from the mass of oral material that was in circulation in the postexilic years, arranging it in a series of six independent discussions around topics of special concern to himself.

Regardless of whether 'Malachi' is regarded as a personal name or title, the fact is that the one who is here said to have spoken the 'word of the Lord' is essentially an unknown figure. We have no information in the text as to background: was Malachi born in Babylon or one recently returned to Judah? We don't know what his work or function, his pedigree, his family situation if he had one, why he was speaking out as he did, or for how long he functioned as a messenger. Suggestions on these matters are plentiful, but in reality we cannot discover answers from within the text. And the reason for this is obvious—*there is no one individual Malachi*! The eponymous 'Malachi' is representative of all who have been messengers throughout the exilic and postexilic period, a selection of whose messages are here included.

Ultimately, there is no answer to some of the questions we might have as to authorship, but what we can say is that the various 'Malachi', and those who translated and compiled this literary work, were persons very sympathetic with the narrower Deuteronomic worldview and its theology, placing them as members in the more theologically conservative camp of the time (see Malachi's Concerns below).

Date

There are several clues within the text that suggest a range of dates, or better, a period, within which the work came to a conclusion. Mention of the 'governor' (*pechah*) in 1.8 means that Judaea was under the control of one who had been appointed by the Persian authorities, pointing to some time after 538 BCE. Whether the 'governor' was Sheshbazzar, Zerubbabel or some later appointee we have no way of knowing as he is not identified.

References to what clearly is a completed Temple (1.10) mean that it must date to some time after 516 BCE, perhaps during Zerubbabel's administration. Possible allusions to the xenophobic policy enforced by Ezra, namely, requiring those with foreign wives to set them aside, depends on dating Ezra/Nehemiah, however it should not be forgotten that they were simply enforcing a narrow and nationalistic Deuteronomic view that was of long-standing within the exilic and postexilic communities. In other words, we are talking about a period of around half a century during which the material found now in Malachi could have arisen and circulated until fixed in its present format.

What needs also to be recognized is that of the six major divisions in the text (see below) each may come from a different time within the extended period noted above. The fact that all have been assembled in one document attributed to 'Malachi' does not mean that each derived from the same spokesman, the same moment within the overall time frame, nor should one assume that there is a sequential relationship between what are essentially six independent reports. The order in which the material divisions now stand, and the specific issues chosen for inclusion all depended on the final Editor's decision.

From Spoken to Written

Given that the messenger's mission was essentially one of speaking, of communicating with the community on specific issues, one can safely assume that a messenger spoke in what he considered the most appropriate manner. That would imply speaking at a lower language level that most, if not all, audiences could readily understand; it would generally mean simple sentences and a limited vocabulary, together with all the features of informal speech such as repetition, hesitations, voice modulation, even gestures and eye-contact. In the case of 'Malachi', set in the postexilic period when Aramaic had become the *lingua franca* of the Israelite community, it would seem logical that any messenger would have addressed his audiences in Aramaic, the shared language, and used the appropriate level of that language.

What one reads in the now printed text of Malachi, the book, is in Hebrew, not Aramaic, and in a more formal, rhetorically structured, and higher level of language, so it is obvious that between the oral presentations of a Malachi and their recording in the book, a great deal of literary activity, apart from translation, has taken place. All that is the work, not of a so-called prophet, but of the Editor(s). He has elevated the language to conform with the literary style of the traditional and more highly regarded

Hebrew, and abandoned second-language Aramaic in the process. One simple illustration of the sophistication of the written text is in the opening vv. 1, 2d-3a where a chiastic structure has been used to great effect. Elevated rhetorical elements and embedded sentences are indicative of a considered and deliberate writing style, so different from the less sophisticated common spoken language.

Readers of the text today need to recognize that they are not reading the words of the Messenger as originally delivered.

Structure and Contents

The structure of Malachi, the book, is generally recognized as consisting of six major but unequal parts following the Title in 1.1: they are, 1.2-5; 1.6–2.9 (or 1.6-14; 2.1-9); 2.10-16; 2.17–3.5; 3.6-12; 3.13–4.3; and a closing, 4.4-6.

Supporting this schema is the special feature of the book, its use of a form that almost certainly originated with the Editor since it does not appear elsewhere. It is a sophisticated rhetorical form that provides the framework into which the six sections have been inserted. That construction is hardly to be expected of Malachi speaking publicly to the community at large. The form is: (A) a statement of a fact or situation, seemingly a statement by God, followed by (B) a responding rhetorical question that challenges or counters statement A (see 1.2, 6-7; 2.17; 3.6-8, 13). This leads into (C) a discussion of the issue raised. See below for a discussion of the book's Literary Characteristics.

The contents of the book cover a number of different subjects, indicating that the work overall is a composite one, as is 'Malachi'. There is no sequential relationship between the six major divisions in the book for they are what one commentator has called 'haphazard'. For example:

A. the opening section 1.2-5 deals with God's love for Judaea in the context of Edom's despicable act. It may well reflect an historical situation shortly after 587 BCE when there were further Babylonian incursions in the region, or the Nabatean invasions of the fifth century BCE. Information is insufficient to allow any certainty.
B. the section 1.6–2.9 consists of two distinct issues regarding priestly activity in Judaea—1.6-14 and 2.1-9, perhaps even 1.6-10, 1.11-14 and 2.1-9—that cohere around the Lord's 'name' issue, and that of polluted offerings in a conspiracy of priest and worshiper that presumably date after 516 BCE when the Temple was completed.

C. 2.10-16 raise the question of marriage to foreign women, a concern of long-standing within the Deuteronomic cohort (see Ezra 10) but not an issue with Zerubbabel and Joshua, so perhaps early fifth century?
D. 2.17–3.5 are concerned with the refining of the Levitical priesthood, a post-538 development.
E. 3.6-12 relate to the practice of tithes and the threat of poor harvests that reflect the period when Haggai was remonstrating to have the Temple repaired in 520 BCE.
F. 3.13–4.3 question the value or benefit of serving God, a relatively timeless issue, but one that was particularly relevant during the hardships of the early days following the return—see Haggai.
G. The collection concludes in 4.4-6 with a timeless call to remember Moses' teachings, along with a final promise of a return of 'Elijah' and the avoidance of a divine curse.

In short, each section can be treated as essentially independent both in terms of its content as well as its specific moment in time. The collection as a whole represents oral material from an extended period c. 587–500 BCE. This perspective may suggest that Malachi the book offers a summary of some of the issues that were of concern during the postexilic period, and thus was a suitable concluding statement for the Prophets/*N'vi'im*?

The format of the book is often spoken of as a series of dialogues between Malachi and the people, or Malachi and priests. The nature of these dialogues has been called Disputation, with Malachi making a formal statement and the people questioning its logic or validity, then to be explained in his or God's response.

This reader questions the Disputation categorization. What is clear is that the Editor responsible for bringing these component parts together has developed a unique personal form or editorial style in which Malachi makes a statement that is 'questioned' by those addressed. Each of the six topics has been placed into identical frameworks. The questions asked as part of the frame are rhetorical rather than questions seeking information. As rhetorical questions they imply a denial of the statement or charge. The form calls on the messenger to explain the validity of the statement made, to justify that statement, and then to expound it as a word from the Lord. The statement may be very brief, such as in 1.2—'*I have loved you..., but you ask, "how have you loved us?"*'—or longer, but it is a form unique to this book. (See 1.6a-d + 6e; 1.7a + 7b; 2.10-13 + 2.14a; 2.17a + 2.17b; 3.7b + 3.7c; 3.13a + 3.13b.) The final main section, 3.13–4.3, illustrates the nature of the book well as it questions the perceived unfairness in society that relates closely with the issues contemporary wisdom was asking—see Qoheleth.

In terms of its didactic purpose, 2.4-9 offers another clue when it speaks of the priestly office as one in which preserving knowledge and teaching was its primary responsibility. The Levitical priesthood had a special role within the religious community, requiring it to ensure that all knew what God expected of them in terms of 'integrity and uprightness' and 'turning away from iniquity'.

There are twenty-four references in Malachi's total of fifty-five verses in which the Messenger-form, traditionally linked with the prophets, is used. That phrase is: '...*says the Lord (of hosts)*' (Heb., *'amar yhwh ts'ba'oth*, rather than the usual *n'um yhwh*—found only in 1.2). While the initial component of the traditional Messenger form, '*Thus says the Lord...*', is used only once, in 1.4b, what is noticeable is that every one of those twenty-four references to '...*says the Lord (of hosts)*', is used for emphasis rather than as formal markers concluding an argument. This is a peculiarity of the Editor's reporting style. It is similar to the usage found in the report of Haggai, where the closing form also appears throughout to be primarily for emphasis rather than as the formal end of an argument. Whether this would suggest some Editorial relationship between Haggai and Malachi would be interesting to explore. This possibility is further raised by both prophet's use of the phrase 'lay it on your heart' (Mal. 2.1-2; Hag. 1.5, 7; 2.15, 18)

While there are many allusions to what God will do that are presented using first-person grammatical forms, many other references to God are in the third-person—see e.g., 3.1 '*See, I am sending my messenger to prepare the way before me, and the Lord whom you seek....his temple*'. The personal pronouns here render the statement opaque and ambiguous. Even more confusing is the text of 1.9 where God appears to be the better choice for the subject of the phrase '*Will he look on you favourably?*' then followed by the phrase, '...*says the Lord of hosts*'.

The pronoun issue in the book as a whole can be confusing, as it is with Nahum. This situation is not surprising given that what we are faced with is an Editor who has gathered six disparate messages that have been passed down orally, and perhaps with some parts already in an initial written version, then fitted into the Editor's framework. At each stage of this complex process the relevant pronouns have been used, but when placed within the overall framework and with the numerous '...*says the Lord of hosts*' phrase added, confusion has entered.

Literary Characteristics

In addition to the rhetorical pattern of Statement–Question–Response that forms the basic frame of the major divisions of the book, there is an extensive range of literary or rhetorical features found in Malachi.

One of the more significant rhetorical features in Malachi is Hyperbole. Throughout the prophetic canon, promises or statements with regard to the imminent future, frequently are set within exaggerated language, promises that could never be fulfilled as literally given. Many such statements were never fulfilled in actuality. It raises the question of the purpose and intention of such hyperbole. Presumably the speakers and audiences knew what was intended by these kinds of statements—offering some hope for those in distress, encouraging those who were facing challenges whether of faith or livelihood. Malachi is no exception as it records numerous potential promises that are hyperbolic—1.11, for example, the Lord's name is said to be known and honoured throughout the world, and incense is offered to the great name of the Lord by all nations. Or, 4.1 in speaking of the arrogant and evildoers who will be 'burned up' as Judaeans tread down the wicked under their feet.

Other obvious rhetorical examples are:

a. Rhetorical Questions. In presenting his material, whether the speaker is God or the people, RQ's are basic throughout—1.2, 6, 8, 9, 13; 2.15 etc. Also on occasions, Malachi answers his own questions (1.13-14; 2.15)
b. Parallelism. E.g., 2.6 *'True instruction was found in his mouth, no wrong was found on his lips'*. See also 1.6a, b, 8a, b; 2.2, 10; 3.2, 6, 10-11 etc. Ascending parallelism: 2.2 (I will send the curse on you, and I will curse your blessings; indeed I have already cursed them…)
c. Exclamations. Expressing positive and negative reactions—e.g., 1.5 (*Great is the Lord beyond the borders of Israel!*), 10a (*Oh that someone among you would close the [Temple] doors…!*), 13 (*What a weariness this is!*); 2.12 (*May the Lord cut off from the tents…!*)
d. Metaphors. 2.16 (*covering one's garment with violence*); 4.1-2 (*the day is coming, burning like an oven…*) Metaphors are applied mainly in references to 'the day of the Lord'.
e. Chiasm or reverse parallelism. The most obvious is the Hebrew text of the opening statement in 1.2a *(I have loved you…(how) have you loved us)* and in 1.2d-1.3a *(I have loved Jacob, but Esau I have hated)*.

f. <u>Contrast</u>. Malachi was at pains to show the contrast between what God will do and what others will do: 1.4b (*They may build, but I will tear down...*); 2.8-9 (*...you have corrupted..., and so I make you despised...*).
g. <u>Assonance</u>. See the repetition of *'ayin* in five Hebrew words in 1.4c.
h. <u>Inclusion</u>. The discussion about the priests despising the Lord's table binds the commentary in 1.7c–12b.
i. <u>Conditional clauses</u>. Parallel conditional or potential situations are offered in 1.6b, c; 1.8a, b; and 2.2.
j. <u>Repetition</u>. The phrase, '*accept an offering from your hands*' (1.10, 13); references to the greatness of the divine name: '*my name is great/revered among the nations*' (1.11, 14).
k. <u>Sarcasm</u>. In the encounter with the priests who are accepting the people's offerings of defective animals, Malachi suggests they offer such to the governor and realize how offensive such offerings are (1.8c).
l. <u>Lord of hosts</u>. Like other postexilic writings such as Haggai and Zechariah, Malachi predominantly uses the phrase 'Lord of hosts' throughout to refer to God.

As a fine literary composition, it is clear that this book of Malachi represents a high degree of literary sophistication far beyond that of an oral presentation.

Malachi's Concerns

Malachi the book contains material deriving from a period when the Judaean leadership was in the hands of a Persian-appointed governor and a chief priest, both of whom were thus committed to ensuring Persian interests were prioritized at all levels. That is not to say that every Judaean agreed with such policies, as Haggai illustrates, but that within the community of returnees who were rebuilding what was left of the old Kingdom of Judah, there were differences of opinion on many matters, including religion. Some were open to Persian ideas and were international in outlook, while others were hardline tribalists with more of a Deuteronomic approach to religious practice, a more simplistic or black-and-white view of the divine at work.

A. The opening section of the book, 1.1-5, focuses on a general issue to do with the claim that God had a special relationship with Judaeans over against Edomites. Despite the opening words as presented having no specific context, the question as to whether Judaea was really God's chosen and beloved suggests that some event or some matters had arisen forcing the question to be asked quite widely. The section reflects community doubts about God's relationship with them since they had been over-run by the Babylonians and been betrayed by their Edomite cousins. These doubts were addressed by the messenger drawing attention to what had happened to Edom. However, the manner in which that doubt was addressed was answered in a very unusual manner; it was answered so indirectly, namely, claiming that by destroying Edom, God was manifesting his special love for Judaea. Who could have imagined that that was what God was intending by destroying Edom? Why had no prophet arisen to explain what was happening? Only when the messenger Malachi sought to untangle the divine thought-process and 'explain' the situation could the community begin to understand such a disconcerting reverse action!

B. A second and perhaps major concern was priestly activity and whether the priests and people were functioning in accordance with the Law as set down. Behind this concern for Law-keeping there may lie some tension between various elements within society and especially within the priestly ranks, for during Joshua the Chief Priest's regime it is clear that the prophet Haggai was strongly opposed to Joshua at the personal as well as the theological level. Much to the chagrin of people like Haggai and his Deuteronomic friends like Ezra, priestly attitudes to the laws and regulations around sacrificial offerings were clearly relaxed. Whether this was due to the fact that Temple activity had been in abeyance for fifty years, or perhaps that Persian attitudes and influence had been allowed to creep into Judaean religion, is hard to say, but clearly Malachi was deeply concerned about this trend.

C. In 2.10-16 a clear anti-foreign note is struck as the issue of marriage to foreign women is considered an act that flouts the 'covenant of our ancestors'. Presumably this was an issue largely but not exclusively confined to those who had returned from Babylon with their 'mixed' family members. These were seen by Malachi as potentially having a corrupting influence. It is here that readers can detect Malachi's anti-foreign view, similar to that of Ezra, that Judaeans were an exclusive community under their God. It was a view held very firmly by the Deuteronomic cohort. It was also a strongly contested view, as Judaean leaders such as Zerubbabel and Joshua were not so troubled, being open to a wider and more international perspective.

D. A further concern was whether there was any positive value in serving God, for the experience of many was that they saw no obvious advantages therein; unjust people seemed to reap the benefits of their injustice, suffering no negative consequences (3.13-15). See also Hab. 1.2-4. Furthermore, the material promises associated with obedience to the Law as embedded in Deuteronomy, such as guaranteed good harvests, did not flow as expected. A sign of divine 'love' for Judaeans surely would have been that their relationship with God assuredly brought the promised benefits, both religious and material; the simple 'blessings for obedience and curses for disobedience' outlined in Deuteronomy 27–28 were clearly not implemented so strictly, leading to deep questions about divine justice. This age-old issue of divine inscrutability and seeming unfairness or injustice was taken up especially in Qoheleth and by the Sages more generally, and it became a point of tension between Prophet and Sage in Jerusalem.

E. A deeper concern is around God's 'name' or reputation. It features in 1.5, 11, 14; 2.2, 5; 3.16; 4.2. In a very real sense, concern for God's name, and/or God's concern for his own name, underlies the messenger's concept of the divine and thus the message of the book as a whole, together with the claim of God's universally acknowledged greatness or power in 1.5, 11, 14. The theme of a strong God who demands people reverence, adore, stand in awe of God and bring God pleasure is an important starting-point for assessing the theological underpinning of Malachi.

Relationship to Deuteronomy

There are sufficient echoes in Malachi of Deuteronomy's language and the concepts informing the Deuteronomistic History (DH) to assume that the Editor was very familiar with the ethos of the Deuteronomic cohort in postexilic Judaea, and that he was in fundamental agreement with the views and theology that it represented.

A. As already noted, the preference for 'the name' as a way of referring to God recalls the preferred way of speaking of the divine presence in Deuteronomic circles (Deut. 12.5, 11, 14 etc.; 1 Kgs 8.16-20).

B. The use of 'Horeb' (4.4) when referring to the sacred mountain, as throughout Deuteronomy, rather than 'Sinai'.

C. The Deuteronomic binary, 'blessing' (2.2; 3.10) and 'curse' (1.14; 2.2; 3.9; 4.6), are responses used widely to describe God's reaction to people's conduct.
D. There is agreement that crop failure, plague and drought are curses that result from divine intervention (3.10-11) as set out in Deuteronomy 28–29. Alternatively, crop spoilage due to insect infestation, vineyard failure and similar agricultural problems are all preventable if one is obedient to the law (3.11). Deuteronomy's view of a strict relationship between obedience and blessing, disobedience and curse is followed explicitly.
E. One point of difference, however, is that Malachi does not use a key Deuteronomic term 'obey' though he does use a similar verb 'keep' with reference to the statutes (3.7).

On Reading Malachi

1. One of the major concerns for one reading an ancient document that has arisen within a culture and language alien to one's own, is seeking to understand it within its own context rather than reading it, evaluating it, interpreting it in light of a different culture and experience. While one does hope that there is some level of correspondence between its past and one's present, there is also much that differs, that hides, within another's cultural and linguistic world, leading the modern reader to think, and even believe, that they have grasped the essence of that ancient document, when in fact they have essentially placed over it a new frame of reference or paradigm, a range of values and notions that can distort its original context. In doing this, they distort its assumed significance to both the original and subsequent audiences. An awareness of these challenges is a basic requirement that hopefully will limit the potential for a surface-reading that fails to plumb the depths within the text or a reading that skews the content towards a particular predetermined goal.
2. It is important to remember that in reading the Hebrew Bible we today are looking at a body of material that was the treasured memory of an ancient community, that held that community's identity and offered its diverse ideas or ideologies to the descendants of that community. It has been adopted by a subsequent community that centuries later emerged from its Judaean origin to be set within a more global context and culture. This community that became known as the Church, regarded this body of material as Scripture,

and to it they added some writings of their own that became the New Testament. Those new writings cannot frame a faithful reading of the Hebrew Bible without downplaying its significance as something 'old' and something different that had to be expanded and updated to meet a different world and time.

3. A Christian paradigm for reading the Hebrew Bible generally regards the Old Testament as having a *teleological* plan and purpose, that is to say, it assumes that the OT portrays the human disaster, which is identified as Sin, a disaster that demands a rescue plan. Thus, Genesis 3 becomes the starting point from which all divine activity is said to represent God's plan for that rescue; the biblical story in this view travels from Adam the Sinner—seen now as an actual historical figure—through to Jesus as Saviour. Paul is the major exponent of this reading that presents the disobedient Adam over against the obedient Christ—see Rom. 5.12-19. This manner of reading must be acknowledged as a much later one and an imposed partisan one that cannot represent any original contextual meaning found in an individual scroll. Only after the entire collection of scrolls is brought together as one document with a fixed order are there potential grounds for (mis)reading it teleologically, as one would a novel.

4. A further but closely related issue has to do with reading Malachi and other OT documents from within the thesis of a 'canonical reading', meaning, in the context of the entire Biblical canon, Old and New, as something called 'normative Scripture'. It is, like the above, a Christian reading, one that gives priority to the way in which the Old has been viewed through the prism of the New. The use of *midrashic* reading of the OT text, searching the OT for material that can be interpreted without regard for its original context, is problematic in that it applies an alien set of values and purpose to the original OT text.

5. Any reading of an ancient OT text must strive to read it in its several contexts, literary, cultural and theological, seeking to avoid imposing a modern overlay that could not have been part of its original setting and purpose. That does not mean that later writers could not re-use or adopt some of the literary features of the earlier Hebrew text, whether specific vocabulary items or wider conceptual ideas. However, there is a vast difference between borrowing or re-using items from the past as illustrative, and on the other hand claiming that in these latter usages one finds the complete or planned realization of what the earlier material

intended. Borrowing the concept of animal sacrifice as a means of thinking or speaking about the death of Jesus, for example, with all its inadequacies and differences, does not mean anything other than using a culturally appropriate and familiar concept to talk about a later event. That later re-use cannot be imposed on the original OT text as somehow 'predictive' of an event or situation centuries later.

6. It is also important to acknowledge that the materials of which the book of Malachi is composed were delivered orally and in Aramaic, and then discussed within the community where they were preserved. None of the six component parts were sermons presented on one occasion only; each presents a frequent, varied, and community-discussed round of talk over a shorter or longer period of time, and in one case—3.16—the Lord is said to have been a keen listener! Subsequently, from those oral versions circulating throughout the extended period from c. 587–500 BCE, materials were gathered and edited into what we now read in a 'frozen' form. Given the low level of literacy, it is almost certain that the words and ideas were brought together by a literate Editor(s) who then determined the report's shape and form. This is clear in the way the third-person narrative presents Malachi and the encounters with his audiences—a series of reports of issues the Editor selected from those known to him, using 'Malachi' as the eponymous spokesperson for them all. The material has passed through many hands before reaching the form in which we appropriate it today.

7. When reading Malachi, the book, or other orally-derived material, the reader must acknowledge certain realities with regard to the text. One such is that the literary form and structures are those chosen by the Editor, and that the material existed in various versions within the community prior to being fixed in one written form; another is to recognize that hyperbole is a rhetorical form basic to the formal prophetic record, that it is not historical reporting in the modern sense; yet another is the very generalized nature of comments made—for example, in Malachi all priests seem to be assumed to be corrupt, along with all the people making offerings. There is no attempt to discriminate between priests and Levites, all are assumed to be guilty of corruption and negligence. This issue may have arisen because what was originally directed at a specific and limited audience is now set in a more broad context of a word to Israel (1.1).

8. A further concern that needs to be addressed is the nature of the messages and their source. By attaching his personal version of part of the Messenger form to the material, the Editor adds weight to the claim that the material originated with God. While moments of inspiration, whether in dreams, auditions or visions, are important to the prophetic mission, a prophet's own personal insight into problematic aspects in society—be they questions of justice, purpose, hypocrisy, 'false' religion and the like—do not usually require, nor do they arise from, a divine prompting. A prophet/messenger, like others in the community, can see what is right or wrong in society and challenge the community accordingly. To think that a messenger has little or nothing to say unless moved by the divine spirit creates an unrealistic impression of that ministry. In the case of 'Malachi', who is never identified as a prophet in the text, seeing what was happening around the Temple forecourts, for example, was all that was required to move him to speak against what clearly had become a flawed religious practice.
9. See further in the Conclusions.

Access to Malachi the Book

My copy of the Hebrew Bible (*BHS*) is on the desk. I open to Malachi that begins at p. 1081; it is a separate 'book' sandwiched between Zechariah and Psalms. Its relationship with the other eleven documents that make up the old Scroll of the Twelve is not clear, nor its relationship with Psalms that follows. Did it ever have an independent existence before being attached to the end of the Scroll to make up the mystical number 'twelve'? A naïve reader would not even think to ask questions relating to this order. Modern readers may have a preconceived view of Malachi and its place arising from its availability in modern book-form, and especially of its location as the final book in their OT and its proximity to the NT.

The materials in Malachi the book are derived from the oral traditions of the postexilic period and while some of the many traditions were presumably generally known throughout the community, access to a written version was severely limited. Literacy levels were extremely low, while access to a physical copy of any such hand-copied document was even more restricted, to say nothing of the transfer from spoken Aramaic to a written Hebrew.

It was inevitable that Malachi was not widely known for some considerable time after its oral materials were compiled and then attached to what became the Scroll of the Twelve. This reader assumes that very few knew of its existence, and even those individuals who were aware of a written document may have been limited to a region or group dedicated to copying manuscripts, such as the Dead Sea community. More would have known of the traditions circulating orally about Malachi, but apart from some central scroll repository, there were very few places that held copies of <u>any</u> of the individual scrolls, including the Scroll of the Twelve, that came to form the Hebrew Scriptures.

The number of books in the Hebrew Scriptures and their order in known lists varies from 22 (Jerome second century CE) to 24. The number of 'books' also depends upon whether a smaller book had been included on a scroll with others, such as Lamentations as part of Jeremiah, or Ezra and Nehemiah as one book etc. There seems never to have been a decision on a final list of authoritative books apart from the five books of Torah. The Old Testament as we now know it, readily available to all with its thirty-nine books, is a very recent and modern phenomenon, but it is the point from which most, if not all, modern readers and scholars begin their thinking about the OT—seeing it as a completed body of ancient texts, rather than as it was for most of its life, twenty-plus individual scrolls each available only to a very select few who were literate. A modern reading from Genesis to Malachi teleologically was never possible until all individual scrolls could be combined into one volume, and for this we are today largely dependent upon the Leningrad MS of c. 1008 CE for what we now read as the book of Malachi.

The role of the priests as teachers was vital in communicating what was required of the Israelite community at all levels with regard to its religious life. Oral instruction, whether formal at specific festivals, or informal at family gatherings, was the means by which any and all religious ideas were shared. Prophetic messages and Sages' instructions to the coming generation were all dependent on the community having some access to those who were the keepers of such oral traditions. The degree and extent of such instruction was therefore limited by one's location and personal interest.

Nature of the Book

Is Malachi really a prophetic work? Does its inclusion in the Scroll of the Twelve define its nature? We are reminded that the Book of Jonah is not 'prophetic' in any traditional sense, yet it has found a place in that Scroll. Is Malachi similar? Or is it, as many commentators have suggested, a series of Disputations in which God's messenger and the audience participate? Is its purpose more instructional and didactic? As is to be expected, the answer(s) is complex, so it is vital to allow the text to inform. It is important to bear in mind that the framework of the book is the creation of the Editor into which he has placed the six material reports from his oral sources.

While the close of the book (4.5-6) does have the air of a prophetic promise involving the 'day of the Lord', in 2.4-7 and 4.4 the call is for more attention to be paid to teachings and instruction, so it is also clearly didactic. The rhetorical question forms, in the reading being offered, are seen not so much as Malachi and/or God disputing the people's actions, but rather as the people questioning and, by implication, denying the charges being made against them. That then becomes an opportunity for some instruction and/or discussion to bring the Judaean community back to the Deuteronomic ideals as seen by the Messenger. Perhaps the most telling fact is that Malachi is never identified specifically as a prophet. The classification of this book as *massa'*, noting its links with both prophet and sage, points to a new class of literature, one with didactic purpose. See the exegesis of 1.1 below and the Introduction to Nahum.

Outline

1.1	Title	
	1.2-5	God's Love-in-Reverse
	1.6–2.9	On Priestly Failures
	1.6-14	Priests and Offerings
	2.1-9	The Levi Covenant
	2.10-16	Opposing Foreign Marriages
	2.17–3.5	Refining the Community
	3.6-12	Guaranteeing a Land of Plenty
	3.13–4.3	Is Serving God of Benefit?
	4.4-6	In Conclusion

EXEGESIS

1.1 Title

A Massa': the word of the Lord to Israel by Malachi (my messenger).

Apart from its use as a personal name (Gen. 25.14), the Hebrew nominal form *massa'*, has traditionally been thought to be derived from the root *ns'*, 'lift up'. It is found a number of times in the OT narrative with a basic contextual meaning of 'burden' (e.g., Isa. 22.25). This has led to it being interpreted in the same vein when found at the head of small prophetic collections, e.g., Isa. 13.1; 14.28; 15.1, or when introducing Nah. 1.1; Hab. 1.1; Zech. 9.1; 12.1 and Malachi. Commentators have often suggested that the prophetic word therefore is a 'burden' placed on the prophet and/or the people This interpretation is both negative and misleading. From the linguistic point of view, the noun *massa'* as used in these three books is a *homograph*, referring to a new form of literary style, an Anthology. It is vital to affirm that it is *Context that determines meaning, not Etymology.*

Many of the uses of the title *massa'* in the prophetic books are introductory to the so-called foreign nations oracles—see Isaiah 13–23 especially—so it is interesting to note that Malachi opens with a reference to Edom as the one unloved in 1.2-5.

The second component in the Title is its identification as '*A word of the Lord*' (Heb. *d'bar-yhwh*). This phrase is a traditional one, used constantly throughout the prophetic literature by Editors to signal that the word now recorded comes with what is claimed to be divine authority, a word from Yahweh, though the phrase also means 'a word about Yahweh' (objective genitive) without defining its source. Linking the *massa'* to the 'word of the Lord' as happens in Malachi and Zechariah, for example, is an attempt to note the close connection between the two traditions of prophecy and wisdom for the purpose of Instruction or Advice.

Unusually, perhaps, the word is addressed '*to Israel*', in this context a vague inclusive term, but given the extended time-period covered, it may refer to the entire post-exilic Judaean community, despite the fact that not everyone in Judaea is the focus of the issues raised. On the other hand, by using the term 'Israel' here, the Editor appears to allude to links back to the original Jacob/Israel name-change tradition recorded in Gen. 32.29. The first component in the message, 1.2-5, with its focus on the Jacob-Esau tension, highlights the fact that in the tradition, Jacob/Israel is the blessed or beloved son, and Esau the 'hated' outsider.

Malachi is identified as one through whose agency the word came; he is the messenger, but does that make him a prophet? Why is he not so identified in the text? And what is the distinction, if any? On the name/title Malachi, 'my messenger', see the Introduction.

The Editor provides no other information as to possible dates, events or personalities with which the various messages of the book might connect, other than the shared link to the eponymous Malachi, 'my messenger'.

1.2-5 On God's Love-in-Reverse

1.2-3 'I have loved you', says the Lord; and you asked, "In what way have you loved us?" 'Was Esau not Jacob's brother?' the Lord asked. 'Now, I have loved Jacob, and I have hated Esau, and have made a ruin of his mountain lands, turning his inherited land into a desert for jackals.'

1.4 If Edom was to say, "We have been smashed, but we shall rebuild what has been ruined," the Lord of hosts says, "They may rebuild, but I will tear down. And they will be called a region of evil, the people with whom the Lord is permanently angry."'

1.5 'May you yourselves see it and say, "The Lord is great beyond the borders of Israel!"'

1.2-3 The introductory statement ' *"I have loved you", says the Lord*' is without context, a peculiar way perhaps in which to begin what is claimed to be the Lord's initial message. Who is being addressed? Where are they? Does the statement aim to address a smaller target audience, or is it rather a national broadcast to all Israelites, even to all Judaeans? What has prompted the assertion? The strong assertion is followed by an equally mysterious '*And/But you have said, "In what way have you loved us?"*' Clearly there is much unrecorded background to these two assertions. Are we to assume that the Editor was aware of some discussion passing between Malachi(?) and the community in which it has expressed serious doubt about being loved by God? Who would represent the community and give voice to this concern? And would 'love' be the verb normally used in such a context? Communal Laments might express disappointment and bewilderment about being abandoned by God, but 'unloved'? There must have been some grounds, some event, some disaster giving rise to them doubting that they were the object of divine love, but what could that have been? Was it the overthrow of Jerusalem in 587 BCE? Was it, as with Haggai, another disastrous harvest around the year 520 BCE?

The question supposedly asked by the community may have been a literal question, but one has to consider that it is more in the nature of an Editor's way of presenting an issue intended as a matter for instruction, not a question for information. It becomes clear as one reads further that the Editor has developed a specific formula, namely a statement followed by questions from the audience that are rhetorical, leading into the issue(s) with which he then deals.

The form is: Statement–Question–Response (see 1.2, 6-7; 2.14, 17; 3.7-8, 13). Given that there is no dispute in these verses, no question of God's love for his people, the syntax takes on a very different nuance. Here, it is the Editor's way of saying something like: 'God has said he loves you, and you are expressing your doubts about that claim'. What follows is an attempt to prove God's love for Judaeans over Edomites.

The Editor adds an immediate and unexpected response by means of the rhetorical question about the sibling relationship between Esau and Jacob. The question '*Is not Esau Jacob's brother?*' has an obvious answer: Yes, Esau was Jacob's brother—everyone knows that! The normal closing phrase '*…says the Lord*', seems out of place here, but the assertion continues: '*Now, I love Jacob, but hate Esau…*' This sudden change of subject, however interpreted, picks up the theme of love, explaining to a degree the opening assertion of God's love for 'you'. It is as though this (traditional) fact should have been known and embraced by the audience, never doubting God's love, despite what might have caused the community to question it.

On the contrast between 'love' and 'hate' in this context, the use of binary terms to emphasize that contrast is typical of the Deuteronomic outlook and its accompanying language (Deut. 4.32-34; 10.14-15; 23.5), perhaps best seen in its blessing-curse binary (Deut. 27–28). The extreme language here is code for 'chosen' and 'not chosen', illustrative of Deuteronomy's narrow worldview and tribal exclusivism. It should not be read or interpreted literally, but seen as indicative of the messenger's location on the theological spectrum of the day.

The description in v. 3 of God's destructive actions having been visited upon mountains and tribal lands-turned-desert, lacks any identification of those mountains as being Edom; the Editor assumes that his readers will make the connection between Esau and Edom, and then that they will understand that the destruction of Edom that must have taken place and become known to Judaeans has demonstrated that God does love and has loved Judaea.

The line of argument here is not only oddly indirect, what I have called 'Love-in-Reverse', it leaves a reader with many questions. Claiming one's love for person A by claiming hatred for person B, A's enemy or opponent, is a perverse way of showing love for A. Even if one accepts the strange thought process involved in the argument, it is devoid of all personal and emotional commitment to A. Asserting God's love for the Judaean party is supposedly proven by asserting an alternative fact—his hatred for Edom—under normal circumstances carrying little conviction and raising deep questions about the nature of that so-called love. Several crucial steps seem to be missing for this reader from the explanation Malachi is said to have offered.

As for the note about Edom's destruction, it is clear that it has taken place already, although there is little evidence in the text allowing readers to identify exactly what event is being referred to and who the agents of this destruction might have been. It is possible that it refers to Babylonian incursions into the region that continued after the 587 BCE invasion, or to a later Nabatean takeover in the fifth century. The point however is that it is something that has happened and the note here post-dates that event.

1.4 Having taken credit for the destruction of Edom, God's messenger records a further divine threat. '*If Edom were to say, "We have been smashed, but we shall rebuild the ruins", the Lord of Hosts says, "They may rebuild, but I will tear down."*' The conditional clause and its apodosis express in another manner the divine action that the reader is asked to accept as demonstrating or proving God's love for Judaea.

In v. 4b a further ignominy threatens Edom, namely '*they will call them (Edomites) a land of evil, the people with whom the Lord is angry in perpetuity*'. The subject of the clause is not defined but the text implies that all tribes in the region will look upon the Edomites as evil or as 'the wicked' (see also Hab. 1.4). Edom would remain a devastated land, as a sign of its evil, clear evidence of the Lord's 'hatred' towards it, and, in reverse, demonstrate his love for Judah. The abstract noun 'evil' may refer to religious or moral failure, or to general national failure. This kind of hyperbole appears to be a promise, but it is rather a further element in defining the threatened reaction of God that is God's love for Judaea.

In referring to the Edomite territory the text has used the noun *g'bul*, technically a reference to a border or border region, but in other post-exilic texts it has been used to depict the entire country (Obad 7; Zeph 2.8). Among the rhetorical tools used by this Editor, repetition of Hebrew sounds is a feature—here in this statement there is the regular beat as five of the ten words feature the consonant *'ayin*. Rhetorical questions are the

Editor's favoured way of raising issues addressed in the book, as well as in the didactic components—see e.g., 1.8; 2.10.

1.5 Verse 5 serves as a conclusion to the demonstration of divine love implicit in Edom's demise. The initial verb is an imperfective form (*tir'eynah*) and can be and has been understood as a future possibility, namely 'your own eyes will see...', predicting that Judaeans will acknowledge what has happened and take it as proof of God's love. However, the more convincing interpretation is to regard the verb form as a jussive 'May your eyes see...', for the messenger wants Judaeans to grasp the fact that they are loved despite their doubts. By placing the subject ahead of the verb, the Editor has drawn special attention to 'your eyes', i.e., you yourselves. In this way the Editor has emphasized his desire to have the Judaeans acknowledge Edom's fall, read it as evidence of God's love, and proclaim the Lord's greatness. '*May your eyes witness it and (may) you say/confess that great is the Lord beyond the border of Israel*'. This is not a Disputation but a chance for Judaeans to learn; it is something the Judaeans hopefully will recognize as evidence of God's wider power.

Here 'Israel' is a geopolitical term presumably referring to the idealized extent of Israel's former territories. It is to be noted that the greatness of God and of his name, along with reverence for that name, become vitally important themes throughout the book (1.5, 11, 14; 4.5), to the extent that it may be considered a primary purpose or motivation in compiling these sayings. God is presented as personally deeply concerned about his name, his reputation (1.6, 11, 14; 2.2, 5; 3.16; 4.2) and about being honoured; it is a very human projection of the divine character.

1.6–2.9 On Priestly Failures

The concerns in this section are entirely independent of those expressed in the previous section, 1.2-5; there is neither a sequential nor a topical connection between them. There is only a structural relationship given the Editor's application of his Statement–Question–Response format throughout the book.

The section may be further divided—1.6-14 relating to priests and people and unacceptable offerings; and 2.1-9 with its focus on the priestly failure in the area of teaching and instructing the people as required in the covenant with Levi.

Given that 1.10 refers to the Temple with doors as a completed building, and priestly activity being carried on there, it can be assumed that the issue taken up here dates from sometime after 516 BCE when the Temple is said to have been completed. That means that there is a significant gap in time—perhaps as much as 50 years—between the Edomite context of the preceding section, dated some time shortly after Edom's betrayal of Judah, and the issues now being raised following the return from exile. Temple activity had resumed, but not in full accordance with what the Levitical law demanded.

1.6-14

> *1.6 'A child honours its father, and a servant (honours) its master.' Now, the Lord of hosts asks you the priests who despise my name, 'If I am a father, where is the honour I am due? If I am Master, where is the respect I deserve?' Then you asked, "In what way have we despised your name?"'*
>
> *1.7 'You have been offering polluted food on my altar.' And you then ask, 'How have we been polluting it?' (You polluted it) when you "said" the Lord's table is despised.'*
>
> *1.8 'And when you continued to offer blind animals for sacrifice thinking there was nothing wrong, and when you were offering those that were lame or sick and thought there was nothing wrong there either. Offer one such to the governor if you will. Will he thank you for it, or look favourably on you?' says the Lord of hosts.*
>
> *1.9 'But now, beg divine favour that he may be gracious towards us! This is your doing! Will he (God?) show favour to any of you?' says the Lord of hosts.*
>
> *1.10 'If just one among you would close the (Temple) doors! and not set fire (on) my altar to no purpose! I have no pleasure in you', says the Lord of hosts, 'nor will I accept an offering from your hands'.*
>
> *1.11 'Truly, from the rising of the sun to its going (down) my name is great among the nations, and everywhere incense is burned to my name, and pure offering(s), because my name is great among the nations', says the Lord of hosts.*
>
> *1.12 'But you are profaning it when you say that my Lord's table is polluted, and the food, the produce (we offer) is to be despised'.*
>
> *1.13 'And you say, "Look, it is tiresome!" and you sniff at it' says the Lord of hosts. 'You continue to bring violated (animals), the lame and the sick, and you bring them as an offering. I will not accept what you bring?' says the Lord.*
>
> *1.14 'Cursed be one who cheats, having a male animal in his flock and vowing to offer it, but who sacrifices to my lord a blemished one. Truly, I am a great king', says the Lord of hosts, 'and my name is fearsome among the nations'.*

Malachi's statement about honour in v. 6 makes the point that within society there is a hierarchy with attendant mutual attitudes and expected behaviour. The analogy is then applied to God; God commands respect as does any master, but such due respect allegedly has not been shown by the priests (Heb. *koh'nim*) in 1.6-12 or by the people (1.13-14). The animals people bring as offerings are blemished and the priests consent to sacrifice them. God is displeased and the people are wearied by the legal demands (1.13). In order to receive the divine blessing and avoid the curse for cheating (1.14), revering the divine name, as do the nations, is required.

The priests are being challenged as those who despise the divine 'name', doing so by 'despising the Lord's table'. It is a theme that serves as an inclusion for vv. 7c-12b, while vv. 13-14 then focus more on the people who bring their defective animals for the priests to offer. The theme verb 'revere' (Heb. *yr'*) functions as an inclusion for the entire section.

The format follows the same rhetorical pattern as in 1.2-5. As was the case with the first section that concluded in v. 5 with a reference to the greatness of God, so also here in vv. 11 and 14 we note similar claims by the Lord who is so concerned about his reputation and about his greatness as King, revered by the nations. An important theme here is the contrast drawn between the Judaeans' despising of God's 'name' (1.6) and the alleged reverence shown by the universe of nations (1.14), all of whom revere this God—an amazing claim (vv. 11, 14).

God's messenger uses formal questions to make the point that there are issues between God and the priests and people. The basic issue is that the priest, the more accountable party, has been ignoring the law's demand that all animals offered for sacrifice be without blemish. The priests and people question the charges against them, implying that they are not valid. Did this charge apply to all priests or only some? The language used makes it appear as though none of the priests, none of the people, adhered to the principles of sacrifice as required. Such language is of course hyperbole. The wider context is God's desire for honour, to be respected, otherwise the implication is that God will not 'show favour' or 'be gracious' to the worshipper (1.9). Failure to offer in accordance with the law's demands is seen as disrespectful, and thus God will withhold blessing.

In terms of Instruction, the messenger claims that the nations give God the honour that he deserves in contrast to the dishonour shown by Judaeans. The people must again realize that such an attitude is unacceptable.

1.6-7 Here the initial and general statement about society values at the time is that: '*A son honours the father, and the servant (respects) his master*'. None present would dispute this arrangement. This opening gambit is followed by two parallel conditional clauses, each presuming to report what the Lord has said: '*Now, if I am a father, where is my honour? And if I am master, where is my respect? (or, how am I respected?)*'. The question of God's relationship with the Judaean community is expressed analogically.

The questions are rhetorical, given what follows. Interestingly, the Hebrew noun rendered 'master' (*'adon*) is then used in the analogy in its plural form, literally 'lords' (*'adonim*), the form that underlies the divine substitute reading for YHWH, namely *'adonay*, 'my Lord'. Frequently in commentaries the plural *'adonay* (literally, 'my lords') when referring to Yahweh is said to be a 'plural of majesty' or similar, a misleading European cultural import into ancient Hebrew semantics.

The rhetorical questions imply that God, who demands respect and honour, has not received it. The statement and questions are general until it is revealed that this is what the Lord of hosts has said '*to you*' (pl.). The objects of God's dismay are '*you, the priests who despise my name*'. The material throughout deals with priests whose actions God finds offensive because they transgress the *torah* and sacrificial legislation.

Who were these offending priests? The charge against them sounds like a universal one, the report appearing to embrace all priests, along with all who brought their offerings. In other words, Malachi presents the entire sacrificial system as corrupted. To view this charge as one leveled against all Judaeans is surely unwarranted! The pronoun object '*you*' in v. 6d may limit the charge to a specific group (unidentified more closely). And surely the chief priest (was it Joshua at the time?) should have been careful to discipline those who served under him, whether in the Jerusalem sanctuary or in any local site, who were derelict in their duty. The charge made against the priests uses such hyperbolic language that to read it as meaning that every priest broke every rule or tradition and had such a complete disregard for his role and work as a priest is overstated; a literal interpretation of the Editor's hyperbole is clearly misleading. (See the Introduction for the note re the use of pronouns in Malachi).

Many among the priestly cohort would demur and ask: '*In what way have we despised your name?*' That question form is rhetorical; it is a denial of failure. The Editor then adds a clarification as to how he believes God has been despised: '*...by offering on my altar polluted food*'. There is then a second formal response by priests to that charge: '*and you ask, how did we pollute (it) you?*', a further denial, to which Malachi's reply was: '*when you say, the Lord's table, it is despised*'. The phrase '*when you* *say...*' (Heb. *be'ᵉmorkem*) is used in conformity with the formula developed throughout for presenting the response to the challenge or initial statement. It does not refer literally to spoken words; it is their actions that demonstrate their alleged despising of the altar.

The phrase '*polluted food*' does not describe food that has become contaminated with some virus or microbial infestation, but food that does not accord with the strict sacrificial guidelines—no sick or injured animals, or animals defective in any manner. To offer something that is blemished was an offence against God. The '*Lord's table*' is a phrase unique to Malachi and in this sacrificial context refers to the altar, though the Hebrew term is that for a regular table.

It is the matter of the Lord's table being despised that remains the focus through v. 12.

1.8 The Editor's opening statement in 1.8a, b is set out in two parallel and essentially identical abbreviated sayings:

> <u>Now/and if/when you bring near</u> blind to/for sacrifice <u>it is not evil/defective;</u>
> <u>now/and if/when you bring near</u> lame and sick <u>it is not evil/defective.</u>

What does the Editor have in mind? Repetition is an effective way of emphasizing one's point, but what is that point?

The questions this verse raises have to do with the nature of the verbs and the clauses' syntax as well as the specific meaning of Hebrew *ra'* that can describe something as evil, wrong, defective, painful or injured. Is it, as most translations and commentators believe, (1) descriptive of the priests' actions and their belief that they have done nothing wrong? Or, (2) that there is nothing wrong with the animals being offered? The two clauses are conditional and suggest two possible circumstances.

The meaning of the two negative phrases in v. 7c, '*...there is not evil*' (Heb. *'eyn ra'*), is seemingly problematic. They are considered to be questions in many translations, not statements, perhaps influenced by the LXX text. If the negative phrases, though occurring only here, are correct textually, they are generally read as '*there is nothing wrong*'. That is to say, the priests consider such defective sacrifices acceptable so there is nothing wrong with their actions. However, if the concluding negatives relate to <u>the state of the animal,</u> it is possible to read the conditions as follows:

> (1.7c) '*...when you say the Lord's table has been despised...* (8a) if you were to bring a blind (animal) for sacrifice, (you are saying that) it is not defective; (8b) if you were to bring one lame or sick, (you are implying that) it is not defective.'

Here the adjective *ra'* is read as a reference to the defective condition of the animal rather than the priestly action itself. An animal that is injured or blemished in any manner is banned from being offered as a sacrifice; it can be killed and eaten (Lev. 22.22; Deut. 15.21) but not offered sacrificially, yet here the priests are treating the blemished offering as <u>unblemished</u>—it surely can't be read as 'evil'—and therefore as acceptable. A current priestly practice is here judged as offensive and requiring correction.

The apodosis in v. 8c is then Malachi's sarcastic challenge:

> '(If that is the case, then) *Offer that* (the injured animal) *to the governor. Will he be pleased with you or show you favour? asks the Lord of host*s.'

Even though an injured animal can be legitimately killed to be eaten, the rhetorical question here emphasizes that it would be an obvious insult to present the governor with one such animal, and if it is an insult to him, then how much more is God despised when he is offered a defective animal?

Use of the Persian term 'governor' points to this section of the text as post-dating 538 BCE and the return from exile. Just who that governor might have been is uncertain, but the fact that he is not named suggests that the Editor knew not who was in view, or more likely, that there was no specific authority figure in mind; it was just a general comment on 'despising' anyone in authority. The rhetorical question implies a strong negative response.

1.9 Within this section, v. 9 turns in a new direction, marked by the adverb '*And now…*', with an imperative verb calling the community, priests and people, to turn to God. The Hebrew expression is literally, '…*entreat the face of God ('el), and may he (God) be kind to us*'. This is followed by a phrase '*from your hand was this*', seeming to blame the priests for having done wrong, leading to the charge of priestly failure. However, the vague expression does not specify what 'this' refers to, while the placement of the adverbial phrase before the verb clearly seeks to emphasize whatever it was that the priests had done. The phrase '*from your hand*' occurs three times in this section (vv. 9b, 10c, 13d), each time referring to a sacrificial act. Here in v. 9 it is used figuratively and in vv. 10, 13, used literally.

We have to assume that Malachi is the reported speaker, and that it is on behalf of elements in the community—the 'us'—that he is criticizing those priests who act poorly. He asks whether God will '*lift up from you his face*' (Heb. *hayissa…panim*), i.e., that God show some level of kindness. Thus far there has not been mention of any negative reaction from

God with regard to the priests' and peoples' failures. It is the unexpected phrase rendered in NRSV as *The fault is yours* that appears to carry very negative connotations but has little context. A less pejorative rendering is probably required—perhaps, 'This is your doing!' for the Hebrew is literally, '*from your hands was this*' with 'this' apparently referring back to the attitude of the priests in making offerings regarded as polluted. The rhetorical question about one showing favour in v. 9d—'*will he show favour?*'—does not identify the subject, but the most obvious possibility is that the subject is God. However, by then appending the messenger form '*...says the Lord of hosts*', the Editor muddies the waters completely.

The rhetorical question asked by Malachi, '*will he lift up from you his faces?*' in v. 9d is actually a statement denying the possibility. The overall point being that if one is certain that the governor is being disrespected when offered a defective gift, a similar offering to God will be seen in a similar manner, resulting in divine disfavour. So '*this*' in the current context refers to that action, offering defective animals for sacrifice. Once again, a concluding '*says the Lord of hosts*' is inserted for effect, though adding to the pronominal confusion.

1.10 The messenger now asks the question about locking the doors of the Temple so that sacrificial activity is prevented, and thus further offence avoided. '*Which one of you (pl.) will shut the doors?*' implies a reference to the two doors of the Temple—the noun 'door' is a dual form—and the question-form is actually exclamatory, a call for someone in authority, anyone, to prevent access to the altar where the animal, having been slaughtered in an outside court, can be brought and offered. Which doors might be shut is immaterial in terms of the point being made about preventing further insult to the Lord. Burning any offering under the present circumstances would be useless, a vain exercise, as it would not result in any benefit to the one making the offering. God, says the messenger, '*has no pleasure in you*'. This phrase about God's 'pleasure' recurs in 2.7, 3.1 and 3.12.

God is said to make plain that '*I will not accept an offering from your hands*', the repetition adding emphasis to the divine disfavour.

1.11 One reason for the heightened divine disfavour, according to the messenger, is the claim that God's reputation, his 'name', actually has universal significance and wide recognition—his name is '*great among the nations*'. The initial Hebrew particle, *ki*, is most likely the emphatic, 'Indeed', rather than the introduction of a result or purpose clause. In a very poetic form—'*Indeed, from where the sun rises to where it sets...*'—the messenger contrasts the world acknowledging Judah's God with the disregard and dishonour shown by those Judaeans who claim to revere that God, but according to the messenger, fail to do so.

There is something quite challenging in these words and in the hyperbole that is used to magnify the divine name. While it may be a fact that the name of the God of the Israelites—was it 'Yahweh'?—was well-known to other nations and empires in the region, in the same way that Israelites knew the names of competing gods such as Marduk, Baal, Hadad and the like, it is quite another thing to claim that those nations were so in awe of that great 'name' that incense and acceptable/pure offerings were made to that 'name'. What is the purpose of such hyperbole? Was it spoken ironically? Was it a deliberate overblown claim that sought to shame the Judaeans into doing the right thing? Reading this statement as literally true, and then seeking possible explanations for such an amazing situation such as foreigners or exiled Jews worshipping Yahweh in a manner consistent with Israelite custom and law, fails to acknowledge that this is hyperbole, as in so many other prophetic claims. To suggest that Gentile nations were offering pure worship out of well-intentioned ignorance is also clutching at literal straws. Reading Malachi as a religious universalist in light of this verse, seeking to identify communities to whom it applies literally, and failing to acknowledge the intended hyperbole, simply shows a lack of linguistic and cultural awareness. What can be said about the language of this verse is that it presents a highpoint in the messenger's challenge to the priestly community and the hyperbole plays into the contrast being drawn between Judaeans and others.

1.12 The verse begins with a forceful statement '*But you...*' with a participle '*are profaning it...*' to contrast the priests' current attitude to the divine name with that of the nations who are said to be honouring it.

The charge is that God's name or reputation is being profaned when it is said that '*the Lord's table is polluted*'. The altar was considered 'polluted' because defective sacrifices were being offered on it. The phrase that literally reads '*its fruit/produce is despised its food*' refers to the material gifts or offerings placed upon 'it', i.e., the altar.

Here the verb 'said' denotes an attitude of mind rather than a spoken utterance.

1.13-14 The focus now moves a little—from the priests who conduct the sacrificial rituals to the people who bring their offerings, though the charge is general. The charge is '*But you have said "Look, what a nuisance!"*' The Hebrew *matt'la'ah* is a *hapax* but is generally thought to be an abbreviated exclamatory *mah-t'la'ah* with a possible meaning '*what a weariness!*' It is a general outburst, but probably more that of the priests who are finding the requirements for sacrifices to be something of a nuisance, a bother. The negative attitude of both parties to the obligations around offerings is then emphasized by the addition of an unusual charge that '*you sniff at it*!' Presumably the 'sniffing' reference relates to their attitude to the whole matter of sacrifices, the detailed requirements for offering at the altar, the Lord's table, though some read as '…sniff at me'. The figure of 'sniffing' implies utter contempt for God and his *torah* demands, with the clarification of the contempt charge to follow. The Editor has indicated this comment as from God by adding yet another '…*says the Lord of hosts*' phrase. It is as though God knows exactly how the community feels about the requirements surrounding 'right' sacrifices, implying that God is thereby deeply unhappy.

Interestingly, this same verb '*sniff at*' is found in Haggai, though in Hag. 1.8 it is <u>God</u> who does the sniffing, expressing contempt for the people's attempt to prepare for rebuilding the Temple.

The messenger now resumes in v. 13b with the charge that defective animals have been brought as offerings; those ravaged by wild animals, or having gone lame or become diseased, implying that they have lost their usefulness to the one making the offering; they are brought to the priests to be sacrificed contrary to *torah* regulations. The rhetorical response '*Shall I accept that from your hands?*' underlines God's refusal to accept such defective offerings, making all such offerings vain and ineffectual (1.10).

Furthermore, a curse is issued in v. 14 against those who have not kept their vow to present the first-born male of the flock to God (see Lev. 22.18-20), and in lieu have brought a blemished animal, a cheap substitute. This charge is linked to the fact that the Lord is not only master, but claims to be a '*great king*' whose name is honoured internationally, but not, by implication, in Judaea. This claim that is said to be made by God, as in 1.11, again emphasizes the underlying theme in Malachi about God's concern for his 'name'. There is something unsettling about this very human emphasis on the concern of God regarding his reputation; a projection of human concerns onto the divine?

These priestly and popular failings that have earned the divine curse reflect the Deuteronomic mindset of the Editor. What form the curse might have taken is not specified, but in line with the Editor's theology it would imply withdrawal of some form of material benefit.

2.1-9 The Levi Covenant

2.1 'Now this command is for you, the priests'.

2.2 'If you do not listen, and if you do not take it to heart to glorify my name, says the Lord of hosts, then I will send among you the curse, cursing what you have blessed; I have already cursed it because you are not taking my name to heart.'

2.3 Look, I am about to rebuke your seed, and rub dung on your faces, the dung of your festivals, (and he will carry you to him?).'

2.4 'Then may you know that I have sent you this command: that you should be(?) my covenant with Levi', says the Lord of hosts.

2.5 'My covenant was with him (a covenant of) life and peace (shalom), and I gave both to him, reverence that made him fear me, and before my name he revered me'.

2.6 'True Torah was in his (Levi's) mouth and no injustice was on his lips; in peace and in uprightness he walked with me, and many he turned back from doing wrong'.

2.7 Indeed, the lips of a priest preserve knowledge and you may seek Torah from his mouth; may he indeed be a messenger of the Lord of hosts'.

2.8 'But you have turned aside from the way; you have made many to stumble in the matter of Torah, you have corrupted the covenant of Levi', says the Lord of hosts.

2.9 'And even I have made you despised and made lowered you in the eyes (for) all the people; because you have not been observing my ways but being partial in (teaching) Torah'.

Malachi now offers a separate word, a command (vv. 1, 4), to the priests to uphold the covenant made with Levi, outlining their responsibilities as teachers or instructors of the people. Rather than fulfil those responsibilities, the priests are here charged in a summary statement that closes the section (2.9), with having 'shown partiality' in what they have taught. They have failed to fulfil each and every obligation laid on them by virtue of their membership of the community bound by the covenant with Levi. The focus moves from the priests' responsibilities with regard to offering sacrifices (1.6-14) to their role as failed instructors of the people—they have failed in that they have actually 'corrupted the covenant of Levi'. Whether those addressed in this section are the same as those criticized in the previous section (1.6-14) is uncertain because the Malachi text simply condemns each and every priest and Levite as guilty of whatever problem he has chosen to highlight.

Although the object of this command is the priestly class as a whole, there is no specific connection between the issue dealt with in 1.6-14 and that being considered here. The Editor has simply located this additional matter of priestly failure within the general treatment of all matters priestly—1.6-14, 2.1-9 and 2.10-16. Furthermore, it is not set within a new Statement–Question–Response format, but simply marked as a separate concern by its introductory '*And now…*'. As for any temporal connection with the other priestly references, little can be discerned other than to note that there is no record of priestly activity during the exilic period itself, so it is probable that this challenge is to be dated some time between 538–520 BCE.

This section also raises the issue of whether there is a role distinction between Priest and Levite, for here no distinction is evident; Priest and Levite are treated as one. Priests (*koh'nim*) were to be holy, set apart, with duties ranging over various aspects of community life; they presided over the sacrificial rituals, prayed, assured forgiveness to those who sought it, pronounced a person free of certain illnesses that would prevent that person joining in worship, supervised the use of 'lots' when seeking divine guidance, as well as having administrative duties relating to the Temple and treasury. Theoretically, priests should come from the tribe of Levi, be a descendant of Aaron, but during the reign of Solomon the Zadokite clan appears to have established a new order, and non-Levites also served. Levites appear to have taken over daily and routine tasks within the Temple following the exile. Malachi makes no mention of the position of Chief Priest, one member of the ruling pair after the return from exile in 538 BCE.

What Malachi does stress is that the priestly role had two dimensions; one was cultic or sacrificial, the other was educational. In the Mosaic blessing of Levi noted in Deut. 33.8-10, both roles are referred to, and this is yet another indication of the close relationship between the Editor of Malachi and the Deuteronomic cohort. The section presents Levi as having been the ideal priest, the standard to which the rest of the priestly community should aspire. Failure to fulfil the twin ideals regarding sacrifices and instruction allegedly will invoke a curse upon the priest, and also turn the blessings they utter into a curse. Once again, the Editor reverts to the notion of curse and blessing, as binary notions, to speak of God's reaction to their failure to glorify the divine 'name'. The image of God noted in this threat is concerning if taken literally and out of context.

2.1-2 The introductory '*And now…*' marks another component in the material relating to the priests and their failure. Although the section heading (2.1) is expressed as a commandment (Heb. *mitswah*) repeated in v. 4, what follows in 2.2 is not a command but two brief conditional clauses: '*IF you will not listen/obey, and IF you will not <u>place it on your</u>*

<u>heart</u> *to give glory to my name (says the Lord of hosts), THEN I shall send upon you the curse, and I will curse your blessings and also I have cursed it because <u>you are not placing it on your heart</u>'*. Malachi speaks of a threatened curse upon the priests if they fail to take seriously the need for God or God's name to be glorified. The phrase '*lay it on your heart*', used twice in this charge for emphasis, recalls similar usage by Haggai (Hag. 1.5, 7; 2.15, 18)—this clearly was a current oral expression for both Editors. We note again the strong emphasis on the need to enhance God's name/reputation as one driving concern in this book.

The question that must be asked is, What was this commandment that needed to be taken so seriously in order to avoid the divine curse? The context in 2.1-4 would suggest that it was that they reverence the divine name by following whatever the covenant with Levi demanded of them. No specific details are given as to the means by which they are to glorify the divine name other than a very general call to follow what was originally required of the Levites under covenant.

The blessing-curse binary that recalls so vividly the Deuteronomic viewpoint is applied here as the divine response to the priests' failure to bring honour to God's 'name', another of the Deuteronomic keywords. Deuteronomy 7.12-16 sets out in some detail the material benefits of obedience, and thus the losses implied in the curses. These categories will apply to the priests who presumably are in danger of losing some of their material support, as are those whom the priests have blessed and who might have expected similar benefits to flow.

2.3 Three threats are pending should the priests continue to fail to bring glory to the divine name: 1. Their offspring (?) will suffer rebuke; 2. God will smear faeces on their faces; 3. Uncertain (a textual problem hides any meaning, so best not to speculate)

Apart from the disgusting action alleged to be God's way of responding to the priests' failure, the question of who is to be rebuked needs clarification. That it refers to the priests' own descendants (Hebrew *zera'* is literally 'seed') is almost certainly what is meant, though some have taken the word literally and see a threat to crops—one problem with that suggestion is that priests did not have land on which to grow crops! Also, crops being rebuked doesn't make much sense, so it obviously has to do with priests' descendants, unless the Hebrew text is emended to *zero'a* to conform with the LXX and to refer to one's 'arm'. Again, this seems unlikely. As for the faeces to be smeared on their faces, apart from the stench and the shame, the reference is to the entrails of slaughtered animals. These had to be removed from the sacrificial animal as unclean, then to be burned separately (Lev. 4.11-12). Contact with the dung would make the priest (temporarily?) unfit to participate in cultic rituals, so this is a reference to both being shamed and defiled. Hyperbole or colourful speech? No matter which one, as a punishment supposedly from God, it would have to be administered by some person present if meant literally, making that person equally defiled. The language used represents a very earthy reaction to the call for the protection of the divine name.

Verse 3c presents a Hebrew text that is problematic—literally '...*dung of your feasts and he will carry/lift you to it/him*'. When dealing with ancient texts there are many occasions that leave readers with unresolvable problems, usually arising from copyist errors—this appears to be one such. NRSV's suggestion that it means '*I will put you out of my presence*', like all guesses, is arbitrary, and driven by the need to say something consistent with the translator's theological presuppositions and the need to avoid leaving a blank space in the text.

2.4 The theme of a command in v. 1 is repeated in this verse with the additional information that it has to do with a covenant with Levi. Using the verb 'send' with the notion of a word or command seems a little unusual, but it is not unknown—see Isa. 9.7. Together with the preposition *'el*, indicating who gets to hear the command, it seems that the priests are being reminded that they are to recall (Hebrew *yada'*, 'know') '*my covenant with Levi*'. There is no record of such a specific covenant within the OT. The closest potential reference is in Exod. 32.26-29 where Levi and 'sons' reacted against the making of the golden calf and killed a mass of those who had worshipped it. Moses is said to have told them that '*you have ordained yourselves to the service of the Lord*'. Deuteronomy 33.8-11 also refers to the Levites being blessed and given a special ministry. Perhaps this is what Malachi's Editor had in mind. If the Levites uphold that ministry, then the relationship with them will remain. The text here, on the other hand, focuses on the person of Levi rather than the tribe and recalls certain traditions about his individual service.

2.5 God is said to have established with Levi personally '*a covenant of life and well-being*' (Heb. *shalom*). The Hebrew *hachayyim*, a plural, literally 'the living (ones)' is also a way of speaking of a vibrant life itself, so along with *shalom* the Editor highlights two very positive aspects of Levi's service. Two further attributes that were integral to this relationship from Levi's side were reverence and awe of God. Although the Hebrew text is somewhat unclear (as '*fear (noun) and he feared me*'), it is generally understandable; fear/awe was the attitude to be shown towards God.

In addition, the text adds literally *'and before me my name in awe was'*. These attitudes towards God are upheld as the ideal, the ideal from which priests are said to have fallen. Again, it is the divine 'name/reputation' that demanded respect, and such was given by Levi according to this report.

2.6-7 The theme in these two verses is the teaching responsibilities of all priests. In poetic metaphors of 'mouth' and 'lips' the Editor states that true or reliable instruction in *torah* was what Levi provided; no false or misleading teaching did he advance. Furthermore, his 'walk' or manner of living, was *'with integrity* (Heb. *shalom) and uprightness'*. This latter highlights Levi's exemplary behaviour that is then said to have *'turned many from iniquity'*. Our Editor asserted that the moral and personal integrity of Levi had the profound effect of changing many people's lives in a positive direction. The Hebrew term rendered as 'iniquity' refers not just to actions that are morally wrong, but actions that leave one with a sense of guilt.

Based on this example of Levi, the Editor then turns to the priests to emphasize that in their role as teachers and instructors in *torah*, a similar standard was required of them. Verse 7 uses a chiastic structure—*Truly, lips of the priest guard knowledge; torah they seek from his mouth*—repeating the metaphors of 'lips' and 'mouth', to highlight the role of all priests as guardians and teachers of knowledge of *torah*. While some commentators have questioned whether this verse is a secondary addition or not, given that it seems to repeat v. 6, one should note that the verbs involved here are imperfectives; they stress the on-going nature of the priests' responsibilities to 'guard' knowledge and to 'seek' or pursue Torah instruction.

The final clause in v. 7c may be interpreted as referring both to Levi as well as to all priests collectively—*'for he was/is the messenger of the Lord of hosts'*. See also Hag. 1.13. There are commentators who see this statement as somehow alien to Malachi; in fact, *BHS* suggests the entire verse is a later addition. Yes, it is unique, but when one places the book within that postexilic period of fifty and more years in which Editors of Jeremiah, Obadiah, Joel, Haggai and Malachi are all drawing on the vast supply of oral materials relating to contemporary issues, there is so much that is shared. Referring to Levi and/or the priest as *'messenger (mala'k) of the Lord of hosts'* cannot be so arbitrarily excised.

2.8-9 The unit begins with a firm contrast between the ideal of v. 7c and the current situation with the priests—'<u>But you</u> have turned aside from the path…' The result was that many people have stumbled or fallen '*in* *torah*'. The repetition of the adverb 'many' from v. 6 adds to the contrast and thus to priestly failure. It is further emphasized by the phrase '*you have corrupted the covenant of Levi*'. The verb in this phrase is the same as the root used in 1.14 to describe offerings that are blemished and thus unacceptable; this generation of priests is charged with debasing the covenant of Levi, the standard to which they are to be held accountable. Keywords here are 'way/path' and 'in *torah*' that serve in vv. 8a and 9b as inclusions for the unit.

God's response is to humiliate and belittle them—perhaps a little more face-saving than having faeces smeared on their faces! The first half of the verse reads: '*And also I, I appoint/make you despised ones and fallen ones to/for the people*'. It is a strong statement with the personal pronoun 'I' placed before the verb to emphasize that it was God's doing to cause the priests to be despised, reversing their despising of '*the name of the Lord*' (see 1.6). A second verb is used to describe God's actions and that is the unusual Hebrew *shaphal*, 'fall', or 'to be made low'. It is '*all the people*' who are the intended witnesses of these actions, using the generic term *'am* that here could include foreigners as well as Judaeans it would seem.

The reason that people have turned from the way and many have stumbled is here given as '*you have not been keeping my ways, nor (have you been) lifting up faces in/by torah*'. The metaphor of 'lifting up the face' recurs from 1.8 and is idiomatic for granting requests or offering favours. Thus, the priests are here to be humiliated because of their failure as instructors and administrators of the *torah*. What constituted 'partiality' is not more closely defined, whether in enforcing requirements or allowing certain people a more lenient treatment, not insisting on *torah*'s demands.

2.6-9 deals specifically with the priestly failure as instructors in the Law; they have failed to live and work by the terms of the covenant of Levi and will be dealt with accordingly, in order that the covenant may be upheld (2.4).

2.10-16 Opposing Foreign Marriages

2.10 'Do we not all have the one father? Has not the one God created us? Why then are we unfaithful one with the other in profaning the covenant of our fathers?'

2.11 'Judah was unfaithful and abomination has been done in Israel and in Jerusalem; Truly, Judah has profaned the Lord's sacred place which he loves and has married the daughter of a foreign god'.

2.12 'May the Lord cut off (completely?) from the tents/community of Jacob any man who has done so, and who brings an offering to the Lord of hosts'.

> *2.13 Another thing you have done: covering with tears the Lord's altar, weeping and groaning because he no longer looks with favour on your offering, nor does he happily accept it from your hand'.*
>
> *2.14 Then you ask, "Why does he not?" It is because the Lord has witnessed the marriage between you and your young wife in which you have been unfaithful to her, but she is your consort, your covenanted wife'.*
>
> *2.15 (* He did not make (you?) one, but the remainder of spirit for him, and what does the one seek seed of God so may you take care in your spirit and with the wife of your youth do not be faithless'.)*
>
> *2.16 (For he hates to send away, says the Lord the God of Israel, and he covers with violence on his clothing, says the Lord of hosts, and may you take care in your spirits and not be unfaithful'. *)*
>
> * Translation uncertain.

The third major division of the book, 2.10-16, has to do not with priests but with the populace as a whole. The Editor has marked it as another discrete unit by providing the initial rhetorical questions (2.10) that are unique features in this collection, while its contents raise a religio-social question about intermarriage with non-Jews and the demand that foreign partners be set aside.

2.10-16 is a portion of the collection that has caused scholars the most difficulty in terms of both translation and interpretation; for example, in vv. 13-16 with the phrases '*wife of your youth*' and '*your wife by covenant*', and also an issue with v. 16 and the possible rendering of the Hebrew *as* '*I hate divorce*'.

Relationships with foreigners was a fraught issue with many Israelites, especially those who were of the Deuteronomic cohort. In exile the question of those relationships became acute as many Jews adopted foreign ways, began speaking the local Aramaic language, and generally found an acceptable accommodation to Babylonian culture and life. Marriages involving foreign women was one inevitable result. It then became a major issue within the postexilic community causing increased tension between those who adapted to international life and those who held doggedly to a more nationalistic view. A number of those who then returned from Babylon with their 'mixed' family were opposed by those who upheld the more exclusivist views of the Deuteronomic cohort. Following the 538 BCE release of Judaeans allowing a return to Jerusalem, they were led initially by Sheshbazzar, then by Zerubbabel and Joshua (520 BCE) who, as Persian appointees, were quite definitely not anti-foreign. Zerubbabel's foreign name is one small indication of a broader perspective with regard to identity in the case of his family. The Persian leaders would not have appointed Zerubbabel and Joshua as leaders of the returning Jews had they not been open to foreign ideas and able therefore to positively represent Persian interests in the empire's most southerly province—Joshua's family included some who had married non-Jewish women—so the issue that was of concern in this section must post-date those early postexilic years. The Editor here reports against the background of an old Deuteronomic exclusivism and antipathy towards foreigners (see Deut. 7.1-6; 1 Kgs 11.1-8), a view shared by Haggai and later enforced by Ezra in the early fifth century BCE (Ezra 10; Neh. 13.23-31), despite it being a view not shared by many of those who had experienced life in exile. It is tempting therefore to locate this particular message in the late sixth to early fifth century BCE.

A key Hebrew verb *bgd* in 2.10, 11, 14, 16 draws attention to the theme of Judaeans' past 'unfaithfulness' (as defined by a certain Deuteronomic cohort, represented here by the messenger) with a warning not to be unfaithful in the future. Here, unfaithfulness is placed in the context of marriage to foreign partners and the impact that that it is said to have had on Judaean religious life by *'profaning the sanctuary'*.

One note generally missing from commentaries is that the 'problem' of foreign marriages is set in the context of Judaean *men* marrying *foreign women*—nothing is said about *Judaean women* marrying *foreign men*! The cultural bias is overwhelming!

2.10-11 Three rhetorical questions introduce this section. They revolve around the question of tribal unity that is allegedly threatened by certain individuals due to their 'profaning' of an ancient covenant made with the ancestors. The questions themselves stress that all Judaeans are one family, created by God, but that unity has been severed by divisions, arising especially from intermarriage with foreign women (v. 11). Strong language, using words such as 'faithless' (*bgd*), 'profane' (*chll*), and 'abomination' (*to'ebah*), describes the messenger's deep concerns about the state of affairs in society. The breakdown of the covenant with the ancestors is linked with profaning the Lord's sanctuary, presumably because foreign brides are assumed to lead Judaean men astray. This 'weakness' that Judaean men show has a long tradition in Deuteronomic ideology with none other than Solomon as the prime example—1 Kgs 11.1-8.

The pronoun 'we/us' throughout v. 10 suggests that the speaker is Malachi himself, with no reference that this is a message from God. Malachi includes himself in these two opening statements.

The phrase '*covenant of our ancestors/fathers*', is a vague and general reference to a covenantal relationship established in the past. The notion of a covenant (Heb. *b'rith*) with the past is usually linked to the belief that God entered into a special relationship with the Jacobite clan that became the Exodus community (Exod. 19.5-6; Deut. 29), but the reference to 'fathers' is ambiguous and could in fact take the reference all the way back to Abraham and his successors (Gen. 15; 17). Malachi claims that that relationship with the idealized past has now been broken on a grand scale—not just by 'Judah' (everyone in Judah?) but in Israel and especially in Jerusalem, the site chosen by God for his dwelling, his sanctuary. That sanctuary is said to be 'loved' with the Hebrew text reading *'aheb*, 'he loves', that could only be a third-person reference to God, a kind of Editorial aside. The underlying problem here is that of Judaean men marrying non-Jewish women, a practice that to Malachi constitutes a profaning of the Jerusalem sanctuary, meaning either that these 'problem' marriages are bringing unacceptable—read 'unclean' idolatrous—practices into Temple worship or not participating in Temple worship at all. When referring to these marriages, the Editor has used the verb *ba'al*, 'to become master of...', that in noun form means 'master, lord', but is also the name of the Canaanite god Baal. Equating marriage to non-Jewish (or 'stranger') women is tantamount to marrying Baal in the eyes of Malachi (see Hos. 2.17-18). Tradition and law stood in the way of marrying foreign women—Exod. 34.12-16; Deut. 7.3-4).

The girls taken as brides by the Jewish men are described as '*daughters of a strange/foreign god*'. The phrase here is unique. Defining them in terms of their intimate relationship to the gods can only be read as negative. Jewish men who so married are here regarded as weak, unable to resist the temptation to follow their wives in worship of their gods—a view projected by the Deuteronomic cohort who saw such dangers all around them (Deut. 7.4).

2.12 Imploring the Lord to '*cut off*' those who marry foreign women, Malachi shows his commitment to Deuteronomy's exclusivist perspective. He calls for '*certain ones who have done this*' to be removed '*from the tents of Jacob*', an expression that would have those who married non-Jewish women removed from the community altogether, whether figuratively or literally. Those identified here are further described in a problematic Hebrew phrase as *'er w''oneh*, seemingly relating to two personal qualities(?). Translations, and thus interpretations, are various, meaning that nobody quite knows what the phrase means, assuming that it is textually correct. Whether the phrase belongs with the verb 'have done it' or with the phrase 'the person who…' is also unclear, and suggested solutions are arbitrary, uncertain, and thus far from helpful.

The *'tents of Jacob'* is figurative for more than just the residents of Judah; it incorporates all who are actually descendants of the ancestor Jacob—surely, a case of hyperbole. Separation from the elect as punishment is perhaps all one can say about the plea here.

2.13-16 This section of Malachi is the most contested in terms of translation and interpretation; it is the Hebrew text itself that presents the greatest challenge.

An additional charge against the community is raised, but whether the pronoun 'you' addresses the entire community of Judaeans, or just those with foreign wives, is initially uncertain. On the other hand, the issue raised here was not universal—it applied to only one segment of the population, and a small one at that, namely, those who had married foreign girls and brought them back to Judaea.

What is clear is that there were individuals who were deeply troubled, weeping and groaning—or was it feigned distress?—that their offerings were not accepted by God. They at least were able to access the altar, so it would follow that they had met all cleanliness requirements to reach that point. How they knew that their offerings were not accepted by God is always a mystery to many readers, but one practical 'proof' would have been that what they had sought by their offering was not realised; for example, that promised blessings such as rescue from harm, or for drought relief and bountiful harvests, had failed. On the basis of Deuteronomic theology, such disappointment would show that God was not pleased with their offering, with the conclusion then drawn that the offering must have been inadequate or deficient in some manner. Figurative tears and wailing aside, God was not persuaded to bless. However, the question is: who were those who believed that their offerings were not acceptable to God? Surely this was not confined to those with non-Jewish wives and children. The opening v. 10 envisages the entire community as the addressees in this section; this is a community problem regardless of individual marriage arrangements.

The reason advanced for God's displeasure here is the cryptic statement about them being unfaithful to *'the wife of your youth'*, their *'wife by covenant'* (vv. 14-15), along with the two phrases generally rendered as *'I hate divorce'*, and its companion *'covering one's garments with violence'* (v. 16).

If there is an over-riding theme for this section, it is that the community addressed is accused of having been faithless; the Hebrew keyword throughout is *bgd*, 'unfaithful'. However, the possible reference to divorce in the final verse seems to have dominated commentary discussion, skewing the debate.

Verse 13 uses hyperbole to picture those addressed as *'weeping and groaning'* over the altar because their offerings have not been accepted. The language is heightened and can be read as mocking those involved or dismissing their feigned feeling of rejection. The reaction to a failed transaction with God allegedly has left them devastated, raising the question as to why (Heb. *'al-mah*) their offering was unacceptable. The weeping and groaning does not apply only to those married to non-Jewish women according to the text.

Verse 14 attempts an explanation. The Lord has observed that they have been unfaithful to the *'wife/woman of your youth'*. Does this simply mean some girl they had married or taken when younger—a literal sense? Or, is this a figurative expression for a former relationship with God? Most commentators and translations take the phrase as literally a former wife/companion under the covenant of marriage to which the Lord was the official witness. The phrase *'your wife by covenant'* seems to be parallel to the *'woman of your youth'* phrase. Part of the problem for modern readers is reading this text from within a modern notion of marriage rather than an ancient one. Most ancient households consisted of one male and more than one female. Whether there was ever some formal marriage ceremony and a 'covenant' entered into is also uncertain, even in the case of the politically driven 'marriages' of kings and the like. In other words, *'wife of your covenant'* is unclear, and *'woman of your youth'* most likely referred to only one of the females in a man's household.

The key verb *bgd* is noted as highlighting the issue throughout this section vv. 10-16—those addressed are said to have been <u>unfaithful</u> to a 'wife' and probably not the one taken when the man was young since that wife usually became the dominant one in the household as ever younger ones were afforded. The very word 'unfaithful' has to be understood from within the cultural world in which the man shared his bed with numerous 'wives'.

Nowhere does the text of 2.14 imply that the men spoken of have divorced or abandoned a wife. The fact that many have returned from exile with mixed families and perhaps several foreign 'wives' is the basic problem for the Deuteronomic hardliners in Judaea—they are seen as having not been true/faithful to Deuteronomy's demands.

Verse 15 presents a Hebrew text that from any perspective, text or syntax, is meaningless, apart from the reflexive jussive that is literally *'may you look after yourself in your spirit'*, a call repeated in the v. 16

as well. Translators struggle to provide some contextual content, but it is arbitrary and subject to individual preconceptions, so in the end, unhelpful. Unfortunately, the custom is to provide some wording rather than leave a blank space in a translation, but any suggested translation should be enclosed within brackets and be identified as guesswork.

Verse 16 similarly opens with a cryptic phrase, literally *'for he(?) hated send (away)'*. No subject is identified nor does the verb 'send' have an object. NRSV follows others who suggest '*I hate...*' but in doing so it puts words into the Lord's mouth uncritically and unjustifiably. If the initial *ki* is causal, i.e., 'for/because...', then it may offer an explanation for God's rejection of offerings made. More likely is it that it is asseverative, 'Indeed,...' introducing a strong independent statement. Deuteronomy 22.19, 29 uses the verb 'send' (Heb. *shalach*) in the context of divorce or expelling a wife, but as such it differs from the central issue here of one being unfaithful. More to the point, in the context of Judaean men having married non-Jewish girls while in exile being called to abandon them along with any children, the statement 'I hate divorce' makes absolutely no sense—if that is what the Hebrew is thought to mean. Many read this problematic text as men having divorced their <u>Jewish</u> wives whom they married when both were young, in order to marry foreign girls, that such is the problem. Again, there is absolutely no evidence for such a conclusion, and with men having numerous wives it becomes even more problematic an interpretation. (N.B. The verb *shalach* is also used in 3.1 in a positive mode!) The traditional translations and interpretations available are unacceptable and driven by factors other than what, admittedly, is a confusing text.

The additional phrase '*covering one's garment with violence*' is likewise opaque and uncertain with LXX and other texts suggesting that 'violence' (Heb. *hamas*) is the subject rather than object of the verb 'cover' and the noun 'garment (Heb. *l'busho*) of uncertain meaning. Commentators make guesses as to possible meanings, but again, whether they are reasonable guesses is questionable. Whether the text is to be viewed as literal or figurative is another complicating factor for interpreters who try to pin down the meaning of a text that is syntactically and textually confusing. Is the real issue divorce or unfaithfulness? The underlying Deuteronomic ideology was anti-foreign, opposing 'marriage' or living with non-Jews, that is to say, viewing 'unfaithfulness' as defined by a nationalistic Deuteronomy. The Editor has perhaps omitted material that would clarify, or the oral tradition to which he had access was quite confused, giving a text that is deeply problematic. As a result, modern readers are left with a text that may never reveal its true intentions.

The section ends with two jussives—'*May you take care of yourselves*' (as in v. 15), and '*May you not be unfaithful*'. These exhortations are the section's final and positive thoughts. The final call not to be faithless brings one back to the keyword, the focus—unfaithfulness, not divorce.

The topic of inter-racial marriage obviously was, for the Deuteronomic cohort, a very sensitive subject. They clearly opposed such 'marriages' or domestic arrangements and for religious as well as xenophobic reasons, but the reality was that many returnees brought their integrated families with them and did not abandon wives or children. It was Ezra and Nehemiah in the early part of the fifth century BCE who sought to enforce such family break-ups, but this section of Malachi must date some time before that policy was enforced. The Messenger who reported on this discussion was a spokesperson for the narrow anti-immigrant cohort.

2.17–3.5 Refining the Community

2.17 'Your words have wearied the Lord, but you say "In what way have we wearied him?"' 'When you say that everyone who does evil is good in the Lord's eyes, and that he is pleased with them. Or (you ask) "Where is the God of Justice?"'

3.1 'Look, I am about to send my messenger to prepare the way ahead for me. He will come suddenly to his temple, the Master whom you are seeking. And the messenger of the covenant in whom you take pleasure, look, he is about to come', says the Lord of hosts.

3.2 Now, who will endure the day when he/it comes, and who will remain standing when he/it appears. Truly, he/it is like a refining fire, and like a washer's soap'.

3.3 The refiner will sit and refine silver and cleanse the sons of Levi, purifying them like gold and silver, and they will belong to the Lord, bringing offerings with justice.

3.4 Then the offering of Judah and Jerusalem will be sweet, as in the days of long ago and as in the former years'.

3.5 And I will draw near to you for judgment and I will swiftly witness against the sorcerers, against the adulterers, and against those who give false witness, against those who oppress worker's wages, the widow and the orphan, who turn aside the stranger and do not fear me', say the Lord of hosts.

The fourth major division of the book is a further independent message. Although it does refer to the descendants of Levi (3.2), there is no other reason to link this section with the section 1.6–2.9 and its concerns about priests who fail in their duties. There the theme is one of judgment; here it is one of refining and encouragement in face of doubts about God's justice. See also Hab. 1.2-4.

In terms of the structure chosen by the Editor(s), it begins with the usual Statement–Question–Response form in 2.17. The statement speaks of divine weariness caused by the people's questioning God's justice. The response from God speaks of future actions that will demonstrate that divine justice is at work. While some commentators wish to separate 2.17 from 3.1-5, from a rhetorical perspective there is good reason to accept that the unit is of a piece, with *mishpat*, 'justice', in 2.17 and 3.5 serving as an inclusion and identifying the theme.

Following the formulaic introduction, the sending of 'my messenger' (*malachi*) is announced, whose arrival is compared to fire as a refining agent. First of all, he will refine the 'descendants of Levi' whose offerings will then be pleasing to the Lord, as in the past, and secondly, act against all manner of social ills. There is a decided switch from the people's complaint about a God who does not deal with injustice and evil (2.17) to the promise of a messenger who will actually do something about the matter (3.1-5). The latter is a response in didactic mode—as if to say, 'Now you will see God in action!'

This reading will acknowledge the function of the title of the book that the Editor has provided (1.1), namely that this work is a *Massa'*, A Word of Advice, as in the Wisdom mode. What it seeks to do is to advise the audience that their complaint about God's apparent failure to bring the evildoer to justice will be resolved when the messenger/angel comes—the injustices that trouble the audience and reflect badly on the divine one will demonstrate that God is just. The keyword 'justice' (Heb. *mishpat*) from 2.17 closes the circle in 3.5.

Although 2.17–3.5 are the traditional boundaries most commentators set for this section of the book, one could make a case that 3.6-7a are also integral to this section, as some have suggested. The determiner is the view one takes of the initial adverb *ki*—is it introducing an explanatory 'because' at the beginning of 3.6, or is it the asseverative 'Truly/Indeed' that begins an independent matter? Whichever view is taken, one can regard 3.6-7a as a link between the fourth and fifth divisions in the book. The Statement–Question–Response form does not really begin again until 3.7b, leading into the discussion about short-changing God.

As for the unit's focus, there is a clear concern over the matter of divine justice as noted by the Inclusions in 2.17 and 3.5, but also interest in the divine pleasure (2.17; 3.1, 4). One mystery to be resolved is the identity of one called the 'messenger', referred to twice in 3.1, and his remit.

The issue of social justice and divine judgment is a timeless one that concerned a number of the prophets and sages—see Hab. 1.2-4—so the concerns expressed in this section cannot be identified with a specific time, place or agent.

2.17 The opening statement by Malachi addresses a community with the charge that they have made God weary by his having to listen to what they say. It is then clarified that they have been complaining about divine justice not being evident—their query about how they have been wearying God is not one seeking information; it is simply an element in the literary form the Editor has developed. The question form itself is rhetorical, implying that God, who is supposed to be just and fair, obviously is not seen as such. They do not believe justice has been meted out upon those who are evil; rather, the evil ones are the 'successful' elite. The audience, according to the messenger, has claimed that those in the community who do evil things are regarded by God as being good—a natural conclusion they have drawn from their experience of life. Not only is this God seen as favouring the evildoers, the community feels that God actually delights in those evil ones and in what they do. So, where is this just God when he should be bringing justice down upon those who are evil? Where is he? Nowhere! The sarcasm is palpable in the strong contrast expressed—the people's continuous questioning that wearies God contrasts with the delight God is assumed to feel towards the evil ones. It echoes the concern of Hab. 1.13.

The Messenger presents God as being 'wearied' by this community questioning the perceived absence of divine justice, so what does it say of the messenger's view of God? If God is really tired of hearing their complaints, what kind of God is he? Disinterested? Unconcerned? Unable or unwilling to respond to evil? The perceived lack of justice can only mean one thing—God favours the evil ones. If this Editorial assessment is read as a message from God, then the implications are devastating.

3.1 What follows is the Editor's attempt to rescue the situation—a promise that God will send his messenger/angel, *malaki*, to deal with the problem and set it to right. It partially answers the question of 2.17—Where is this God of justice? It is clearly didactic in intent and begins with an attention-getting marker *hinneh*, 'Lo' or 'behold', followed as usual by a participle—in this case *sholeach* 'sending', that here does not mean 'divorce' or sending away as some have argued is the sense in 2.16. This messenger/angel will prepare the way for 'me', i.e. God himself, who will suddenly appear in his Temple. The sentence features a mix of pronouns—first-, second- and third-person pronouns in the one sentence—and all refer to God. In terms of syntax it is messy, but perhaps reflects the Editor's struggle to put his received information into a meaningful form. (See the note on the use of pronouns in Introduction) Interestingly, the text uses the noun *'adon*, 'master/lord', with the definite article, rather than the divine name when suggesting that he is the one for whom the community 'is seeking'. The Editor has not provided any further information as to this matter of '*seeking*', of its origin or motivation. The messenger's appearance is also said to be sudden.

What appears clearly to be a parallel version of the first sentence in the verse is the statement that the '*messenger of the covenant*' has come, or is about to come—the verb form can be either. The Editor was aware of different oral versions circulating, and has included both for emphasis. Who or what is the '*messenger of the covenant*', and of what 'covenant'? are questions to which commentators have a myriad of answers, including that the messenger here is Elijah of 4.5. The common association of God with the angel of the Lord and the mix of pronouns in the first half of the verse suggests that God is also the emissary whose arrival will be sudden. As for the 'angel of the covenant', the more likely definition is that the angelic emissary is the 'covenant angel' who upholds the relationship established between God and the covenant people as a whole, i.e., God alone. Who then will be the agent to effect the purification policy outlined in 3.2b? God's messenger/angel must take some concrete and identifiable form, but none is identified as fulfilling such a role. As happens with most 'prophetic' promises, hyperbole is used and rarely are details elaborated, leaving readers to speculate on the basis of their own assumptions.

To then describe this 'messenger of the covenant' as someone the people 'delight in' seems most unusual, as though it is someone they already know, or perhaps it is the covenant relationship itself that is the source of such pleasure—the latter seems more meaningful, given the dire warnings that follow.

3.2-4 Two rhetorical questions make the point that when the messenger arrives, 'he' and/or his mission cannot be resisted; none will be able to oppose what he seeks to achieve by way of refining the community. The 'day', as a widely-used concept, generally refers to some future but unspecified event(?), here said to begin with the messenger's appearance. (See also Amos 5.18-20.)

Two metaphors are applied in the description of the messenger's mission—fire and soap, both cleansing or purifying agents. Fire will refine in the manner of the intense heat used to refine metals by removing the dross to leave behind the pure metal, be it silver or gold. The second metaphor is 'fuller's soap' using the analogy of washing raw materials such as wool prior to weaving it into fine fabrics. In both cases, the fire and the soap simply remove unwanted or contaminating elements in order to leave behind the finer product. The process should not be interpreted as judgment, as some commentators insist, but as elevating what is the good and useful. Reading the metaphors that promise action by the messenger as punishment misreads the analogies completely. Refining is for the purpose of improving or of increasing the value of what is latent. But, how will God do the refining?

The initial verb in 3.3 is literally '*he will sit*'. While this may seem an unusual descriptor of the refiner's position, it does picture the silversmith or goldsmith seated before a small smelting apparatus in the process of making some hand-worked silver or gold object. The Editor advises that such a refining process is the aim of the messenger's mission vis-à-vis the '*descendants of Levi*', those who are currently serving as Levitical priests. Details of the refining process itself are not given.

In this postexilic period, Levitical priests other than those descended from Aaron took on many Temple-related responsibilities. They were descendants of Levi's first sons; some were 'singers' who were related to the second son, and then the 'gatekeepers' or temple functionaries descended from the sons of Korah. It appears that they were not involved directly in offering sacrifices, the responsibility of which fell to the Aaronide priests as outlined in Lev. 6.8–9.24. Levites could teach and take care of the practical aspects of Temple life. Were these the only priests envisaged that required 'refining'? or was it more widespread? Whichever it was, the Editor saw that there needed to be some purifying of the way they fulfilled their responsibilities to ensure that they were done as expected, '*as in the days of old*', that idealized past that never was.

The refining process is said to result in the Levites being bearers of offerings for YHWH '*in/with righteousness*' (Heb. *ts'daqah*). The preposition describes the manner in which the gifts will be brought, presumably meaning that all the requirements set down for an offering will be met.

As a result of the refining, the Editor foresees offerings made throughout Judaea to be once more a source of pleasure for God. This contrasts with the first issue in this section. In 2.17 the people have accused God of delighting in those who do evil, whereas the point being made here is that those who actually cause God delight are those whose offerings are done in accordance with all the law's requirements. Seeking to please God is clearly one of the purposes ancient Israel intended in its religious or cultic activities, especially in the area of sacrifices. Sweet smelling offerings, either of incense or of the burning of animal flesh, were seen as giving pleasure to God, and thus ensuring God's favour.

3.5 This verse answers the deeper question of God's alleged lack of concern for justice, the charge that God delighted in those who did evil (2.17). They are linked by the literary Inclusion, *mishpat*, justice/judgment. The text here literally says: 'I will come near to you for judgment', the meaning of which is ambiguous. Who is to do the judging? It is generally understood to be God who does all the judging, but here I suggest that it is the people—they finally will see evidence that enables them to decide whether God is just or not. I suggest a translation: 'Now I am coming to you for your judgment!' By seeking the people's assessment of what God is about to do, the people finally will know whether God is in fact just, that God does not favour the evildoers, as they currently allege.

Since the Editor believes that the messenger is about to come (3.1), an imminent event, the phrase '*I will be a witness hastily ('ed m'maher) against…*' expects a quick decision to be made. God intends to demonstrate to the people that he is just by acting against a range of social ills. The Editor then offers a list of those against whom God will take action: against sorcerers, adulterers, those who are false witnesses, against oppressors of workers, of widows and of orphans, against those who are anti-foreigner, and those who do not 'fear' him.

'Sorcerers' refers to those who engage in religious or cultic practices associated with non-Israelite religions—see Dan. 2.2; Deut. 18.10. Adulterers are condemned for destroying families as in Deut. 5.18. Those who give false witness and so, for whatever reason, seek to undermine the justice system are condemned (Exod. 20.7). Others in the list are more familiar social ills that show a lack of compassion for the disadvantaged and defenceless, including for the alien who is an itinerant or temporary resident of Judaea (Exod. 22.21). Many of those who suffer injustice fall into more than one category as the wealthy take advantage of widows, orphans and aliens by cheating them out of wages due. All of those listed as offenders here are caught up in the final phrase as '*those who do not fear me*', those who do not respect YHWH.

Once the community sees justice done, they will have their doubts about God's justice answered—so, 'Where is the God of justice?' He is about to appear!

3.6-12 Guaranteeing a Land of Plenty

3.6 'Truly, I am the Lord, I have not changed; and you the sons of Jacob have not perished'.

3.7 'From the time of your fathers you have turned aside from my statutes and failed to keep them; return to me and I will return to you', says the Lord of hosts.

3.8 'Would a person rob God? Truly, you have been robbing him! And you have said, "In what way have we robbed you?" In the matter of your tithes and offerings'.

3.9 'You are being really cursed and I am the one you are robbing, the whole nation of you!'

3.10 'Bring into the storehouse the entire tithe, that there may be food in my house; put me to the test in this', says the Lord of hosts, 'and see whether or not I will open heaven's windows and pour down an abundant blessing'.

3.11 'I will rebuke the devourer (locust?) so that it will not destroy what the land provides; the grapevine in your field will not fail to fruit for you', says the Lord of hosts.

3.12 'May every nation be happy for you, and may you truly be a land of delight', says the Lord of hosts.

In 520 BCE the prophet Haggai sought to explain Judaea's current agricultural crisis and drought as the direct result of the community's failure to restore the Temple; it was God's way of reminding the people that God needed a 'house' in which to dwell, he said. It is therefore quite conceivable that this new section of the book has this as its historical context, although drought and harvest shortfall was a regular feature of life in this agriculturally marginal region. While there is a concern here for correct cultic observance, 3.6-12 has no other connection with the issues raised elsewhere in this book. Its special focus is the community's failure to observe certain statutes regarding tithes that are causing God, in the Editor's mind, to withhold blessing such that a locust infestation and poor harvest ensues. The use of 'blessing' and 'curse' as descriptors of the situation points to the same Deuteronomic theological underpinning (see Deut. 7.12-16) as is evident in Haggai.

The section begins with a statement about the community's past failures with regard to God's statutes and calls for the people to 'Return' with the promise that God would 'return' to them, a mutual turning back, such that the original relationship might be restored. The formal rhetorical question 'How...?' that follows suggests the practical step to be taken that will demonstrate a 'return', namely paying the tithes that are due. In the middle of the section, 3.8-9, the metaphor of 'theft' (Heb. *qbʻ*) is used as a keyword describing the people's failure to pay the tithe required. The Editor assures the people such theft will mean that the present hardships of poor harvest, lack of rain and the locust plague will continue—God's blessings will not be showered on the land. When they 'return', the land will become a land of 'delight', with the nations recognizing the people's new-found joy.

With regard to the formula developed by the Editor for this book, this new section does not quite follow the basic pattern but offers a more complex version. The statement portion covers 3.6-7ab and incorporates a call for action. The people's question in 3.7c initially is a response to the statement that is then followed by a second statement about robbing God. That is then followed by the rhetorical question in which the people deny having robbed God. The remainder of the section explains what is to happen that will restore the land and guarantee the harvest, bringing delight to all.

As noted above, there is what some consider a good reason for regarding 3.6-7a as the conclusion to the previous section, 2.17–3.5, reading the introductory particle *ki* as 'because' and providing the explanation for the divine activity noted especially in 3.5. On the other hand, 3.6 is a well-constructed introduction to a section that has its own theme calling on a return to mutual obligations and related to a theme similar to that found in Joel—see Joel 2.12 and the divine response to the locust plague.

3.6 This verse and section begin with the particle *ki* that in this context is assuredly the asseverative 'Indeed'. The content is structured as a statement in parallel halves: literally, '*I YHWH not change; (and) You children-of-Jacob not perish*'. The relationship between the two halves depends on the interpretation of the connecting 'and/but' that some read as 'therefore', the second half expressing the result of the first. What God's immutability has to do with the people not perishing is open to discussion, but as an opening statement without other context it is, for the Editor, simply a statement of two accepted facts—God and the Israelites are extant. The syntax of each half places the emphasis on both YHWH and 'you' by setting them before the verb.

The two verbs concerned, '*have not changed*' (Heb. *shanah*) and '*cease not/not destroyed*' (Heb. *kalah*) may be read as close in meaning, that God and the people are both operating as consistent with expectations. Some read this to mean that God's relationship with Israel has not diverged, and that explains why Judaeans remain as a people; this is a positive reading. Others prefer a negative sense, namely, that while God has not changed, nor has the tendency to rebellion on the part of Israel changed/ended. Those who opt for the negative reading generally see Judaea's situation as set out in 3.7 and proceed from the perspective of human sinfulness. This involves reading the verbs in 3.7b as calls for repentance when they are merely a call for a 'return' to God to which God in turn will 'return' to them, a restoration of an earlier relationship. It speaks of <u>mutual</u> turning as the verb is applied to the action of <u>both</u> parties.

3.7 The verse proceeds with God as the assumed speaker and an accusation against the forefathers for their 'turning', with the verb (Heb. *sur*) meaning that it is a 'turning aside', a rejecting of God's statutes. How far back does this turning aside extend? And who are the 'fathers' involved? It is quite apparent from Josh. 24.14-15 that the 'fathers' up until the entry into Canaan were polytheists, worshipping a variety of gods, and later reports such as Ezekiel 20 confirm that such practices were the norm. The charge here paints a picture of a never-ending 'turning aside' from what God's statutes required so they have not been 'kept'. The combination of the Hebrew verbs *sur* and *lo' shamar* are characteristic of Deuteronomy (see e.g., Deut. 17.19-20). 'Turning aside' presumes an initial loyalty to the statutes set by YHWH, from which the present generation and their forefathers had constantly departed. So the negative situation addressed was nothing new! It is a salutary reminder that popular Israelite religion throughout the OT period was never ideal in the eyes of religious authorities, and that monotheism was a theory that developed very late—see Isaiah 40–55. In terms of the postexilic community being addressed in Malachi, monotheism was still a very new concept, one that may not have influenced many at the popular level.

There is then a call for a 'return'. In this it echoes other postexilic prophets who called for a 'turning', a turning also linked to the actions of the forefathers. Beginning perhaps with Joel (2.12-13) and found again in Zech 1.3-4, it is obvious that a postexilic concern shared by these later prophets is expressed by the same verb *shub*, 'return/turn around', found in the oral forms to which all had access. While frequently the call to 'return' does imply repentance, that cannot apply in these examples where the 'turning' is to be a mutual 'turning towards', though it does imply a change of attitude by <u>both</u> parties in order to bring about a reconciliation. The expression may imply that the community must take the first step and then God will respond in like manner, but it should never be reduced to Judah having to 'repent' while God simply responds. (There is a tendency among some commentators to simplistically reduce every human exchange with God to 'repentance' in accordance with a narrow theology of human sinfulness.)

The question '*in what (how) shall we return/turn back?*' in v. 7c follows the formula used by this Editor and appears to be a serious question with an underlying denial that any such action is required of them.

3.8 It is at this point that the Editor applies his formula for the exchange with the community by asking a question that is rhetorical: '*Can/should humans (*Heb. *'adam) rob/deceive God, because you are robbing me?*' The question form is actually a statement to which the community responds with its question that is a firm denial that they are robbing God. The Editor reports their response using his usual formula—*wa'amartem...*, '*but you say...*'—as the community challenges the accusation.

There is some question about the rarely used Hebrew verb *qb'*; it may mean 'rob', but there is some doubt as to whether this is correct, except that its use three times in this section rules out the possibility of a simple copying mistake. The verb *'qb* with a possible meaning 'circumvent, cheat' is suggested as more appropriate, but it depends on a metathesis or switching of the component letters. We note that the LXX reads a verb meaning 'to cheat', that may indicate what was intended here. As a response to the question about 'turning towards', this opening question about cheating God presumably refers to the practical step needed to show evidence of a 'turning'; the topic changes to a discussion of tithing.

The Editor now explains in the briefest of answers what was meant by 'robbing' God—simply put, 'the tithe and the offering'. That is the topic that will be explained in the following vv. 9-12.

Tithing was a common practice in the ancient world. An annual tithe, a tenth part of crops harvested or of other material gain, was a form of tax that supported both the cult and the government. While tithing was not part of the legal demands initially, being absent from the Book of the Covenant (Exod. 20.22–23.33) it was seen negatively as a policy that kingship might introduce (1 Sam. 8.15). 'Offering' was a more general term for the entire range of material goods that were required of the gods—sacrifices, incense, first-born animals, etc.—some of which were to be shared with the poor as well as with the priests who had no land with which to provide food for themselves.

Nehemiah spoke of the need to pay tithes (Neh. 10.32) and found after a visit to Babylon around 444 BCE that the matter had lapsed (Neh. 13.6-10), so this section may well relate to issues that the Messenger reports on at that time.

3.9 Malachi begins his explanation with a warning: '*With the curse you are being cursed, and (it is) me you are robbing, the nation, all of it*'. The use of participles suggests that this is something current, that the community is enduring difficult times in terms of their crops, with inadequate rainfall along with a locust(?) plague (vv. 10-11). The mention of 'curse' as a descriptor of what is happening derives from the Deuteronomic view that failure to keep divine statutes will be met with one of many 'curses'—see Deut. 7.12-16; 28.15-24.

With an agricultural crisis facing the people currently, it is conceivable that this section takes up an issue that is at one with similar complaints made by Haggai (Hag. 1.4-6, 10-11), suggesting that this message is contemporary with Haggai. Although drought, locust plague and shortage of harvest was a perennial problem in Judaea, attributing it to non-payment of the tithe in this case may well be another perspective on the crisis of 520 BCE.

3.10-11 With God again as the supposed speaker, the Editor urges the people to '*Bring the whole tithe into the treasury...*' suggesting that they have been short-changing God, not paying the full tithe as required. The additional reason is '*and it will be food in my house*'. This latter is of some significance: the noun *tereph* generally refers to prey, the torn flesh of an animal (see also Nah. 2.12 [13]), but also was later used more generally of food, as here. The more interesting matter in light of this reader's contention that *Massa'* (1.1) placed this book in more of a didactic mode, is that the phrase '*food in my house*' occurs elsewhere only in Prov. 31.15 and refers to the provision of food for the family. So, the concern in this verse is for the full tithe to be paid so that the community itself can benefit from what is held in store. In this case, the tribal treasury is within the Temple, God's 'house'—see also Haggai.

The community is then challenged to '*test me in/by this*' (Heb. *bchn*), emphasized by the insertion of another '*said YHWH of hosts*'. If they begin now to pay the full tithe, says God, then they may see God respond positively—they will see '*whether or not I will open to/ for you the windows of the heavens...*'. The figure of the 'windows of the heavens' opening to allow the rain to fall is more than just a figure of speech; it is grounded in the ancient worldview that above the earth's blue dome there is 'the water above the earth' (Gen. 1.7; 7.11) and the dome's windows can be opened to allow some to fall as rain. The rain is then spoken of as an '*overflowing blessing*'—literally 'a blessing until there is no more'—that God will pour down upon the land. Whether it rains or not is, according to this worldview, totally dependent upon the divine decision.

The use of 'curse' and 'blessing' in this section indicates the close ties the Editor has to the Deuteronomic party—his vocabulary and worldview are derived directly therefrom.

The verb *g'r*, 'rebuke', is used in 3.11 again to portray God's response in judgment of a situation, as in 2.3. Here the reaction could have a positive impact and bring about the removal of an agricultural pest, perhaps the locust—the Hebrew is literally, 'the eating one' (*ha'okel*). (See also Joel 2.26-27 the central verse in that book.) If this were to happen and God passes the test set for him, it will guarantee that the '*fruit of the ground*' will not be ruined. In a parallel statement, the vines planted in the fields '*will not be childless*', a figurative use denoting no lack of fruit. If the people are willing to pay the full tithe, then they may see whether or not God removes the present agricultural difficulties—but they must first pay up. The challenge is emphasized by the addition of the 'says YHWH of hosts' formula.

For some commentators these two verses are regarded as a promise, no doubt because they are convinced that Malachi is a prophet. However, the full context would regard this as the testing challenge; with the larder full of their tithes, will they see all problems relating to their crops removed and a good harvest gathered in? Will they learn this lesson, and will God be able to do as he claims? Time will tell!

3.12 If YHWH of hosts passes the test set for him and he responds to the tithes filling his 'house' then there is the confident hope that the world may affirm that Judaea is a truly blessed community. The verbs here can be viewed as jussive rather than simple imperfect or equivalent. This expresses hope again in universal terms, as usual using hyperbolic language.

Whereas in section two (1.6–2.9) the focus was on God's name and reputation among the nations, here it is the people and land of Judaea that will be acknowledged—they will be seen by their international neighbours as a 'delight' (Heb. *chephets*) as in 2.17, 3.1. This contrasts with the response in 1.10 in which God is said 'to have no delight' in the community's defective offerings. Offering the full tithe may result in an international response, as nations recognize the wonders of life in Judaea—another example of the Editor's hyperbole.

3.13–4.3 Is Serving God of Benefit?

3.13 'What you have said about me is hard', says the Lord, 'and you said, "what have we been saying among ourselves about you?"

3.14 'You said that serving God was pointless, and asked what gain was there when keeping his commands, or when going about mourning before the Lord of hosts?'

3.15 'Now, we ourselves regard the insolent as being happy, they both build acts of evil, also they put God to the test, but they escape.'

3.16 'Then those who feared the Lord discussed among themselves. The Lord noted and listened in then a remembrance book was written before him for those who feared the Lord and who were mindful of his name'.

3.17 'They belong to me', says the Lord of hosts, 'for the day I am to make them my special possession; I will have compassion on them just as one has compassion on a child who serves him'.

3.18 'And you will change your mind when you see (the difference) between the righteous and the wicked, between the one who serves God and the one who does not serve him'.

4.1 'Look the day is imminent, burning like an oven, and all the insolent and all the wicked will become stubble, and it will consume them on the day that comes', says the Lord of hosts, 'leaving them neither root nor branch'.

4.2 'But for you who fear my name there will come forth a sun of righteousness, and there will be healing in its wings, and you will emerge leaping like calves released from the enclosure'.

4.3 'You will tread down the wicked ones for they will be like dust under your feet on the day when I take action', says the Lord of hosts.

This final main division of the book turns again to the general topic of divine justice, raised first in 2.17–3.5, but now set in the context of a discussion of one's personal benefit in keeping the divine command. It begins with the messenger's charge that the community, or at least a certain portion of the community, are said to have spoken in the strongest of terms against God, claiming that serving God was ultimately of no personal benefit. Their complaint arose because they saw evildoers escaping recrimination from 'testing' God. Questioning the perceived injustice in society is surely a justifiable matter to raise, but here it seems to be regarded as causing great offense, and the charge is presented as more contentious than the 'wearying' of God in 2.17. To render the Hebrew *chazaq* as 'harsh' (NRSV) places a very negative connotation on the people's complaint. The adjective *chazaq* refers to something as hard, strong, or powerful. The question the community asked was a hard question, one difficult to resolve and one motivated by disappointment rather than intending sharp negative criticism.

What benefit or profit were people expecting to derive from being obedient? According to Deuteronomic ideology, a clear line could be drawn between obedience and material blessing (Deut. 7.12-16), while its corollary was that disobedience must result in divine curse. Here the people complain that this thesis is demonstrably untrue—the unjust never suffer the consequences.

There are two possible scenarios here: 1. A crisis had passed and the righteous and wicked have both shared in the better outcome, meaning the wicked were just as well off afterwards as were the righteous; 2. The crisis had passed but the righteous did not see themselves more advantaged because the wicked were not penalized for their wicked ways. Whatever the reality, the righteous saw this as unfair in terms of the Deuteronomic ideology that was operative—the wicked were not punished and/or the righteous were not rewarded or alternatively, the righteous had suffered the same traumas as the wicked. The binary terms 'righteous' and 'wicked' are typical of both Deuteronomy and the Wisdom tradition. Note also the use of these binary terms in Hab. 1.4 and the Lament's Complaint.

What the setting for this section might have been is uncertain, but whatever the crisis, it had left the entire community, righteous and wicked equally 'blessed', a situation that the righteous found grossly unfair and grounds for complaint. Could it have been the disappointment felt by those who considered themselves righteous following the recovery Haggai spoke of once the community began restoration work on the Temple in 520 BCE, or alternatively, the full restoration promised by the whole community in Joel 2.18-29? With the crisis over, if all enjoyed the benefits of better times, the righteous obviously felt cheated; it was to them unfair if the wicked escaped retribution and the righteous did not benefit sufficiently!

An early question here has to do with those addressed in a charge that, as written, encompasses all members of the community. So many of Malachi's charges are expressed in the most general of terms—see e.g., 2.1, 17. However, there was also present a group referred to as *'those who revered the Lord and who thought on his name'* (3.16). Who these folk were, and how many, is not further elaborated, but they almost certainly were those who are spoken of also as the righteous (3.18), rather than being yet another segment of the community. (When the Editor throughout uses such generalized and binary terms, it becomes difficult to define specific or exceptional elements within the society). The conversation this group engaged in was of particular interest to the Lord who had tuned into their discussions—a novel notion if taken literally. The Lord took note of the opinions they expressed and responded positively to those who revered his 'name'. Their names were then recorded in the Lord's 'book of remembrance'. This group so described were nevertheless the ones asking tough questions of God, yet for which they were being criticized. They were 'the righteous' who considered themselves disadvantaged and their obedience inadequately rewarded. However, at the coming 'day' such persons would be 'spared' the traditional punishment promised for that terrifying 'day', when the distinction between the righteous and the wicked would be made plain. Whether 'being spared' was to be their only 'profit' (3.14) or not, is unclear.

The phrase '*the service of God*' (Heb. *ᵃbod-'elohim*) in 3.14 is echoed by '*serving him*' (Heb. *ha'obed 'otho*) in 3.17-18, functioning as literary inclusions for the section.

3.13-14 Malachi's unique formula of Statement–Question–Response initiates this section with the charge that 'your words have been strong upon/against me'. The assumed speaker is God, and the audience is the righteous who have a serious question to ask of the God whom they serve. The verb 'be strong/hard' itself is neutral, in the sense that it can have positive or negative connotations; here it is assumed by most commentators that the Hebrew preposition *'al*, 'upon/over/against/concerning', carries a decidedly negative tone, though it could also mean nothing more than that the questions asked were difficult or challenging ones for God to answer. To render the Hebrew *chazaq* as 'harsh' (NRSV) places a very negative connotation on the people's complaint. The adjective *chazaq* refers to something as hard, strong, or powerful. The question the community asked was a <u>hard</u> question, one difficult to resolve and one motivated by disappointment rather than intending sharp negative criticism. The addressees responded with 'what have we said upon/against/about you?', asking for clarification and at the same time implying their denial of the charge. The verb-form used here is Hebrew niphal suggesting a reflexive sense rather than passive, so the people are presented as talking among themselves around this topic.

What they then are said to have agreed amongst themselves was that: '*It is of no value to serve God*'. Serving God, they say, offers them nothing special or concrete (*shaw'*, empty, nothingness); that is their lived experience. The parallel statement is that they saw no profit (*betsa'*) in keeping the laws. This Hebrew term usually denotes an unjust or undeserved gain, but that implication would not seem appropriate here. In light of the Deuteronomic stance of Malachi, the complaint about the lack of benefit would suggest that they have not derived any material advantage from serving God, none of the benefits that could be anticipated (see Deut. 7.12-16). It is important to note that the question being put to God is being asked by the 'righteous', those who are on God's side, not the 'wicked'. So there is nothing wrong with their question or complaint; it must not be viewed negatively. On the other hand, those folk who did not comply with the covenantal demands, 'the wicked', were the ones whom the righteous believed were enjoying the privileges/blessings promised to those who obey! That group within the community against whom the current charge is levelled, the righteous, considers that they have a legitimate question to put to God, what the Editor has named '*hard words*'. If they have seen and experienced injustice, or what they consider unfairness, in the community, then they certainly have questions to put to which there were no simple answers.

They additionally complain that there is no value in their '*going about as mourners before the Lord of hosts*'. Commentators often take this figure quite literally to mean that they walked about in sackcloth, as though in mourning. Admittedly, the Hebrew term *q'dorannith* is unique, but it derives from a root *qdr* that speaks of darkness or dirt. It can refer broadly to one's appearance, suggesting a gloomy facial expression, sullenness or even anger. See Ps. 38.7; Job 30.28. In the context of a communal complaint, this can only refer figuratively to their state of mind, their deep disappointment at seeing what they consider injustice or unfairness triggered by their Deuteronomic worldview. The phrase '*before the Lord*', seems to imply religious activity, so even in the conduct of their religious duties these community members felt that they were missing out on some benefits. To read the latter phrase as implying that the various ritual acts themselves served no purpose, is a distortion of a legitimate complaint about unfairness in society, and, from their perspective, the obvious failure of the Deuteronomic promises.

3.15 The reason this community feels cheated of the benefits expected from obeying the divine commands is now related, as in 2.17. From third-person description the text moves to a first-person inclusive form. It opens with an attention-getting '*And now, we…*'. Who is this 'we'? There seems to be no obvious link with the rest of the sentence which simply says, '… (*are*) *being happy arrogant ones*'. It is a terse statement in which the 'we' are not those arrogant ones who are said to be finding joy in their callous disregard of God's commands. The happy arrogant ones are described in two parallel clauses each one introduced by the Hebrew particle *gam*, 'also', that sets out two situations: 'they both…, and…'. In this case:

'*they both build acts of evil, also they put God to the test, but they escape*'. The figurative use of the verb 'build' in this context suggests action that builds them up or enhances them in some self-serving manner, while putting God to the test and disregarding God's demands. The claim that those who do so are not penalized or cursed is the issue. 'Testing' God, as the audience had been challenged to attempt (3.10), in this clause carries a negative sense, that is, tempting God.

The underlying problem is that those described as arrogant and evildoers are seen as untroubled and prospering in defiance of the Deuteronomic code. Despite the generalized challenge, it is clear that the issue of 'benefits' promised by Deuteronomy to the obedient is deeply flawed.

3.16 Here we are introduced to another phrase, namely, '*those who feared the Lord*'. They appear to stand apart from the undefined 'we' of the previous verse but who are later described as 'the righteous'. The God-fearers are said to have discussed together a matter of great concern, presumably it had to do with whether serving God was or wasn't beneficial—what advantage was there in following the law? The actual content of their discussion is not recorded but the context suggests it was to do with their sense of injustice. The God-fearers are also referred to as '*those who thought on his name*', that is those for whom God's name and reputation were held in high esteem, by honouring and obeying the demands of Torah. The section then has three different phrases for describing the righteous—each perhaps arising in the oral traditions that were in circulation.

The initial word in this verse—Hebrew '*az*—is the temporal marker 'then/next', though some early textual variants such as LXX have 'these things…'. It simply marks another element in the unfolding report. It is that the Lord actively '*inclines (the ear)*' to listen in to their conversation and then, pleased with what the Lord hears, responds by having their names inscribed in his '*book of remembrance*'. This figure of a book in which names are entered is not an uncommon one—see Exod. 32.32-33; Isa. 65.6—and means that individuals and their fate are preserved by God for posterity, a positive and comforting thought for those who find themselves so listed. Another name for the book is 'the book of life' (Ps. 69.29). The picture presented uses very anthropomorphic language.

3.17 The notion of belonging to God underlies the simple phrase '*They will be mine*', implying protection in the face of a coming 'day' that could spell trouble. That claim of ownership or lordship is emphasized in the parallel phrase '*my special possession*' (Heb. *s'gullah*). While the noun may describe material possessions or property, it appears in Deut. 7.6,

14.2 and 26.18-19 as a way to describe Israel's special relationship with its God based on the notion of God's having chosen them. The syntax of the verse is unusual in the sense that the noun *s'gullah* is detached, appearing to be the object of the participle 'do/act'. It is an example of the reversal of word-order, found throughout late writings. Here the concept of ownership is highlighted by the placement of the *s'gullah* noun at the end of the phrase, where least expected.

We note that the opening criticism in this section (3.14) was that there was no advantage in 'serving God', while here in v. 17 'serving God' is the basis for differentiating the righteous and the wicked.

The notion of a 'day', when God is about to act (Heb. *'ani 'oseh*), is one found frequently throughout the prophetic canon and is the focus here in 3.17–4.3. 'The day' or occasion lies in the future and is only ever vaguely defined, usually using highly figurative language. However, for it to have meaning to any present audience, that vague future time cannot be so far off that it does not have some application to them. In general terms it implies divine judgment that has benefits for the righteous, and corresponding disaster or punishment for the wicked, and all such is imminent. The promise in this context must imply soon-to-be experienced material benefits to those who are outraged at the apparent lack of justice and fairness in their world.

The particular form in which 'the day' is described here uses a simile—God will have compassion on those who are his, who belong to him, '*as/like a man has compassion on his son who serves him*'. The relationship of father-son is applied analogically to that of God and the righteous. The example reflects the patriarchal culture of the time and of the nature of the relationship between the patriarch and his children—they were for his service! There are echoes of the social pattern from 1.6.

3.18 The verse opens with the Hebrew verb *shub*, 'return/turn around', often used as a metaphor for repentance, but also, as here, some more general change of mind or attitude (see 3.7). NRSV renders it as '*Then once more...*' which misses the point; here the verb indicates a reversal of attitude, a change of mind, in the folk complaining—they will move from believing there has been no benefit in serving God to become witnesses of divine justice at work. The text speaks of God 'doing' something that unfortunately is non-specific, but that will see the arrogant and evil duly punished, i.e., the Deuteronomic rewards in action. The Editor assures them that serving God will have its reward—once again demonstrating the didactic nature of the Editor's response, combining wisdom and promise in accordance with the nature of the literary *Massa'*.

4.1 (3.19) The focus turns now to 'the day' itself with a strong expression, literally 'Indeed, behold, the day comes', stressing the imminence of the event, though its actual form or manner is hidden behind the similes used. 'The day' is the focus word, the inclusio, for this and the next three verses in the context of distinguishing the righteous and the wicked.

'The day' will be '*burning like an oven*'. This is not a weather report but an attempt to portray judgment under the figure of consuming fire. The *tannur*, 'oven', was made of clay and was used for cooking and heating a home. The burning chaff or stubble placed at the base of the stove drew heat upwards, cooked the bread attached to the side of the oven, as in a modern 'tandoor'. It is the burning itself that is the focus, for stubble burns fiercely and leaves little or nothing behind.

The metaphor of stubble or chaff being burned is found elsewhere in the postexilic material (Isa. 47.14; Joel 2.5; Obad. 18) to indicate punishment and destruction, made more emphatic here by the addition of the unique phrase '*leave them neither root nor branch*'. A plant without roots or branches is an oxymoron, but as imagery it is a powerful one pointing to an imminent and complete annihilation of those seen as arrogant evildoers (see 3.15). There was an ancient Near Eastern curse that used similar imagery and may be seen behind Amos 2.9; complete destruction is intended—used here, it is another example of hyperbole.

4.2 (3.20) By way of contrast, for those who '*revere my name*' there will '*go forth*', i.e., there will appear, what is described as a 'righteous sun'(?). The syntax in this clause is unusual—literally '*and it will come forth to/for you (who are) fearers of my name sun (of) righteousness*'. It is unclear whether it is the sun (Heb. *shemesh*) or righteousness/justice (*ts'daqah*) that will come forth, or whether righteousness describes the sun. The LXX suggests 'sun of righteousness'. While the notion of the sun rising or coming forth is literally what the sun does each morning, behind the phrase may lie the widespread ancient Near Eastern convention of portraying the sun as a disk with wings. When the sun's function is added, namely, coming '*with healing in its wings*', it paints a picture of something restorative happening. It is possible that the figure is meant to portray the shedding of light on justice that will see the righteous rewarded and the wicked properly dealt with, as in 3.18.

There is a question about how to interpret the imperfective verb forms in 4.2a, b. Assuming that Malachi is a prophet, it is traditional to render the Hebrew verbs *w'zarchah*, 'arise, come forth', and *witsa'them* 'you shall go out...' as future actions, as prophetic promises. However, given that there is a basic question about the book's 'prophetic' nature, it is valid from the point of view of syntax to regard these two parallel verbs as jussive forms—they are both speaking of the wish or longing that something may appear. This gives a rendering of 4.2a and 2b as *'may... the sun appear..., and may you go out and jump about...'*. So, rather than predicting a certain future event, the verse expresses parallel wishes. See the Postscript for further comments on the relationship between translation and interpretation.

'The day' hopefully will be an occasion when the righteous come to see and experience that there is actually a benefit in serving the Lord, though what that benefit is has to be assumed. In the context, it must be some practical or material benefit for the righteous over the wicked. The whole point of the Editor's response, via this figurative language, is to answer the righteous ones' question and to bring comfort and assurance so that they remain obedient. An interpretation that seeks to identify the sun as a messianic figure, or as Jesus as Saviour, destroys the contextual sense of the Editor's report about those who were complainants—'the day' was imminent, not centuries into the future, otherwise its message was irrelevant.

As a further consequence, the righteous will have every reason for celebration. It is presented in the simile of a young calf leaping out of the stall following a period of enclosure. That imagery appears derived from the practice of corralling an animal for fattening—see Amos 6.4—and its release denoting joy and new opportunity.

4.3 (3.21) Yet another image is used to portray what 'the day' is hoped to bring—this time metaphor is used to describe the fate intended for the wicked. The opening verb likewise can be treated as jussive, meaning *'May you tread down the evil ones...'*, expressing the speaker's hopes. There follows a strong assertion, reading *ki* as the asseverative: *'Truly/Indeed, may they become ashes under the soles of your feet'*. This imagery does not imply or sanction violence, but is a cultural image, like that of stubble being burned, to express complete victory for the righteous ones. This will all happen *'on the day that I act* (Heb. *'oseh)'*. The phrase intends to stress that the one who is about to act—'act' here is a participle, the form associated with an imminent event—though exactly what the action will involve is unspoken. What is typical of the warnings about the coming 'day' is the stress on its certainty, its imminence and divine origination; its reality, what might actually happen, is always hidden in figurative language.

The section is concluded with the '*...says the Lord of hosts*' formula by way of emphasis.

4.4-6 (3.22-24) In Conclusion

4.4 Remember the torah of Moses my servant which I commanded at Horeb concerning all Israel, statutes and commandments.

4.5 'Look, I am about to send you Eliyyah the prophet before the great and terrifying day of the Lord comes'.

4.6 'He will return the minds of the father to the children and the minds of the children to their fathers, otherwise I will come and strike the land with violence'.

What appear to be three independent statements complete the written document. They also give the appearance of being later additions. The first is an imperative, a call to reflect on the *torah* given to Moses at Mt Horeb (4.4). The second advises that God is about to send the prophet Eliyyah (4.5), and the third, if literal, refers to a social revolution within families (4.6). In the case of the two latter actions, they are directly related to the impending 'day of the Lord' as a great and terrifying event with worldwide consequences.

The question about the relationship between this section and the rest of the book shows a diversity of opinion and the matter is probably unresolvable, but it is important to note here that the rhetorical feature that marks the book as a whole, the Statement–Question–Response form, does not extend to this current section. Also, the frequent insertion of the '*...says the Lord of hosts*' phrase elsewhere is notable for its absence from this section. The independence of these final three verses seems certain, therefore. Who wrote these three verses, when they were written, and why they were appended are also questions without answers though speculations are rife. Those addressed in 4.4 could be the Levitical priests whose responsibility was to teach the statutes and ordinances, while the announcements in 4.5-6 are more general. The mention of Moses and Eliyyah, thought to represent the Law and the Prophets, suggests to some that this brief section is editorial and intended to bring to a conclusion those two major parts of the Hebrew Bible. Again, that notion would imply that they were added after all the various individual scrolls were available and in some fixed order, that is in codex form, making them an extremely late addition. Theories that argue that Malachi and the promise of Elijah about to appear were placed last in the collection in order to link to the Gospel of Matthew as their realization, are far removed from the historical setting to which the material belongs. Later additions they may be, but not so late as to place Malachi in such a Christian context.

4.4 (3.22) The call to remember or reflect on '*the torah of Moses my servant*' is perhaps addressed in particular to the priests whose prime responsibility it was to instruct the community in *torah*. The verb '*remember*' is also a more general call to the entire community to live by *torah* as instructed, not just to recall it. The following relative clause is slightly ambiguous and can be read as referring either to Moses— '(*my servant) whom I commanded...*', or to the *torah* itself '*...which I commanded...*'. *Torah* is defined more closely by two prepositional phrases; it was given '*at Horeb*' and was '*concerning all Israel*'. *Torah* is then explained further as '*statutes and judgments*', parallel terms for the legislation in the Sinai covenant. The syntax is complex and connections vague, but the overall sense is clear. The use of the place-name 'Horeb' in lieu of 'Sinai' indicates the Deuteronomic connection. This is a call that looks back to earlier traditions, contrasting with the following two verses that are more forward looking.

Referring to Moses as '*my servant*' affords Moses a special role alongside that of Abraham, Joshua, David and Zerubbabel, and links with the role of the Servant of the Lord as found throughout Isaiah 40-55. It is a term of honour for those in the closest relationship with God, whether individual or as the collective form 'servant Jacob' (Isa. 45.4).

4.5-6 (3.23-24) An opening '*Behold...*' alerts readers to the announcement that God is about to send '*Eliyyah the prophet*'. Elijah the prophet, whose exploits were described in the DH (1 Kgs 17–2 Kgs 2), appears to be the one here identified, though some have suggested that 'Elijah' is more a representative of the prophets in general, so to some looking for a revived version of the original Elijah is not necessary. The original Elijah had 'died', or at least was taken up into the Heavens, perhaps 400 years prior, so if on the other hand this is the Elijah in view rather than another of the same name, then a resurrected Elijah is promised as returning shortly— again the participle used (Heb. *sholeach*) indicates something about to happen or currently in progress. His return will mark the period before 'the day of the Lord' comes, as a preparatory mission. Here 'the day'—or is it the Lord?—is further described as '*great and fearsome*', a phrase also found in Joel 2.31.

The imminent prophetic mission, if understood literally, is to be that of bringing about a social revival, a return to the traditional social pattern of father-child relationships in which the child honours the father—see 1.6. How it is to be achieved is not clarified. Here the initial verb form can be read as jussive rather than predictive—'*And may he cause the heart/*

mind of the fathers to turn back...'. Such a restoration of social harmony brought about by the prophet will mean that God will not need then to strike the earth with *cherem*, usually understood to mean 'violence/ anathema/taboo'. It is a term associated with the 'holy war' motif, as when God places a 'ban' on certain actions—a good example is in the description of the ban/taboo (*cherem*) placed on material goods in Jericho demanding that nothing should be taken from the city as spoils once the walls collapsed (Josh. 6.18). Failure to keep the terms of the ban is said to bring disaster, as illustrated when the people then tried to capture Ai and failed. It is a distinctive Deuteronomic concept.

Some commentators wish to see the prophet's mission in terms of a restoration of the covenant relationship with the 'fathers', the ancient forebears of this now generation. If the prophet's social revival mission were to be successful, then the destruction implicit in 'the day of the Lord' would be avoided. That is surely the whole point of the 'promise'— ensuring that 'the day' does not come! The interpretation turns on the understanding and thus the translation of the Hebrew phrase *pen-'abo'*. The particle *pen*, 'lest', here must mean 'otherwise, (I will come…)'—in order to make sense of the threat. Avoiding the coming 'day' by implementing a social revival is a novel idea not found elsewhere.

Whether 'the earth' (Heb. *ha'arets*) that potentially might be destroyed is a reference to 'the world', to the land of Judaea, or to the ground is a moot point; in any event, the Editor, using hyperbole again, sees total disaster possible if there is no positive response to the imminent mission of the prophet. These are words of comfort to the immediate community—social harmony restored when the *Torah* is observed.

It is the word *cherem*, 'ban/taboo', the very final word in the Hebrew text of Malachi that concludes the Book of the Twelve and thus the prophetic canon, once ordered. The thought that a sacred text should end on such a negative note has led to the LXX changing the order of these final verses such that it concludes with 4.4 (3.22) rather than 4.6 (3.24) to have the book end more positively. The MT also seeks a better ending, suggesting that readers read 4.5 (3.23) again following 4.6 (3.24).

And with that, the book of Malachi draws the prophetic canon to an end.

Postscript

This Reading of Malachi began with a question about the provenance of the book. Is Malachi a 'prophetic' work by virtue of its inclusion in the Scroll of the Twelve? If so, what element(s) in the text support that definition, since Malachi is never spoken of as a prophet? If not, what does the initial term in the book title, *Massa'*, suggest as a provenance? The conclusion reached by this reader and hopefully illustrated throughout by the exegesis and attention to the book's rhetorical features, is that Malachi represents a different genre from the 'traditional' prophetic books; it is much more didactic in nature, and exhibits literary and rhetorical connections with both the prophetic and the wisdom literature. The refusal of the Editor to use the noun 'prophet' to describe or refer to Malachi the messenger, means that one should avoid applying the term in this case, or at least qualifying it if it is to be used.

Its Editor has collated six separate issues that were addressed orally during the postexilic period, setting each within his frame of Statement–Question–Response. Each issue is independent and reflects a range of community concerns during the period 587–500 BCE and even later. 'Malachi', a composite figure representing a number of 'messengers' of the period, each with a role as mediators of the divine concern that the community live out Torah. Priests and Levites had a role to play, as did the people as a whole, in ensuring that the requirements of Torah were being met. Other concerns expressed related to God's special 'love' for Judah, to the anti-foreign attitude of some to returnees to Judaea who brought with them their foreign wives and children, to matters of fairness and social justice, and whether there was any practical benefit for the 'righteous' over the 'wicked' (3.18) when seeking to live out Torah's obligations. In each case, the Messenger has sought to explain the problem being addressed and its resolution. It is this latter that approximates what might be regarded as prophetic 'promise', suggesting that 'the day' that is imminent will demonstrate that the community's concerns can be met, and God's 'name' be honoured. And all this in the context of Instruction, as in the Wisdom material.

On Translating and Interpreting Malachi

The following are some of the issues this reader has found that can affect the translation and interpretation of Malachi.

'Harsh' Words

In 3.13 NRSV has chosen to render the Hebrew phrase *chaz'qu 'alai* as '(*You have spoken) harsh words against me*'. The choice of '*harsh*' suggest that the words spoken by those addressed were intentionally bordering on the malicious, that they convey a negative cast, and that as such they give a reader the impression that God took offence at their undeserved or unjustified criticism. That negativity is strengthened by rendering the following preposition as '*against me*'. The Hebrew verb in this case, *chzq*, refers to action being firm or strong, a challenge; the spoken words were words difficult to accept and resolve. The preposition '*al* can mean that they are 'over, above, against, concerning (me)', not necessarily aggressive or threatening. If the latter sense, 'concerning', is decided upon as the preposition's nuance in this context, then an interpretation offered based on a translation such as 'your words concerning me are difficult/hard', simply acknowledges that there is a challenge, but not such as implies criticism or determined rebellion against God. However, by choosing 'harsh' the NRSV translation has skewed a reader's attitude towards what is the people's genuine and apparently justifiable complaint, and a negative interpretation of the community will follow accordingly—they have used 'offensive language' against the Lord, as one commentator has expressed it!

Rhetorical Questions

The question-form is one of the most obvious and central literary forms used throughout Malachi. Determining whether a question genuinely seeks information, or whether it is a rhetorical one that actually intends to make a statement, can be determined from the general context and the translator can then offer a translation that identifies it as such.

In the opening section of Malachi, 1.2a asserts that God has loved Judah, to which the popular response is recorded as *bammah 'ᵃhabtanu* (1.2b), '*in what (ways) have you loved us?*' Similarly, in 3.8 the question is '*How are we robbing you?*' The question-form has generally been regarded as the people seeking information from God for evidence that the allegations about divine love or about robbing God of something are indeed accurate or truthful; i.e., that the community is simply asking for information about alleged activity of which they were unaware. On the other hand, if the question is rhetorical, the stance taken by this reader, then the questions actually deny the claims in the statement—it is a far more subtle use of the question-form by which the community makes the point that they do not believe that divine love has been shown, nor do they agree that they have been 'robbing' God. Consequently, the remainder of each section is didactic, attempting to explain and prove that God has indeed loved Judah, and that they have robbed God of what was due him. Other examples of the question in the community's response to the statements made throughout are all of the rhetorical kind—1.6, 7; 2.17; 3.13—and are denials of the charge made against them. This is a basic function of the question-form as applied by the Editor in his framing of each section.

In an oral context a speaker may have to field questions for information from his audience, or may use questions seeking to have the audience agree with him on some topic. Rhetorical questions draw out the audience to make them consider points a speaker is making. However, when a written report uses third-person reference, and implies that God is the one asking the question, the question-form is largely rhetorical, requiring the reader to think about the matter being raised. There is in 1.2 a rhetorical question-form—*Is not Esau Jacob's brother?*—that is obviously a way of making a strong positive statement and one that the audience would agree with, as all knew the old tradition about the brothers. It can be translated positively as 'You all know that Esau was Jacob's brother..., yet I....!'

In this and the many similar cases in Malachi, to decide that the relevant question-form is rhetorical will then determine how one interprets the sense in the question, and that then allows the translator to consider ways to express the implied sense, rather than simply offering a literal rendering of the Hebrew.

Hyperbole

Failing to identify and understand the use of hyperbole in Malachi and elsewhere in the OT can and does lead to peculiar and unwarranted interpretations. While translation of the texts concerned is relatively simple, it is the interpretation that reveals the extent to which a commentator understands how language is used.

In Mal. 1.11-12, and 14 for example, where hyperbole is used with irony to shame the community for its failure to honour the divine 'name', some commentators have gone to extraordinary lengths to try to identify those foreign nations or alien peoples who are said to have honoured the 'name' and who have done, perhaps unintentionally, what the Lord demanded of Israel in terms of 'pure offerings'. Commentators have developed theories to explain how this 'truth' about the worship of Israel's God was currently happening universally, and they congratulate Malachi for his unique insight and theological contribution. By failing to regard the language as hyperbole, and by reading it literally, the text becomes completely distorted and the Editor's purpose and meaning lost. Hyperbole is and remains hyperbole, a manner of speaking that by its very nature entertains, emphasizes, excoriates or encourages the audience that properly understands its contribution to the communication.

Eschatology

The OT concept of *hayyom*, 'the day', with the definite article, also known as 'the day of the Lord', is important within books such as Malachi, and while its *translation* is never a problem; its *interpretation*, however, certainly is. Although its semantic range is broad and covers a period of time, even an event, not just a twenty-four hour period, 'the day' has become for some readers a much loaded concept. 'The day' is generally accompanied by a Hebrew participle *ba'*, 'coming', to denote an imminent action. While vague when it comes to details, it can spell blessing or salvation for the righteous, and judgment and punishment for the wicked. Other elements are that it is a moment to be feared and that it will come unexpectedly. One thing that is undisputed is that 'the day' is imminent, about to happen, supported by the nuance provided by the associated participle; it is not an event envisioned for centuries into the future—see notes on Mal. 4.5-6. An obvious reason for this is that the audiences to which this challenge of 'the day' is addressed are the ones to whom it applies. If the future envisaged for 'the day' was to lie so far into the distant future, whatever threat or encouragement it symbolized would be completely lost on the present audience as they would all have died long before 'the day' arrived.

To argue, as some do, that there might have been a partial fulfilment of 'the day' at the time spoken of, then to await some final and complete fulfilment, is a reading strategy that makes plain a reader's preconceptions. Many Christian commentators, based on their understanding of the 'prophetic', suggest that the fuller realization of the 'promises' point to the coming of Christ in both his first and then his anticipated second comings. Some go so far as to suggest that the promises hold some kind of eternal value, and so the Church may also be caught up in the on-going realization of these promises. This perspective is driven by a theology totally alien to the real-time context of the books themselves.

Additionally, the language used to refer to 'the day' is usually hyperbolic, making exaggerated claims about 'the day' and what it might bring.

Reading the hyperbole literally and seeking to identify a distant realization is antithetical to the hyperbole's purpose, and leads to the distortion of the text in its OT setting.

That is to say, reading and interpreting a book like Malachi as 'eschatological', as many commentators do, especially with regard to Mal. 3.20, seeking to link its words to events or personalities far, far removed from the audiences to which the messages were addressed, is evidence of that reader's agenda. It is a reading driven by factors other than its immediate textual, cultural and historical context. For some, the eschatological reading is proposed because they are aware that so many of the so-called prophetic 'promises' were not fulfilled, so a subsequent or an end-of-time fulfilment is developed to cover the failure. This was done in both late postexilic Jewish and early Christian circles, with their contemporary events or personalities claimed as the real or final fulfilments intended. However, the very term itself, deriving from Greek *eschaton*, suggests that it is a concept of time foreign to the prophetic notion of 'the day'. The Hebrew time concept, *'olam*, usually but misleadingly translated as 'eternal', also argues against the eschatological view, for *'olam* marked only a long, yet indefinite, period of time, the longest time one could imagine, whether in reference to the past, as in Mal. 3.4, or to the future as in Mal. 1.4, (see also the Davidic so-called 'eternal' covenant in 2 Sam. 7); it was not a philosophical concept of eternity or some end-of-time possibility.

Reading Malachi within its ancient context is what this reader has aimed to achieve, acknowledging that it is a collection of numerous, six in all, different messages representing something of the depth and abundance of the oral materials circulating within the postexilic communities of Judaea. It gives a good summary of some of the issues uppermost in the minds of the leaders of that community as they readjusted to life in their own land again, but under domination by foreign powers that caused them to question the power of their traditional God, Yahweh. Re-affirming a national identity and a distinctive life under Torah, together with Wisdom's guidance, became a key focus for the Editor of the collection known now as Malachi, the book.

Select Bibliography

Commentaries

Clark, D.C., and H.A. Hatton, *A Handbook on Malachi* (UBS Handbook Series; New York: United Bible Societies, 2002).

Coggins, R.J., *Haggai, Zechariah, Malachi* (Sheffield: Sheffield Academic Press, 1996).

Jacobs, M.R., *The Books of Haggai and Malachi* (Grand Rapids, MI: Eerdmans, 2017).
Ogden, G.S., and R.R Deutsch, *A Promise of Hope; A Call to Obedience* (ITC; Grand Rapids MI: Eerdmans, 1987).
Redditt, P.L., *Haggai, Zechariah, Malachi* (NCBC; Grand Rapids, MI: Eerdmans, 1995).
Smith, R.L., *Micah–Malachi* (WBC, 32; Dallas, TX: Word Books, 1984).
Verhoef, P.A., *The Books of Haggai and Malachi* (NICOT; Grand Rapids, MI: Eerdmans, 1987).
Waltke, B.K., and M. O'Connor, *An Introduction to Biblical Hebrew Syntax* (Winona Lake, IN: Eisenbrauns, 1990).

Journal Articles

Boloje, B.O., 'Malachi's Use of Torah in dialogue with the Wisdom Tradition of Proverbs', *OTE* 31 (2018), pp. 243-63).
Muller, H.-P., 'Massa II', *TDOT* IX (1984–1986, Eng. trans., 1998), pp. 20-24.
Wendland, E., 'Linear and Concentric Patterns in Malachi', *BT* 36 (1985), pp. 108-21.

CONCLUSIONS

On Prophets and Prophecy

Neither Nahum nor Malachi have been given a prophetic identity by the Editors of the two books attached to their names. In the case of Habakkuk, on the other hand, he is identified as a *nabi'* (Hab. 1.1), yet the writing style throughout the book shows little use of established prophetic literary forms. When put together with the narrative created about Jonah, a legendary prophet, it becomes clear that within the Scroll of the Twelve as it has developed, the very concept of a 'prophet' has undergone change. No longer was a prophet or prophetic book a signal of a unidirectional word from God via a messenger to his people, if that ever really was an adequate definition; rather, it was becoming clear that the individual concerned had a mind of his own, with personal insights into the world and its workings independent of divine instruction. Individuals like Habakkuk and Malachi could boldly challenge God, speaking to and about God, as did the psalmists and sages, and demand answers to basic questions relating to injustice, violence and evil in society and of God's relationship to them. The written report of their messages has been included in a 'prophetic collection', the minor prophets' Scroll, though who determined their qualification for inclusion is unclear. The very definition of 'prophet' was thus in flux, and with it the range of material, whether oral or written, that could claim to be 'prophetic'. It is the noun *Massa'* that can be associated with this shift.

Concern for the immediate context, rather than some distant future, was a clear element in the reports of these three individuals. From this point of view, the traditional definition of a 'prophet' that biblical scholars have generally used, requires modification in order to accommodate to these shifts. The earliest references to the role of the 'prophet' (*nabi'*) was to identify them as 'seer' (*ro'eh*)—see 1 Sam. 9.9—a perspective that accords with the noun *chozeh*, 'vision', as describing the work of Nahum and Habakkuk. While distinguishing between the roles of 'prophet' and 'seer' in the early records is far from exact, at least with these minor prophets it is possible to suggest that the role of the *nabi'* has begun to coalesce with that of the Sage (Heb. *chakam*) for the purpose of Instruction, and that it involves the prophet's more personal evaluation of a situation rather than a supposed dependence on external 'revelation'.

That the *Massa'* represented a new literary type focusing on Instruction, locating these three books between established prophetic works such as Isaiah and Jeremiah and the Wisdom tradition as in the Book of Proverbs, also testifies to the evolution that was taking place in Israel's literary world at this time. Some of the old literary forms such as '*Thus says the Lord...*' are used very sparingly, while '*..., says the Lord*' is added more to emphasize a point being made than as a concluding device for a divine announcement.

Habakkuk offers an example of a text, in this case a Lament psalm, serving as a literary framework broken open for the insertion of a debate with God about God's role in dealing with injustice, especially as it involves apparently the use of the Chaldeans as a divine agent. Habakkuk is far from satisfied with the response he gets from God. However, the device of borrowing an established tradition/story for another purpose echoes the form of the current Book of Job that uses the legend of righteous Job as a basis for discussing the relationship between adverse circumstances and individual sin. It serves to deny the validity of the Deuteronomic link between blessing and curse based on the obedience-disobedience paradigm.

Within the Scroll of the Twelve's listing of books, there is also clear evidence of books like Jonah and Haggai challenging the view expressed in a book like Nahum with regard to foreigners. The dominant Deuteronomic cohort were an intensely nationalistic group whose 'chosenness' they believed elevated them above others. While Haggai the man and Nahum demonstrate a similar nationalistic attitude, regional events modified the experience of many others like Zerubbabel and Joshua, who were complicit with foreign powers, and like those who intermarried with foreigners, to witness to a more open view in other parts of the society. The narrow theology that was held up as the ideal by priests and some prophets, was being challenged by those with a broader mind. Theological orthodoxy as defined by Deuteronomy was no longer ubiquitous.

A Final Note on Translation and Interpretation

A. The Semitic languages, of which biblical Hebrew is an important family member, are essentially characterized by verbs and nouns that derive from a triliteral root. The three-lettered root identifies the basic concept or idea, and the individuation by means of vowel points, prefixes, suffixes, infixes, abbreviations, intensifications, nominal forms and so on become the contextual applications expressing the state of an action or name of an object related to the root. In the case of Hebrew with its alphabet of just twenty-two letters, the number of possible triliteral roots clearly is mathematically restricted. A quick survey of any standard Hebrew dictionary indicates that there are a large number of roots that can identify multiple values, beyond the subtle contextual variations of a basic sense whether concrete or metaphorical. These are, in BDB for example, simply marked as (I) or (II) and the differentiated meaning equivalents suggested.

For the translator and exegete, determining which sense attaches to any one use of a root within a biblical text is always to be based primarily on the specific context in which it occurs and not on the dictionary-derived meaning(s). For example, the root *brk*, normally 'bless', also has an antithetical meaning of 'curse'—see 1 Kgs 21.10, 13; Job 1.5, 11; 2. 5, 9; Ps. 10.3. How this latter and seemingly contrary meaning is derived depends on cultural and contextual factors rather than strict linguistic or syntactic ones.

The translator and interpreter is responsible for being sensitive to the many elements from culture as well as linguistics that contribute towards discovering an ancient editor's supposed intentions when putting ideas into a fixed written form. Since none of us in the modern period is a mother-tongue speaker of biblical Hebrew, the task of accessing the editorial intent is massively disadvantaged. Whatever meaning we derive from a text is entirely dependent upon a readiness to spend the time 'soaking' in the various texts in the hope that, with increasing familiarity, some of its subtleties, its nuances, can be a little better appreciated and taken into account. Knowing that many triliteral roots may point to very different semantic values is an important first step towards unlocking a text's meaning.

B. A second issue is around what seem, or are assumed, to be 'multivalent' senses of a particular word or root. Many forms are believed to have a broad semantic range and to be applicable to different scenarios both concrete and metaphorical. The root form *kbd*, for example, may describe something as 'heavy', 'abundant', or as 'glorious', even 'burdensome', and the nominal form as one's 'liver'. The semantic range that is covered by this root is determined culturally, and as such may confound a modern reader with its breadth. To take the Hebrew noun *ruach* as another example: the dictionary gives it a range of meanings—wind, spirit, breath, odour. In modern parlance these are each distinctive 'things', so a translator has to choose one of the possible meanings, and an interpreter then expands on that assigned meaning. In Gen. 1.2 the *ruach-elohim* is presented as a core element in the creative process. Many translations render it as 'the spirit of God', some as 'the Spirit of God', others as 'a wind from God', 'a breath from God', even 'a divine wind' (*kamikaze*), each rendering being a personal decision made by a translator based on theological grounds and/or on a notion that *ruach* has one of the several specific values suggested in the dictionary. On the other hand, what the noun conveys culturally is actually a unitary notion—that of something invisible but existentially real, its presence known and experienced only by its impact. The wind is never seen, but its effect is witnessed in the blowing leaves; breath is never visible other than in the heaving chest, the spirit is never seen except in an assumed impact or influence on the individual; odour is never seen, but smelled. I would want to argue that the *ruach* is not multivalent; it speaks of 'that which is invisible but effectual'. Attaching the term to the divine one as a construct unit, *ruach-elohim*, in Gen. 1.2 points to that which is behind the reality of the physical world. It was not a literal wind, or breath, or spirit of God or the gods that 'fluttered' over the surface of the waters. That surface movement on the waters was itself the evidence of an invisible reality behind it. The noun *'elohim* in this context may best be seen as the component denoting Mystery. Putting all that into words is what translators seek to do, but in that very aim one is attempting to concretize what is ethereal, available only to the sensory imagination; none of the suggested meanings found in the dictionary can adequately represent the full notion inherent in the Hebrew term *ruach*.

A modern translator and exegete must be sensitive to ancient cultural ways of thinking, so far as that is available, and not assume that the semantic range of any biblical term has the specific values that a dictionary in a foreign language may assign. The translator's task is made more challenging when one is required to choose a specific meaning when the root expresses a broad culturally-determined value not readily available to a modern and foreign language.

C. A third issue is one to which I sought to draw attention in this commentary; it is the matter of *homographs*. All languages to which I have been exposed have a common feature in that rather than just homonyms and homophones, they feature *homographs*. It would seem that often little attention has been paid to this linguistic phenomenon of written forms that are identical but whose semantic value is very different. Again, it is one feature of language to which a limited number of letters in the alphabet might point, especially in poetic works that can play more creatively with language and forms. Non-native speakers of any language may have no inkling that what confronts them in a written text is a *homograph* and so simply read the word as one found in the dictionary even though it seems not to fit the context. Emendations to 'make it fit' one's misreading are not unknown in commentaries!

The three books that are the focus of this commentary are each identified in their Titles as a *massa'*, a noun that this reader argues identifies a particular and emerging literary type, one with both 'prophetic' and Wisdom connections. To assume that the term derives from the root *ns'*, with the singular meaning 'to rise', then to be interpreted as a 'burden', a specific contextual meaning in some narrative texts, is unacceptable on the grounds of falsely assuming one value for the root and ignoring other possibilities. Given the limited number of triliteral roots possible in Hebrew, the use of *massa'* in the unique context of book titles, and foreign nation oracles, as well as in the wisdom collections in Proverbs 30 and 31, *massa'* must be derived from a root *ns'* that carries a very different value from the current one proposed by standard dictionaries. Its written form, *massa'*, clearly does not mean 'burden' in any sense in these three books; it is a *homograph* with its own distinct value. I would suggest that a <u>second root</u> *ns'* has to do with Instruction or Advice, and that *massa'* as found attached to the books as an identifier, refers to the collected materials, an Anthology, and of its contents as instructional material with both prophetic and wisdom connections.

www.ingramcontent.com/pod-product-compliance
Lightning Source LLC
Chambersburg PA
CBHW051059230426
43667CB00013B/2365